TRAINING FOR SPORTS SPEED AND AGILITY

Speed and agility are central to success in a wide range of sports. *Training for Sports Speed and Agility* is the first evidence-based study of all those aspects of athletic preparation that contribute to the expression of speed and agility during competition.

Drawing on the very latest scientific research in the fields of strength and conditioning, applied physiology, biomechanics, sports psychology and sports medicine, the book critically examines approaches to training for speed and agility. This book further explores the scientific rationale for all aspects of effective training to develop sports speed and agility, comprising a diverse range of topics that include:

- assessment;
- strength training for speed and agility development;
- speed–strength development and plyometric training;
- metabolic conditioning;
- mobility and flexibility;
- acceleration;
- straight-line speed development;
- developing change of direction capabilities;
- developing expression of agility during competition;
- periodisation.

Every chapter includes a review of current research as well as offering clear, practical guidelines for improving training and performance, including photographs illustrating different training modes and techniques. No other book offers a comparable blend of theory and practice. *Training for Sports Speed and Agility* is therefore crucial reading for all students, coaches and athletes looking to improve their understanding of this key component of sports performance.

Dr Paul Gamble currently works as national strength and conditioning lead for Scottish Squash and is also responsible for a number of national-level athletes in a variety of sports, having previously worked in professional rugby union with the English Premiership side London Irish. This is Paul's second textbook and he has published a number of articles on related topics, as well as developing course materials for postgraduate degree programmes.

TRAINING FOR SPORTS SPEED AND AGILITY

An evidence-based approach

Paul Gamble

LONDON AND NEW YORK

First published 2012
by Routledge
2 Park Square, Milton Park, Abingdon, Oxon OX14 4RN

Simultaneously published in the USA and Canada
by Routledge
711 Third Avenue, New York, NY 10017

Routledge is an imprint of the Taylor & Francis Group, an informa business

© 2012 P. Gamble

The right of Paul Gamble to be identified as author of this work has been asserted by him in accordance with sections 77 and 78 of the Copyright, Designs and Patents Act 1988.

All rights reserved. No part of this book may be reprinted or reproduced or utilised in any form or by any electronic, mechanical, or other means, now known or hereafter invented, including photocopying and recording, or in any information storage or retrieval system, without permission in writing from the publishers.

Trademark notice: Product or corporate names may be trademarks or registered trademarks, and are used only for identification and explanation without intent to infringe.

British Library Cataloguing in Publication Data
A catalogue record for this book is available from the British Library

Library of Congress Cataloging in Publication Data
Training for sports speed and agility : an evidence-based approach / edited by Paul Gamble.
  p. cm.
Includes bibliographical references and index.
1. Physical education and training. 2. Athletes—Training of. 3. Muscle strength. I. Gamble, Paul.
GV711.5.T73 2012
613.71—dc22
2011013051

ISBN: 978–0–415–59125–6 (hbk)
ISBN: 978–0–415–59126–3 (pbk)
ISBN: 978–0–203–80303–5 (ebk)

Typeset in Bembo and Stone Sans ITC Pro
by Prepress Projects Ltd, Perth, UK

 Printed and bound in Great Britain by
TJ International Ltd, Padstow, Cornwall

CONTENTS

List of figures   vii
List of tables   ix
Acknowledgements   x

PART I
Theory of sports speed and agility development   1

1 Introduction: what defines sports speed and agility?   3

2 Foundations of speed and agility expression in sports   7

3 Assessing physical parameters of speed and agility   19

4 Athleticism and movement skills development   40

PART II
Developing physical capabilities for speed and agility   47

5 Strength training for speed and agility development   49

6 Speed–strength development and plyometric training   73

7 Metabolic conditioning for speed and agility performance   92

8 Lumbopelvic 'core' stability   103

9 Warm-up methods and mobility training   122

PART III
Developing technical and perceptual aspects of sports speed and agility   133

10 Technical aspects of acceleration and straight-line speed development   135

11 Developing change of direction capabilities and expression of sports agility   142

PART IV
Designing the programme   155

12 Planning and scheduling: periodisation of training   157

References   167
Index   185

FIGURES

2.1	Spring–mass model during stance phase of running	8
2.2	Determinants of sports speed	17
2.3	Determinants of sports agility	18
3.1	Illinois agility test protocol	31
5.1	Single-leg barbell straight-legged deadlift	54
5.2	Split stance bilateral cable press	56
5.3	Split stance dumbbell row	57
5.4	Front-racked barbell alternate knee raise	58
5.5	Loaded overhead single-leg good morning	59
5.6	Front-racked barbell backward lunge	60
5.7	Barbell overhead forward lunge	61
5.8	Front-racked barbell lateral step-up	62
5.9	Front-racked barbell cross-over lateral step-up	63
5.10	Front-racked barbell diagonal single-leg squat	64
5.11	Barbell diagonal lunge	64
5.12	One-arm incline dumbbell bench press	65
5.13	Single-arm cable press	66
5.14	Single-arm cable row	66
5.15	Single-leg cable straight-arm pull-down	67
5.16	Front-racked B-drill	68
5.17	Cable-resisted leg drive	69
5.18	Dumbbell pivot, lunge and return (¼, ½, ¾ turns)	70
5.19	Cable-assisted lateral pivot, lunge and return	71
5.20	Single-leg cable arm drive	72
6.1	Barbell jump squat	80
6.2	Barbell bound step-up	81
6.3	Loaded split bound	82
6.4	¼, ½ and ¾ counter-movement pivot and bound into lunge	86

6.5	¼, ½ and ¾ drop pivot and bound into lunge	87
8.1	Single-leg balance with whole-body rotation	109
8.2	Swiss ball plank figure-eight exercise	111
8.3	Side bridge with hip flexion on domed device	112
8.4	Extended plank with alternate arm raise on domed device	113
8.5	Front plank with alternate arm/leg raise	114
8.6	Swiss ball alternate leg jackknife	115
8.7	Single-leg alternate arm cable press	116
8.8	Front plank with lateral dumbbell raise	117
8.9	Side-on single-leg cable push out	118
8.10	Swiss ball overhead Russian twist	119
8.11	Swiss ball hip rotation onto domed device	120
8.12	Single-leg cable-resisted rotation	121
10.1	Spring–mass model applied to the 'L-shaped double pendulum' model at foot strike and toe-off	137
11.1	¼, ½ and ¾ turns, near lead leg	148
11.2	¼, ½ and ¾ turns, far lead leg	149
11.3	Horizontal jump into reactive 45-degree or 90-degree cut	153

TABLES

3.1	Selected repeated sprint ability protocols	38
11.1	Parameters to categorise change of direction movement	147
12.1	Representative off-season training mesocycle	164
12.2	Representative pre-season training mesocycle	164
12.3	Representative competition or 'in-season' training mesocycle	165
12.4	Representative 'peaking' training mesocycle	166

ACKNOWLEDGEMENTS

The ability to coach speed and agility performance is classically the skill that any strength and conditioning specialist will acquire last of all, as it stems from a great deal of observation and experience. On that basis I must thank the athletes, sports coaches and other practitioners that I have had the privilege of working with and learning from.

But above all else this book is for Sian . . .

PART I
Theory of sports speed and agility development

1
INTRODUCTION

What defines sports speed and agility?

Defining sports speed and agility

An obvious first step when attempting to develop the capacities involved is to first define what constitutes speed and agility in sports. As will be discussed in the following chapter, a number of physical qualities and neuromuscular capabilities can be identified as contributing to speed and agility expression. There are therefore a number of avenues for the strength and conditioning specialist to explore; each of these may ultimately impact upon the athlete's ability to express speed and agility in competition.

It should also be recognised that both speed and agility are expressed in response to and according to the demands of the given situation in a match. The context in which these movements are performed therefore has a critical bearing on both the characteristics of the movement and in turn the nature of the physical, sensory and cognitive input required. Often tactical awareness or 'game sense' and decision-making are decisive attributes in terms of the athlete's ability to express their propensity for speed and change of direction performance.

The nature of the sport is clearly a defining aspect that governs what form speed and agility takes in the context of competition. However, even within the same sport, the types of speed and agility movement required vary according to the role allocated to the individual athlete, for example in a team context. Not only this, even for an individual player, the situation in a contest will further serve to determine the characteristic movement demands – an illustration of this is the different forms of speed and agility movement required when attacking versus defending. Focusing in further still, the unique constraints and demands of a given scenario in a match will ultimately define the specific movement response(s) necessitated by the situation.

Can speed and agility be taught?

The traditional view regarding speed performance has been that 'sprinters are born and not made'. Although some aspects of sprinting performance are dependent upon genetic factors, the consensus on this point has shifted over recent years and it is now acknowledged that speed abilities are trainable. There is much the same ongoing debate with respect to agility performance. Anecdotally, particularly in evasion sports, many coaches and observers are of the belief that the best performers with respect to agility capabilities possess these qualities as a 'natural ability'.

In an attempt to resolve these debates, there is a growing body of data which indicates that both change of direction performance and reactive agility can be developed by means of appropriate training interventions. Various studies have shown that the mechanics of the movements that constitute change of direction activities are amenable to change through instruction and appropriate movement skill practice in a way that reduces injurious lower limb stresses and also confers improvements in performance in many cases (Hewett et al., 2006a; Myers and Hawkins, 2010). Furthermore, the perceptual and decision-making aspects of agility also appear to be trainable even in elite performers. A short-term (3-week) training intervention designed to specifically develop these abilities by requiring the athlete to react to video images on a big screen during reactive agility drills successfully produced improvements in performance on a reactive agility test that were almost exclusively due to improved reaction time and decision-making (the movement time component of subjects scores was largely unchanged) (Serpell et al., 2011). However, despite the growing evidence to the contrary, in the field many coaches still hold the view that quick and agile athletes are born and not made.

What is also clear from the previous section is that what constitutes speed and agility expression in a particular sport and athlete is highly distinct and clearly defined by the unique constraints associated with the sport, the athlete and the match situation. To an extent sports may share common aspects in terms of athleticism or movement skill competencies. To the same extent, athletes in these sports may benefit from a generic approach when training to develop speed and movement skill capacities. However, for the athlete to ultimately realise an improvement in their ability to express their agility in the context of a match, the strength and conditioning specialist must have an intimate understanding of the intricacies of the characteristic movements required and the associated physical, metabolic, perceptual, cognitive and decision-making aspects involved.

Aspects of training that influence sports speed and agility expression

Part of the complexity of training to develop an athlete's speed and agility is that these abilities comprise a host of factors. Therefore a wide array of training aspects can conceivably contribute, individually and in combination, to improving these attributes. An obvious example of physical qualities that have the potential to influence performance is strength training. This training factor can increase the ground reaction force that the athlete is capable of generating, and in turn potentially increase propulsion and therefore running and change of direction speed.

The challenge is therefore not straightforward, particularly as the approach taken for each aspect of physical preparation must be considered and appropriate in order to positively influence speed and agility capabilities. Taking the previous strength training example, a number of different strength qualities are identified to predominate in different phases, even within a sprint in a straight line. Furthermore, conventional strength training modes employed in isolation are shown to have limited transfer to speed and change of direction performance. Similarly, a range of different energy systems and metabolic processes are implicated in sprint and repeated sprint performance.

The sprinting action itself represents a complex movement task – each stride requires execution of several individual aspects that must be coordinated and executed in a sequenced fashion with precise timing. The change of direction movements involved in agility activities feature numerous variations, and the athlete must possess the required movement competencies and underlying physical qualities to execute each of these movements efficiently. What represents sound movement technique may also differ for a given sport. For example, in collision sports the 'ideal' upright posture identified for maximal sprinting must often be modified (along with stride length) in order to allow the player to evade opponents, particularly when in congested space. Athletes from different sports are similarly observed to employ different movement strategies for the same movement tasks (Cowley et al., 2006).

A key consideration when designing training to develop sports speed and agility is the context in which these qualities are expressed during competition. The performance environment in the sport similarly involves perceptual and decision-making aspects that are unique to the sport and provide the context in which speed and agility movements are executed. In many sports, speed and agility activities are initiated in response to an event occurring in the competition environment – for example movement of an opponent. As such, perceptual and decision-making aspects are involved in the timing of the execution of these activities. The nature of the movement itself is similarly dictated by the situation facing the athlete.

An evidence-based approach to developing speed and agility performance

The corollary of identifying the 'physical' factors that might contribute to the expression of sports speed and agility is identifying the best approach to developing each of these individual factors. This is not as simple as it sounds. The strength and conditioning specialist must identify how best to train each of the individual components in the most effective and efficient manner, based upon the available research evidence in the literature. However, this must also be undertaken in such a way that the athlete will ultimately be capable of enhanced speed and agility performance. The latter involves two major challenges:

- identifying the means of developing the particular physical capacity in a way that facilitates transfer of training effects to speed and/or agility expression;
- coordinating all of the different elements of training in order to take account of the interaction between each of the different training stimuli and minimise interference effects.

Although there is growing consensus that the components that comprise speed and agility performance are trainable, what is much less clear from the available scientific literature is what the optimal approach to training speed and agility performance might be. Both 'sports speed' and particularly agility represent open motor skills on the basis that their expression is shaped by and initiated in response to events that occur in the competition environment. The approach taken to training sports speed and agility must therefore recognise the need for the coupling of perception and action, and the aim must be to develop these qualities as adaptive motor skills. There should therefore necessarily be an element of open motor skill learning during sports speed and agility development in order to incorporate perception–action coupling and account for development of perceptual and decision-making aspects, particularly in the latter stages of athletes' training (Serpell *et al.*, 2011).

2
FOUNDATIONS OF SPEED AND AGILITY EXPRESSION IN SPORTS

Introduction

Expression of speed in a straight line and agility each comprise a multitude of factors. This has two major implications for the strength and conditioning specialist when designing a programme of physical preparation to develop athletes' speed and agility performance. The first is that there is a requirement for detailed knowledge of the determinants of linear sprinting, change of direction and agility performance. The second is that developing speed and agility expression will require a multidimensional approach.

There is something of a paradox in that the various measures of change of direction and straight-line speed performance are relatively independent (Little and Williams, 2005) – and as such developing these capabilities will require dedicated training. However, the components of speed and change of direction performance remain inter-related to varying degrees (Vescovi and McGuigan, 2008) and athletes require each of the various qualities that underpin speed and agility in order to fully express these abilities in the context of their sport.

This paradox can be illustrated another way: a number of studies report that scores on measures of strength and power, for example, are correlated with speed and change of direction performance to varying degrees. However, training interventions for any one of these aspects employed in isolation have frequently been found to have only limited transfer to speed and particularly change of direction performance. The process of identifying the physiological and neuromuscular parameters that predict speed and change of direction performance remains important in order to elucidate the properties to be trained to enable the athlete's capacity for speed and agility expression to be developed (Reilly *et al.*, 2009). The inter-relationships between the identified determinants of speed and agility – and how best to achieve transfer of the respective training modes to speed and agility performance – are additional issues that require consideration.

Determinants of speed performance

Running locomotion can be conceptualised as a *planar spring–mass system* (Brughelli and Cronin, 2008). That is, during the stance phase the kinetic chain of joints from the athlete's supporting foot to their centre of mass acts like a spring with the athlete's centre of mass on top – hence 'spring–mass system'. Planar motion is described as a bouncing movement at a given velocity (Brughelli and Cronin, 2008). Thus, straight-line running can be viewed as forward bouncing motion in which the athlete acts like a spring (lower limb kinetic chain) with a mass (torso and head) on top (Figure 2.1).

Classically, sprinting speed is described to be the product of stride frequency and stride length. However, this description can be misleading and might appear to suggest that it is better to over-stride; this is not the case. Foot contact should occur directly underneath the athlete's centre of mass, as placing the foot in front of the body results in excessive braking forces (Nummela et al., 2007). It is therefore more accurate to say that sprinting speed is the product of stride frequency and the distance covered with each step (Weyand et al., 2010). In order to attain higher running speeds athletes are observed to increase both stride frequency and distance covered with each step up until a threshold speed, after which subsequent increments in speed are achieved solely with increased stride frequency (Nummela et al., 2007).

Stride frequency would appear to depend upon the time taken to recover, swing and reposition the limb prior to touchdown during the swing phase. The time taken to execute elements of the swing phase in turn appears to dictate the duration of ground contact during sprinting (Weyand et al., 2010). The distance covered with each step will be the net product of propulsion and braking forces generated during each foot contact and the resultant horizontal propulsion in a forward direction. In addition to horizontal force application the athlete must generate vertical ground reaction forces to counter impact forces and prevent any collapse upon foot contact. However, if the vertical forces

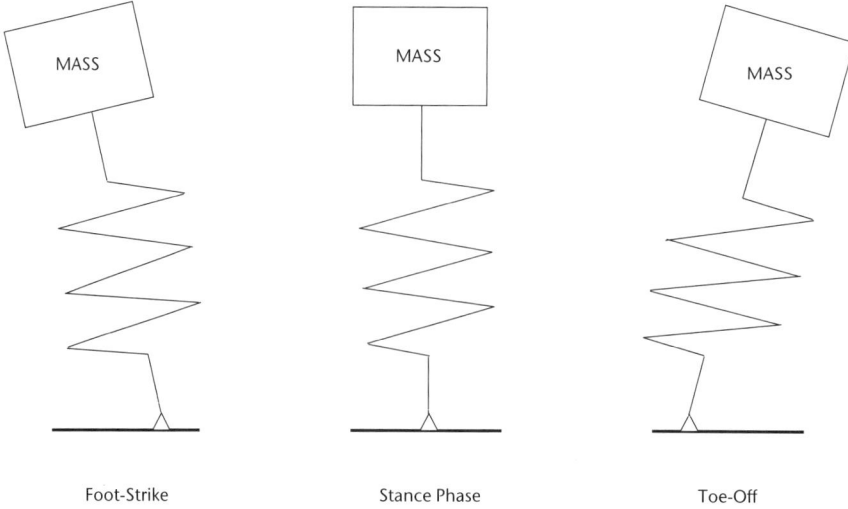

FIGURE 2.1 Spring–mass model during stance phase of running.

generated are excessive this will result in wasteful vertical motion, which is a characteristic of less economical runners. Although not modifiable by training, an athlete with longer limbs would be capable of covering a greater distance with each step (Weyand et al., 2010). Assuming they were also able to execute the swing phase efficiently enough to maintain a similar stride frequency this would confer faster running velocities.

There would seem to be a trade-off between stride frequency and the duration of ground contact with respect to the time this permits to generate propulsion. It has been identified that sprinting performance does not appear to be limited by the athlete's maximum force capabilities. A study of track athletes and team sports players found that these athletes were in fact capable of generating levels of force during hopping movements that exceeded those recorded during sprinting (Weyand et al., 2010). Hence, what appeared to limit the sprinting performance of the athletes studied is that they were unable to develop force rapidly enough within the brief period of ground contact during sprinting.

Faster athletes do, however, appear to be able to exert greater forces relative to body mass in a shorter period of ground contact (Weyand et al., 2010). Similar findings were also reported in a study of elite junior endurance athletes (Nummela et al., 2007). Horizontal ground reaction forces recorded relative to body mass during foot contact were strongly associated with maximal running speed performance. In addition to the association with maximal running speed, it was identified that athletes' ground contact time also strongly influenced running economy during a time trial over longer distance – that is, runners with superior running economy exhibited shorter ground contact times (Nummela et al., 2007). Optimising both force application and duration of ground contact when running and sprinting therefore has implications not only for maximal running speed but also for athletes' economy when performing running activity.

The 'stretch-shortening cycle' during locomotion

The planar spring–mass model of running locomotion described previously illustrates the importance of the storage and return of elastic energy during each foot strike with respect to propulsion during sprinting (Brughelli and Cronin, 2008). The 'stretch-shortening cycle' (SSC) refers to the augmentation of force and power output that is observed when movement is executed immediately following a countermovement or pre-stretch action (Wilson and Flanagan, 2008). This phenomenon is therefore implicated in the generation of propulsion via contractile and elastic elements with each foot strike when running.

The mechanisms underlying the SSC include a mechanical component and can also comprise neural and reflex aspects, depending on the nature of the movement. The mechanical component is associated with the storage of elastic energy by muscle and connective tissue structures during the countermovement or pre-stretch action, which is in turn released at a rapid rate and returned as kinetic energy during the subsequent concentric part of the movement (Wilson and Flanagan, 2008). The neural or reflex contribution to increased muscle activation and force output originates from the 'stretch reflex', which involves local reflex pathways at the spinal level that are triggered when sensory organs within the muscle–tendon complex are stimulated in response to a rapid change in length and tension.

There is a differentiation between 'fast' and 'slow' SSC actions, generally based upon the following criteria (Wilson and Flanagan, 2008):

- the time interval spanning preparatory 'preload' movement and concentric muscle action, or the duration of ground contact (in the case of sprinting and other 'bounding'-type activities);
- the degree of movement or 'angular displacement' that occurs through the joints of the limb(s) involved when performing the movement.

Because of the brief ground contact time and limited movement that occurs through lower limb joints of the stance leg between touchdown and 'toe-off' during sprinting, it is categorised as a fast SSC action (Wilson and Flanagan, 2008). As such, there is likely to be stretch reflex involvement in addition to a mechanical component. Conversely, many change of direction movements that are a feature of agility actions in sports involve longer ground contact times, more extended eccentric and concentric phases, and a greater degree of movement through lower limb joints. A number of these movements therefore fall into the slow SSC category and as such will depend largely on mechanical factors associated with storage and return of elastic energy.

Stiffness of the muscle–tendon unit is modifiable by both acute influences (muscle pre-activation) and chronic effects (training adaptation) (Wilson and Flanagan, 2008). Muscle pre-activation prior to touchdown not only influences stiffness and correspondingly mechanical properties (Belli *et al.*, 2002) but also potentiates reflex-mediated augmentation of power output during SSC activities (Ross *et al.*, 2001). Importantly, this is a learned effect that is responsive to training adaptation with repeated exposure to SSC movements. Similarly, characteristic changes in the mechanical properties of the musculotendinous unit are associated with performing regular SSC activity over an extended period. For example, triple jumpers and long jumpers have been shown to exhibit increased levels of musculotendinous stiffness measured during SSC activity (repeated hopping) (Rabita *et al.*, 2008).

Leg stiffness is associated with enhanced running economy and is also related to shorter ground contact times when running (Wilson and Flanagan, 2008). A relationship has also been reported between musculotendinous stiffness and rate of force development (Wilson *et al.*, 1994). In this way, neural and mechanical adaptations enhancing stiffness through the lower limb kinetic chain during ground contact can contribute to sprinting performance by both increased rate of force development and shorter ground contact times.

Postural control, strength and stability

The orientation of the body is shown to determine the net propulsion forces generated and associated parameters (including ground contact time) when accelerating (Kugler and Janshen, 2010). The ability to manipulate and control the orientation of the body and maintain a stable posture is therefore identified as a key factor that influences acceleration and speed performance over short distances. Indeed, one study identified that the forward orientation of the body was a more important factor than the ground reaction forces generated, in terms of determining horizontal propulsion (Kugler and Janshen, 2010).

It has also been identified that co-contraction of a variety of lumbar and trunk muscles serves to stiffen the spine and abdominal wall, which enables more efficient storage and return of elastic energy during dynamic movements such as running (McGill, 2010). The capacity to control lumbopelvic posture and stiffen the spine and torso prior to and during ground contact can thus influence storage and return of elastic energy during each foot strike in a similar fashion to that described previously for the extensor muscles of the lower limb. When functioning in this way, this 'torso/abdominal spring' might therefore be viewed as an extension of the linear 'spring' that comprises the lower limb, as depicted in the spring–mass model described in the previous section.

The importance of the capacity to stiffen the lumbopelvic region is also emphasised for agility tasks. The scenario described for change of direction movements is that torques generated at the hip are transmitted through a stiffened 'core' (McGill, 2010). Lateral trunk stability in particular has been shown to be a key factor in executing change of direction cutting movements safely and efficiently, particularly for female athletes. For example, a recent study of video captures of knee ligament injuries identified that the female athletes featured exhibited lateral trunk lean in combination with an abducted knee joint position during recordings of female athletes as they sustained anterior cruciate ligament injury on the video recording (Hewett et al., 2009).

Mechanical and morphological properties of locomotor muscles

The contractile properties of individual muscle fibres have been shown to be responsive to training. Increases in both shortening velocity and peak power output measures of single muscle fibres have been reported following a training intervention that employed SSC activities (Malisoux et al., 2006). These changes are related to morphological adaptations, such as myosin heavy chain (MHC) expression, discussed later in this section.

Mechanical properties of the muscle–tendon unit such as the compliance of series elastic components – that is, the relationship between stretch or elongation and force applied to the tendon and aponeurosis – can also impact upon force–velocity characteristics of the locomotor muscles, and thereby influence sprinting performance (Stafidis and Arampatzis, 2007). The relative elongation of series elastic components of knee extensor muscles under a given stretch load was identified as the factor that distinguished 'fast' from 'slow' subjects in a group of sprinters. The authors proposed that this mechanical property of the muscle–tendon unit is advantageous for storage of elastic energy by the knee extensors of the supporting limb during the initial part of ground contact when sprinting (Stafidis and Arampatzis, 2007).

Key aspects of morphology of the locomotor musculature with respect to speed performance include:

- relative proportion of fast twitch (type II) to slow twitch (type I) fibre types;
- length of muscle fibre fascicles;
- cross-sectional area of muscle fibres;
- expression of fibre subtypes and MHC isoforms;
- muscle architecture such as pennation angle.

The first two in the list (muscle fibre types and fascicle lengths) are primarily genetically determined. Elite sprinters are typically reported to possess quadriceps muscle fibre composition in the region of 60–80 per cent fast twitch type II fibres (Maughan and Gleeson, 2004a). Similarly, a study comparing the musculoskeletal structure of sprinters with that of non-sprinters found that the fascicle length measured from the lower leg (calf) muscles of sprinters was on average 11 per cent longer than that of non-sprinter subjects (Lee and Piazza, 2009). This contributed to a 50 per cent larger ratio of fascicle length to moment arm length in the lower legs of the sprinters studied.

Other characteristics are, however, modifiable by environmental factors such as strength, plyometric and sprint training. Preferential increases in cross-sectional area of type II muscle fibres have been reported by longer-term sprint training studies (Ross and Leveritt, 2001). However, these changes might be viewed as a secondary adaptation of strength, power and sprint training. It should be recognised that hypertrophy-oriented strength training is not appropriate for speed performance because of the suboptimal nature of training adaptations that are associated with this form of training, in terms of both force development capabilities and body composition.

Myosin heavy chain isoform expression is of direct relevance to speed performance as this pertains to the contractile characteristics exhibited by the muscle fibre – such as force development capabilities (Ross and Leveritt, 2001). There is some evidence that appropriate sprint training may induce a shift towards greater expression of MHC isoform (and muscle fibre subtype) type IIa. Studies reporting a significant shift towards type IIa MHC expression also report concurrent improvements in sprint performance. However, the form of sprint training undertaken appears to determine the nature of the training adaptation with respect to MHC expression – in particular training frequency and the duration of both work and rest periods employed. Sprint interval training with longer work bouts and incomplete recovery appears to elicit adaptations that are closer to those associated with endurance training (Ross and Leveritt, 2001).

Adaptations to muscle architecture – in particular pennation angle of muscle fibres – can influence force output independently of any changes in muscle cross-sectional area. Changes in muscle pennation angle have been reported in response to a period (14 weeks) of strength training (Aagaard *et al.*, 2001). Such adaptations may be elicited by various modes of training undertaken to enhance speed and agility performance (e.g. strength and power training, plyometrics, sprint training), with corresponding changes in force generating capacity of locomotor muscles.

Strength qualities for speed and change of direction performance

A number of strength qualities have been identified as being important for different phases of speed performance (Young *et al.*, 1995) and execution of change of direction movements (Sheppard and Young, 2006). Based upon kinematic analysis and examination of ground reaction forces during the sprinting action it has been reported that the primary role of both knee extensors and ankle extensors is to impose and maintain high levels of stiffness through the lower limb joints during the interval prior to and during foot contact (Belli *et al.*, 2002). Conversely it is the hip extensors that have been primarily identified as being the major contributors to generating propulsion.

Additionally, all of these muscle groups generate positive (concentric) and negative (eccentric) work at different intervals in the contact and flight phases of the sprinting action, corresponding to the motion of the hip and knee joints (Belli *et al.*, 2002). Indeed, when sprinting, the hamstring muscles that extend the hip and flex the knee are observed to undergo eccentric contraction during the latter part of the swing phase, before contracting concentrically during the early–middle part of the stance phase, and then finally undergoing eccentric contraction once more during the late stance phase (Yu et al., 2008).

Different strength qualities have been reported to predominate in different phases of a 50-m sprint (initial acceleration, speed over short distances, maximum speed) (Young et al., 1995). The importance of concentric force development has been highlighted for initial acceleration (0–10 m) performance (Sleivert and Taingahue, 2004). Sprinting at higher velocities appears to be more strongly associated with speed–strength measures that involve high force outputs over a brief interval of time (Young et al., 1995). Measures that combine reactive strength and fast SSC performance (drop jump height) similarly report stronger statistical relationships with sprinting performance over longer distances (Hennessy and Kilty, 2001).

Measures of speed–strength [hang power clean one repetition maximum (1-RM) scores] were reported to relate to straight-line sprinting speed but not performance on a simple change of direction test for a group of team sports athletes (Hori et al., 2008). These results suggest that the determining strength qualities for change of direction performance may differ from those for straight-line sprinting. Other studies featuring various tests of change of direction performance have similarly reported a lack of statistical relationship with a number of strength and speed–strength measures. That said, more simple change of direction measures involving only one 180-degree turn were shown to be moderately related to strength and speed–strength test scores, a finding similar to what was observed for straight-line speed tests (Jones et al., 2009). The reliance upon various strength qualities may therefore depend on the nature and complexity of the change of direction movements that are characteristic of agility movements in the particular sport.

Depending on the athlete's initial velocity and degree of deviation from their original path, change of direction movements will often comprise braking forces to decelerate the athlete, closely followed by propulsion forces that move the athlete in the new direction (Brughelli et al., 2008). The deceleration component of such change of direction activities and generation of braking forces that this involves demands certain strength qualities of both agonist and antagonist muscle groups, such as eccentric strength. Similarly, overcoming the athlete's own inertia to propel themselves and accelerate in the new direction of movement requires additional strength qualities, for example maximal strength and speed–strength (Jones et al., 2009).

Neuromuscular skill and coordination elements

The sprinting action is a cyclical action comprising sequential contact and flight phases (Belli et al., 2002). There is considerable coordination and skill involved in achieving optimal limb and foot placement at touchdown as well as timing and directing force application prior to and during each foot contact. The positioning of the limb and the foot immediately prior to touchdown strongly influences the braking and propulsion phases of ground contact when running (Nummela et al., 2007). The region of the foot that connects with the running surface at touchdown further influences both braking forces and storage and return of elastic energy during ground contact. The motion of the foot at the point when it connects with the ground is another critical consideration – if the foot is moving forwards braking forces will result, whereas if the foot is moving in a rearward direction at touchdown propulsion forces are exerted. Similarly, pre-activation of knee and hip extensors immediately prior to touchdown influences the stiffness of the locomotor muscles during ground contact, which in turn affects the athlete's ability to utilise stored elastic energy during each foot contact (Nummela et al., 2007).

The relative timing of force application during each foot contact is likewise critical in determining the magnitude of effective propulsion forces versus horizontal braking forces, as well as vertical ground reaction forces. The athlete's ability to maximise forces applied to generate horizontal propulsion during the restricted time window allowed by the brief period of ground contact has been identified as the critical element that determines sprinting performance (Weyand et al., 2010). In addition to horizontal force application the athlete must generate vertical ground reaction forces to counter impact forces and prevent any collapse upon foot contact. However, applying excessive vertical forces at touchdown will result in wasteful vertical motion, which is a characteristic of less economical runners (Nummela et al., 2007). Faster athletes are observed to produce only moderate vertical impulse relative to body mass (Hunter et al., 2005). The key parameter is therefore the *effective vertical impulse*, which should be relatively low and closely married to impact forces in a negative (downwards) direction but still sufficient in magnitude to prevent any collapse at touchdown.

Agility movements in particular involve a critical need for the sensorimotor capabilities associated with mobility, stability and body awareness. Athletes must possess the necessary joint range of motion, intermuscular coordination and strength qualities throughout their lower limb kinetic chain in order to properly execute change of direction movements. This includes aspects of postural stability (e.g. proprioception and kinaesthetic sense of body segments in three-dimensional space) as well as the specific neuromuscular and sensorimotor abilities associated with dynamic stabilisation.

Metabolic bases of speed and agility performance

In view of the brief duration and short distances that are characteristic of high-intensity efforts during intermittent sports, the ability to utilise high-rate metabolic pathways – that is, phosphagen [adenosine triphosphate (ATP)–phosphocreatine] and glycolytic systems – is widely identified as a key determinant of sports speed performance (Ross and Leveritt, 2001). In fact, the respective maximal running speeds supported by aerobic and anaerobic metabolism for an individual athlete have each been identified as significant predictors of that athlete's high-speed running performance capacities. Using the athlete's measured maximum velocity at maximal oxygen uptake (vVO_2max) and the maximum running speed that the athlete is able to sustain for approximately 3 seconds it is possible to predict the athlete's performance for all-out running efforts ranging from 3 to 240 seconds' duration (Bundle et al., 2003).

On the basis that the majority of sports require repeated bouts of high-speed locomotion, the ability to maintain a high level of function throughout successive high-intensity efforts is a critical factor. Characteristic changes are observed to occur with repeated sprints that alter the linear spring properties of the lower limb kinetic chain as described by the spring–mass model, and these changes are accompanied by reductions in propulsion forces and stride frequency in particular (Girard et al., 2011).

Both the *power* – rate of energy (ATP) production – and the *capacity* of metabolic systems are of relevance when performing repeated bouts of speed and agility performance. In addition to the phosphagen and glycolytic systems, aerobic metabolism is also implicated in the capacity for repeated sprint performance (Bishop et al., 2004). For example, the oxidative capacity of the muscle is related to its ability to resynthesise phosphocreatine (Bogdanis et al., 1996). Aside from supporting recovery from high-intensity intermittent exercise, the direct contribution of aerobic metabolism to energy provision can also be significant – particularly when consecutive high-intensity efforts are performed, even if extended rest is allowed between bouts (Bogdanis et al., 1996).

A critical aspect of fatigue resistance when performing repeated bouts of high-intensity running activity is the capacity to counteract the adverse effects of peripheral and central fatigue on lower limb mechanical properties and sprinting mechanics (Wilson and Flanagan, 2008). For example, the capacity to clear lactate and buffer hydrogen ions released as a result of glycolytic energy production is a key aspect that influences the athlete's ability to offset changes in muscle pH and continue to sustain work output when performing repeated high-intensity efforts (Ross and Leveritt, 2001). Muscle buffering capacity is therefore identified as a key determinant of repeated sprint ability (Bishop et al., 2004). Other fatigue mechanisms identified with repeated sprint activity involve the accumulation of inorganic phosphate (Pi) within the muscle cell (Glaister, 2005) and leakage of potassium ions from the muscle cell (Iaia and Bangsbo, 2010). Muscle oxidative capacity and sodium/potassium pump activity, respectively, are the physiological parameters implicated with these particular fatigue mechanisms.

Sensory, perceptual and decision-making aspects of sports speed and agility

A key factor for agility tasks in particular is the use of visual input when executing and coordinating movement. One example of this is the landing activities employed in sports such as netball and basketball for which subjects are observed to employ visual cues to coordinate muscle activation prior to and during touchdown (Santello et al., 2001). This in turn modulates ground reaction forces and lower limb kinematics upon landing. The importance of this visual regulation of preparatory and touchdown phases of landing is illustrated by the observation that when visual input is removed landings are characterised by greater and more variable ground reaction forces and altered joint kinematics (Santello et al., 2001).

The particular movement strategy adopted by an athlete is shown to vary even when negotiating a fixed course – such as a slalom course in the sport of downhill skiing. This appears to be a relatively unconscious process as the movement response that the athlete opts for in a given situation is in some cases contrary to their pre-race strategy (Supej, 2010). Critical factors that will govern the chosen movement response include approach speed and the degree of cut required to make the turn and avoid the obstacle. Perceptual aspects appear to similarly influence movement parameters during running change of direction movements, even when executing a pre-planned movement. This is illustrated by another study which reported that even the presence of a static dummy 'defender' (a model skeleton) markedly altered athletes' movement kinetics and kinematics compared with trials with the same pre-planned movement task but negotiating a cone placed on the floor (McLean et al., 2004).

Executing movement responses under unanticipated conditions presents considerably different sensorimotor challenges to those faced when the athlete is able to predict and plan the change of direction movement. Read and react agility tasks, for example interceptive movements that require anticipating and responding to the motion of an opponent or ball, require the athlete to process and interpret cues from the environment in order to prepare the movement response. There are various perceptual aspects and cognitive abilities such as anticipation and decision-making involved in these processes. The total time required to complete a change of direction movement task is accordingly greater under conditions in which the athlete is required to react and respond to an external cue than under pre-planned conditions (Farrow et al., 2005). Aside from the impact on movement times, the greater complexity of the corresponding neuromuscular control challenge also results in measurably different movement kinetics and kinematics when performing the same change of direction task under reactive conditions (Besier et al., 2001).

The 'information–movement coupling' involved in selecting, initiating and controlling movement responses is dependent upon the athlete's capacity to utilise cues from the external environment. Studies have demonstrated that skilled performers exhibit faster and more accurate movement responses (Holmberg, 2009). This has been attributed to a superior ability to detect, select and process task-relevant cues from the environment in which the movement is performed.

In the case of interceptive movements, there are various sensory, perceptual and decision-making aspects that govern the ability to anticipate, regulate and adapt movement responses. In ball sports, skilled performers have been shown to adopt a 'predictive movement strategy' whereby they select and initiate movement responses in advance based on anticipation of their opponent's shot selection and their expectations of the resulting trajectory of the ball (Gillet et al., 2010). This involves the ability to deduce shot selection from advance cues derived from the environment such as the movement behaviour of the opponent. There are in turn further experiential and perceptual aspects associated with judging the expected flight and bounce of the ball.

It has been observed that these anticipated movement responses are then refined in motion according to the actual trajectory of the ball, and these late adjustments comprise further visuo-motor abilities (Gillet et al., 2010). In this way, information–movement coupling also determines how movement responses are subsequently modified once the movement response is under way (Le Runigo et al., 2010). Finally, expert performers demonstrate superior capacity to react and respond when late deviations occur in the flight of the ball. Specifically, there are measurable differences reported in 'visuo-motor delay', that is, time elapsed between detecting a deviation and initiating an adjustment in movement response. As a result, when these late deviations occur expert players are better able to make the correction required in a timely manner (Le Runigo et al., 2010).

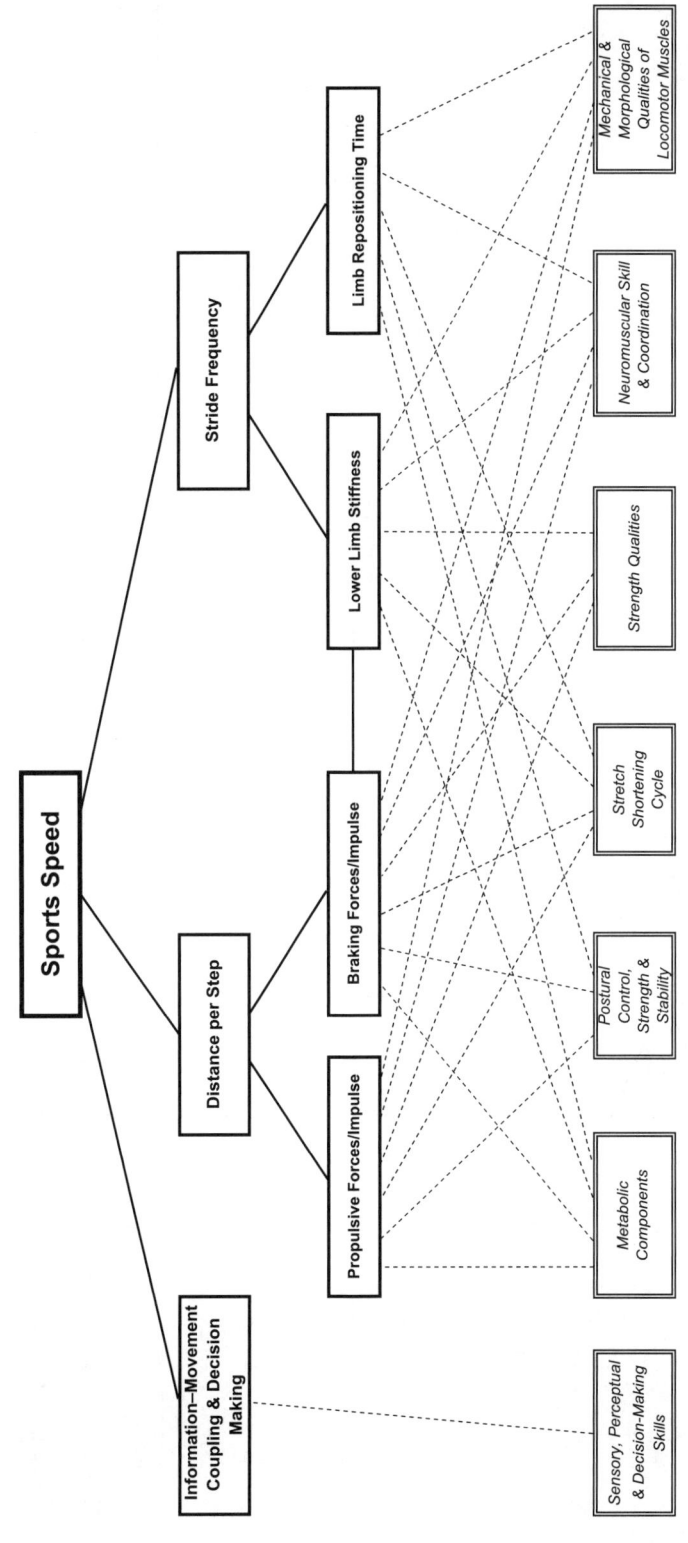

FIGURE 2.2 Determinants of sports speed.

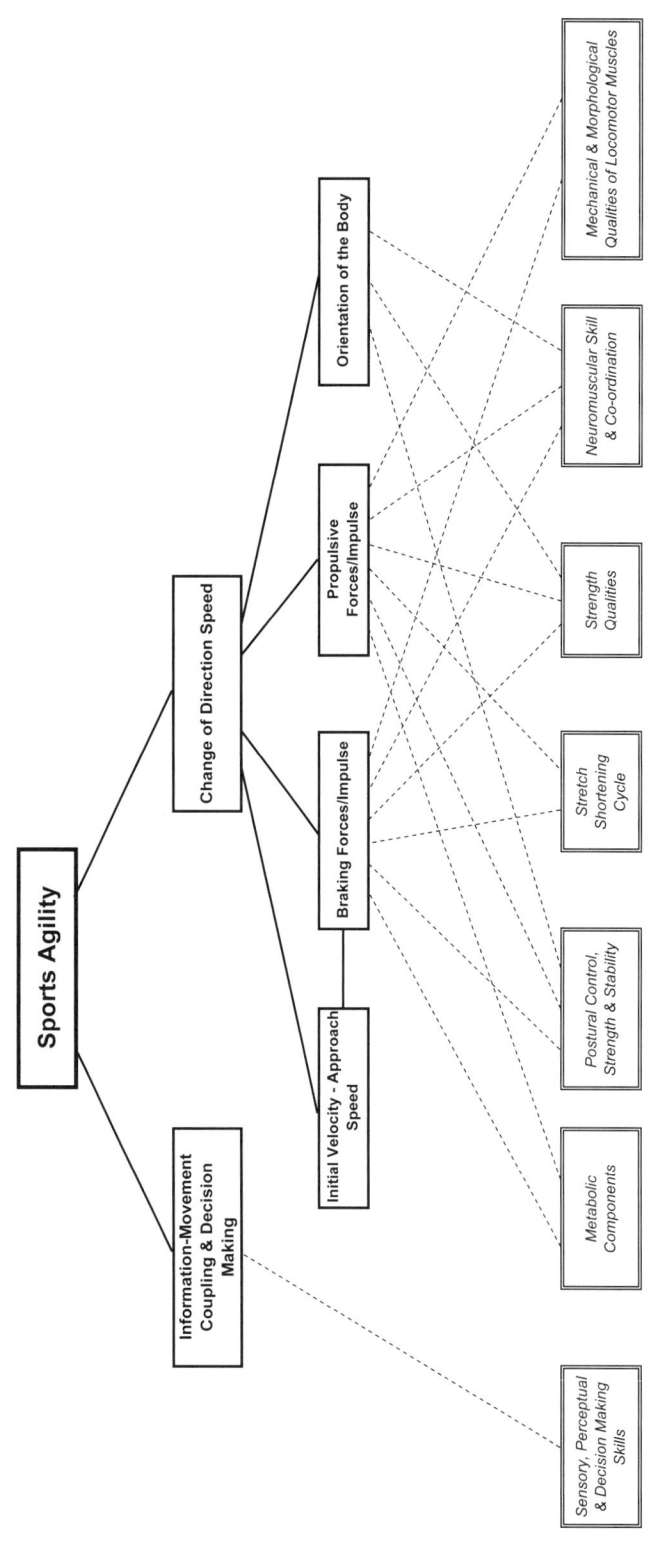

FIGURE 2.3 Determinants of sports agility.

3
ASSESSING PHYSICAL PARAMETERS OF SPEED AND AGILITY

Introduction

Assessment is a crucial adjunct to athletes' physical preparation to develop speed and agility. Testing serves three primary objectives (Reilly *et al.*, 2009):

1. profiling the athlete with respect to the identified physiological and neuromuscular determinants of speed and agility performance, either to identify areas requiring development or for the purposes of talent identification;
2. monitoring training adaptation in each relevant area with reference to the identified needs of the athlete;
3. critically evaluating the effectiveness of the athlete's training with respect to achieving the identified goals of the training programme.

Ultimately, the value of testing can principally be judged upon its utility in guiding or refining the training prescribed to the athlete (Reilly *et al.*, 2009). As such, modes of assessment must fulfil the following criteria:

- prove *valid* in that the test mode successfully evaluates the particular physiological and neuromuscular factors that influence speed and agility expression;
- produce *reliable* results so that there is a degree of confidence that any registered change in test scores represents a real change in performance on the test rather than random variability;
- be sufficiently *sensitive* to detect the relatively small and highly specialised adaptations characteristically observed with highly trained athletes.

Selecting a test battery

There are a large number and wide variety of measures of speed and change of direction that are employed in different sports. Likewise, there are numerous test modes and protocols used to evaluate the neuromuscular and physiological parameters that are deemed to be determinants of speed and agility performance (see Chapter 2). Selecting the most appropriate test therefore represents a key challenge.

Fundamentally, any form of assessment is useful only to the extent that it is relevant to the aspect of performance it is designed to measure, or effective in evaluating the physiological or neuromuscular components that underpin performance. One aspect of establishing the extent to which test scores and performance measures are related is how they vary over time (Nimphius *et al.*, 2010). This is contrary to most investigations, which are based on a one-off measurement with the results subsequently interpreted in an attempt to ascertain a causal relationship. Longitudinal studies tracking a number of tests and performance measures over time highlight that the statistical relationships between test measures and markers of performance may also vary when assessed at different time intervals over an extended period (Nimphius *et al.*, 2010). This raises questions about the wisdom of making assumptions regarding the degree of any causal relationship with a particular aspect of performance based upon a single set of measurements.

Furthermore, it is important that testing be not only systematic but also time efficient: the greater the amount of time a battery of tests takes to complete the less likely it is that testing will be conducted with sufficient regularity to track fluctuations in performance (Gamble, 2009a). Given this, being selective in the number and array of tests that feature in the final test battery is critical from a practical viewpoint (Reilly *et al.*, 2009). The final selection of tests may have further consequences in view of the observation that strength and conditioning specialists naturally tend to design athletes' training in a way that favours improvements on the particular performance measures which feature in the chosen test battery (Brown *et al.*, 2004). In this case the selection of assessment methods assumes greater importance on the basis that it may ultimately influence the training that is prescribed to the athlete.

Assessing strength qualities

Maximum strength

Measures of maximum lower-body strength are considered important to speed capabilities on the basis that running performance depends to a large extent on the ability to impart ground reaction forces during each foot contact, which in turn is related to the maximum force-generating capacity of the lower-body musculature (McBride *et al.*, 2009). Leg strength qualities are also identified as a determinant of change of direction performance abilities (Sheppard and Young, 2006). Modes of strength assessment can be categorised as 'isometric', 'isokinetic' or 'isoinertial', based upon the conditions involved in the test.

Isometric strength testing modes evaluate strength or maximum force output under static conditions: the athlete applies maximal force against rigid and immovable apparatus, and there is no change in joint angle while the athlete (statically) applies force (Abernethy *et al.*, 1995). A force transducer measures forces applied against the apparatus or alternatively a force platform can be used to quantify ground reaction forces applied through the athlete's feet, for example in the case of a (static) squat movement (Wilson and Murphy, 1996). Measured force output is highly dependent upon test conditions, particularly the joint angle(s) involved. Furthermore, isometric strength measures recorded under static conditions provide very limited information about strength qualities under dynamic conditions – hence, the relevance of this form of strength assessment with respect to speed and agility performance may be questioned.

Isokinetic strength assessment involves costly and highly specialised test apparatus (an isokinetic dynamometer) that enables torques generated against a lever arm moving at a preset and constant angular velocity to be recorded. Under appropriate test conditions this form of assessment provides highly reliable results for knee flexion and extension across a range of velocities. However, the validity of these test modes is limited by the fact that they are typically performed seated and involve single-joint movements, with the athlete strapped into the apparatus to restrict any extraneous movement of torso or other limbs. Thus, there is very little biomechanical similarity in terms of both posture and movement characteristics between the test movement and what occurs during locomotion. In accordance with this, isokinetic strength measures were not found to be sufficiently sensitive to detect positive changes in running performance elicited by a successful training intervention (Murphy and Wilson, 1997).

Isoinertial strength testing is therefore the preferred mode of assessment for evaluating maximum strength in a way that bears most relation to athletic performance (Gamble, 2009a). This form of strength testing involves maximal efforts performed using conventional strength training modes – that is, resistance machines or free weights exercises. Of these, free weights-based assessment would appear the most valid on the basis that test modes which employ resistance machines are commonly performed seated and the apparatus restricts the movement to a fixed plane, which reduces the biomechanical specificity in a similar way as described with isokinetic dynamometry. Commonly used isoinertial strength test modes of possible relevance to speed and agility performance include versions of the classical powerlifts (a misnomer), for example barbell squat and barbell deadlift.

The standard isoinertial test measure is the one repetition maximum (1-RM), expressed as the highest load the athlete is able to lift for one complete repetition, although submaximal tests also exist that involve completing multiple repetitions (e.g. 3-RM, 5-RM). It has been suggested that relative strength measures (i.e. expressed relative to the athlete's body mass) are of more relevance to speed and change of direction performance than absolute strength scores, in view of the fact that the associated strength demands specifically involve the athlete overcoming the inertia of their own body mass (Nimphius *et al.*, 2010). In support of this, relative but not absolute strength scores on a 1-RM barbell squat demonstrated a statistical relationship to sprint times over various distances in college American football players (Brechue *et al.*, 2010). Another study of college football players similarly reported significant positive statistical relationships between free weight barbell squat 1-RM scores expressed relative to body mass and sprint performance over both 10 and 40 yards (McBride *et al.*, 2009).

Results of studies investigating the relationship between strength measures and change of direction performance have been more equivocal. A number of studies have failed to demonstrate any correlation between maximum strength measures and change of direction performance (Brughelli *et al.*, 2008). However, one study did report that maximum strength scores on a free weight barbell squat expressed relative to body mass were statistically related to performance on both speed and change of direction tests in a sample of female national-level softball players (Nimphius *et al.*, 2010).

Eccentric strength

In much the same way as concentric strength measures, both isokinetic and isoinertial test modes can be employed to evaluate eccentric strength. Assessment of eccentric strength using isokinetic dynamometry involves similar issues of validity as described for concentric strength assessment. Although less widely used, isoinertial modes of maximum eccentric strength assessment do exist. Field-based isoinertial tests of eccentric strength evaluate the maximum load that the athlete can lower through a predetermined range of motion for a set time interval (e.g. 3 seconds). Other modes of isoinertial assessment employ similar protocols, but incorporate force platform apparatus in order to quantify ground reaction forces. The latter form of assessment requires costly and specialised equipment as well as trained staff to operate, which are not often available to the majority of athletes.

There is currently a lack of studies exploring the relationship between isoinertial eccentric strength measures and speed and/or change of direction performance. However, one study has reported that an isokinetic measure of knee extensor eccentric strength did show a slight positive statistical relationship with performance on a change of direction test (Jones *et al.*, 2009).

Strength endurance

The majority of tests of strength endurance involve performing repetitions to exhaustion with body weight exercises – examples include maximum pull-up and push-up tests. However, tests involving external resistance that employ conventional resistance training modes do also exist, and these similarly involve performing a maximal number of repetitions (through the full range of motion) with a set load (Sierer *et al.*, 2008). Studies relating strength endurance to measures of speed and change of direction performance currently appear to be lacking. However, these strength qualities may have potential relevance to speed performances over longer distances (requiring speed endurance) and repeated sprint ability.

Anaerobic power or 'speed–strength'

It should be recognised that developing propulsion forces when running requires not only the ability to develop high levels of force, but more importantly also the capacity to generate these forces rapidly during the narrow time window permitted during ground contact. On this basis, it follows that specific measures of 'speed–strength' qualities that reflect the athlete's ability to develop ground reaction forces 'explosively' will be of relevance to their speed and agility performance. Testimony to the perceived importance of 'explosive' power or speed–strength with respect to sports performance (Abernethy *et al.*, 1995), a broad range of testing modalities have been employed to assess these qualities.

Isokinetic dynamometry

Isokinetic testing at higher angular velocities has been employed as a measure of both high-velocity strength and speed–strength. As discussed previously the validity of this form of testing for evaluating speed–strength performance is questionable. Indeed, isokinetic measures of knee flexor and knee extensor torques have been shown to bear no relation to sprint times over any distance (0–5 m, 0–10 m or 0–30 m) in team sports players (professional and semi-professional rugby league players) (Cronin and Hansen, 2005). This finding is in keeping with the lack of biomechanical specificity of the single-joint open kinetic chain movements involved in this form of assessment with respect to the coordinated multi-joint movements that feature in athletic performance (Cronin and Hansen, 2005).

Measures of rate of force development

Given the limited time window for application of force during ground contact when running, the rate with which the athlete is capable of applying force is potentially a more relevant parameter with respect to speed performance than standard measures of maximum strength. However, the conditions under which rate of force development (RFD) is evaluated as well as the measure of RFD selected (peak versus mean RFD) both impact upon the validity, reliability and sensitivity of this measure.

A concentric measure of RFD was shown to be capable of discriminating between good and poor performers on a sprint test, whereas the isometric RFD test failed to do so (Wilson *et al.*, 1995). Similarly, RFD scores assessed under isometric conditions failed to register any changes in response to ballistic, plyometric or strength-oriented lower-body training, even though improvements were demonstrated in measures of athletic performance (Wilson *et al.*, 1993).

The measure of RFD selected is another key consideration, particularly from the point of view of reliability. Measures of peak RFD are highly unreliable because this method essentially involves selecting a single point on the force–time curve; as a result there is considerable risk of random error of measurement. As an average value derived from the force–time curve, mean RFD scores represent a more robust and reliable measure. From a practical point of view, measurement of RFD also requires expensive and not easily portable equipment, such as a force plate, as well as trained staff to operate it, both of which are unlikely to be readily available for many athletes.

Jump squat assessment of power output

Jump squat test modes employ a variation of the free weight barbell squat during which the subject propels the load – that is, jumps into the air – at the termination of the concentric phase of the movement. These tests have often employed a Smith machine-type apparatus. This equipment permits only vertical motion as the barbell slides on vertical runners. However, linear position transducer and accelerometer devices are now commercially available that permit this form of assessment to be conducted under unrestricted conditions with standard free weights.

Power output scores for both conventional parallel barbell jump squats and split barbell jump squats performed in a Smith machine reported a statistical relationship with recorded horizontal propulsion forces and 'initial acceleration' sprint times over 5 m from a standing start (Sleivert and Taingahue, 2004). It has been highlighted that the use of

Smith machine-type apparatus that restricts the motion of the barbell may affect the validity of the measure with respect to speed performance. Scores on an unrestricted jump squat (jump squat height and calculated power output expressed relative to body mass) were able to discriminate between 'fast' and 'slow' performers on a 30-m sprint test in a group of professional and semi-professional rugby league players (Cronin and Hansen, 2005). Such correlations between jump squat test measures and change of direction performance have proved more elusive, with the majority of studies reporting no significant relationship (Brughelli *et al.*, 2008).

Methodological issues determining jump squat power output and 'P_{max}' load

It has been identified that the apparatus and calculation method employed when determining power output during jump squat testing have a considerable impact upon the power output values derived (Cormie *et al.*, 2007a). In particular, serious concerns have been raised with regard to jump squat test modes that rely solely upon a linear position transducer attached to the bar to calculate power output values from the athlete plus barbell mass, alongside derived speed–time and acceleration data from the displacement measurements. This calculation method involves various assumptions that are not necessarily valid, the result of which is that derived power output values are found to be significantly overestimated (Cormie *et al.*, 2007a). Other test modes employ a linear position transducer in combination with a force plate, so that power output is derived from both force–time data and a speed–time curve derived from recorded displacement data. This method produces power output values that are closer to the correct values; however, this is the case only if the jump squat test trials do not involve any horizontal motion (Cormie *et al.*, 2007a). In addition, the necessity to incorporate a force plate during testing renders this form of speed–strength assessment less accessible to many athletes because of the cost and difficulty obtaining access to such specialised equipment.

The practice of undertaking jump squat trials over a range of loads in order to plot a load versus power output curve has also become common, in part to identify the load at which power output is maximised ('P_{max}'). However, methodological flaws in the way that power output is typically calculated when using such an approach have been demonstrated to produce inaccurate individual power output values, and this effectively warps the shape of the resulting plot of load versus power output (Cormie *et al.*, 2007b). When values are calculated using the correct method and the load–power output curve is therefore plotted correctly it has been demonstrated that power output for the barbell jump squat is in fact maximised at 0 per cent of 1-RM squat load for both adolescent (Dayne *et al.*, 2011) and college-aged male athlete subjects (Cormie *et al.*, 2007b). The P_{max} load for these athletes therefore equates to the athlete's own body mass without any external load.

The practical importance of this P_{max} value is also increasingly questioned. A study of senior elite rugby union players reported that the difference in power outputs at loads above or below each player's identified P_{max} value was minimal. Power outputs at loads 10 per cent and 20 per cent more or less than the identified P_{max} load on average differed by only 1.4 per cent and 5.4 per cent respectively (Harris *et al.*, 2007a). In terms of practical application, P_{max} values also vary with different lower-body resistance exercise modes (Cormie *et al.*, 2007c); hence, test values cannot be generalised to other training exercises.

Olympic weightlifting repetition maximum testing

Other approaches to speed–strength assessment involving external resistance employ repetition maximum testing using variations of the Olympic lifts. The power clean is generally chosen because of the familiarity of this lift for most players and the fact that it has a distinct end point – that is, the player either fails or manages to catch the bar at the top of the lift (Gamble, 2009a). Although it is possible to quantify power output during these tests, the generation of horizontal as well as vertical forces involved during the movement makes it more difficult to calculate power output values accurately, as described in the previous section.

In a study of college American football players power clean 1-RM test values expressed relative to body mass showed a statistical positive relationship with sprint performance, particularly over shorter distances with an emphasis on acceleration ability (Brechue et al., 2010). Another study similarly found that, when subjects were divided into 'strong' and 'weak' groups based upon hang power clean 1-RM scores expressed relative to body mass, the 'stronger' athletes also exhibited superior performance on a 20-m sprint test (Hori et al., 2008). However, 1-RM hang clean scores relative to body mass failed to discriminate between these subjects' respective performances on a simple test of change of direction performance in the same way.

Vertical jump testing

Vertical jump tests are commonly employed as a standard generic measure of lower-body power, and the actions of jumping and sprinting are identified as having biomechanical, kinetic and kinematic elements in common (Hennessy and Kilty, 2001). Variations of this test can be used to qualify concentric-only performance (squat jump) versus eccentric–concentric performance (countermovement jump). Finally, the drop jump variation of the test (initiated by dropping off a box of a prescribed height) is used to incorporate reactive (speed–)strength qualities (see 'Measures of reactive speed–strength and stretch-shortening cycle performance').

Single-leg versions of the vertical jump provide unilateral measures of speed–strength (Young et al., 2001a), and this also permits comparison of dominant versus non-dominant legs (Newton et al., 2006). Variations also exist to the standard vertical jump test executed from a stationary position, such as the one-step lead-in technique for the (bilateral) countermovement jump (Lawson et al., 2006). A variety of one-, three- and five-step approaches have likewise been employed during vertical jump and reach testing.

Although results of studies differ, countermovement vertical jump measures have been reported to show a degree of positive statistical relationship with performance on a straight-line sprint in college-level team sports athletes (Vescovi and McGuigan, 2008). Likewise, greater countermovement jump height has been associated with faster sprinting performance over various distances in a study of female sprinters (Hennessy and Kilty, 2001).

Both countermovement jump height and 30-cm drop jump height have reported positive statistical relationships with performance on a simple change of direction test (Jones et al., 2009). Positive correlations between countermovement vertical jump height and two (more complex) change of direction tests (Pro Agility and Illinois test) were weak but significant among high school and college soccer and lacrosse players (Vescovi and McGuigan, 2008). Other studies have similarly reported low to moderate positive relationships between standard vertical jump measures and various tests of change of direction performance (Brughelli et al., 2008).

Horizontal jump testing

Standing long jump and standing triple jump are also used to measure lower-body power in a horizontal direction. These tests require generation of both horizontal and vertical ground reaction forces, which would appear to better reflect what occurs during running activities. Hence, it is postulated that horizontal jump ability will be highly related to sprint performance (Holm et al., 2008). Single-leg versions of horizontal jump tests also exist, which would seem to replicate closer still the unilateral horizontal propulsion that occurs during running (Meylan et al., 2009). Finally, in addition to bilateral and unilateral horizontal jump tests in a forwards direction, lateral (single-leg) horizontal jump measures have also been investigated.

Horizontal jump test measures often report higher positive correlations with change of direction performance than those reported with vertical jump testing (Brughelli et al., 2008). However, one study that allows direct comparisons between a bilateral horizontal jump test measure (standing long jump) and a bilateral vertical jump test with respect to 20-yard and 40-yard speed measures and a change of direction test (T-test) reported that, although both measures showed moderate positive relationships with straight-line speed measures, there was a stronger relationship for the vertical jump measure than for the horizontal jump test measure (Peterson et al., 2006). That said, the horizontal jump test measure reported the stronger relationship with T-test change of direction performance in this study.

Performance on a unilateral (single-leg) horizontal jump test was reported to show a significant positive correlation with subjects' corresponding 10-m sprint performance (Meylan et al., 2009). Performance on the single-leg horizontal countermovement jump test measure has also been identified as the best predictor of subjects' performance on a change of direction test out of the three (vertical, horizontal and lateral) single-leg jump tests assessed in this study (Meylan et al., 2009).

Measures of reactive speed–strength and stretch-shortening cycle performance

Reactive speed–strength assessments involve the coupling of eccentric and concentric muscle actions as the athlete decelerates their own momentum prior to initiating propulsion in a positive direction (Newton and Dugan, 2002). In addition to eccentric and concentric contractile properties, these tests also involve a stretch-shortening cycle (SSC) contribution to force output. The most common test of this type is the drop (vertical) jump, whereby a vertical jump is executed immediately after dropping from a box of a specified height.

The height of box selected for the drop jump test will influence drop jump performance. The major factors with respect to the selection of an optimal drop height include the individual athlete's eccentric strength capabilities and previous exposure to drop jump plyometric training. Plotting athletes' jump heights from a range of drop heights is a method employed to evaluate and monitor reactive strength and SSC performance. If a force platform or contact mat is employed during drop jump testing a 'reactive strength index' can also be derived. This is typically calculated as the ratio between jump height or flight time during the jump and ground contact time during the jump (Newton and Dugan, 2002).

In much the same way as described for conventional jump testing, variations of the drop jump test exist that involve jumping for horizontal distance rather than vertical height. These tests therefore assess contractile and SSC performance during the coupling of eccentric muscle action in a predominantly vertical direction followed by generation of a combination of vertical and horizontal ground reaction forces. The single-leg version of the horizontal drop jump in particular has received some attention in the literature (Holm et al., 2008). This test is conducted in a similar way to the drop vertical jump: a 20-cm box is typically used and the athlete aims to jump for maximum horizontal distance (landing on two feet) whilst minimising ground contact time.

Drop vertical jump height has demonstrated a positive statistical relationship with faster sprinting performance in female sprinters (Hennessy and Kilty, 2001). The single-leg drop jump in a horizontal direction has also been investigated and kinetic and kinematic parameters of performance on this test have been evaluated in relation to subjects' corresponding sprint performance. Horizontal distance achieved during single-leg drop jump trials correlated with both overall 25-m sprint performance and the 5- and 10-m split times of regional-level team sports players (Holm et al., 2008).

Triple-hop distance is another measure of reactive speed–strength and SSC performance in a horizontal direction (Hamilton et al., 2008). Executing repeated hops again requires considerable athleticism, balance and postural stability. As such, an extended familiarisation period involving a large number of practice trials will be necessary prior to testing, in view of the finding that subjects' familiarity with the movement will influence the reliability of scores between trials (Markovic et al., 2004). Performance on the triple-hop test was shown to be positively related to vertical jump performance in male and female collegiate soccer players (Hamilton et al., 2008). A five-hop variation of this test was shown to identify differences in performance between dominant and non-dominant limbs among collegiate female softball players (Newton et al., 2006).

Measures of straight-line acceleration

Two distinct acceleration phases have been identified within a sprint test over 40 yards (36.58 m), described by the authors as 'initial acceleration' and 'middle acceleration' (Brown et al., 2004). Initial acceleration or 'first-step quickness' has commonly been evaluated using 5-m and 10-m sprint times (or split times over these distances), whereas sprint times over slightly longer distances (10 m or 15 m) are taken as a more global indicator of acceleration ability. Whereas first-step quickness time over 5 m and acceleration 10-m times correlated closely in semi-professional and professional rugby league players, these measures were reported to be less closely related to players' corresponding maximal speed scores assessed over 30 m (Cronin and Hansen, 2005).

Another consideration is the choice of starting position when assessing acceleration (and speed performance in general). When conducting the test from a stationary start, different starting positions (e.g. split stance versus crouch start) should be considered depending upon the postures from which athletes initiate movement during competition.

Assessment of maximum straight-line running speed

A common practice in the United States in particular is to employ sprints over 40 yards for the assessment of maximum straight-line running speed (Brechue *et al.*, 2010). The 40-yard test appears repeatedly in fitness test batteries, including those employed for selection purposes such as the NFL Combine. Other sports employ total sprint distances of 30 m and 40 m, and this appears to be largely determined by what the convention is for the particular sport. As a result, there is considerable normative data published over these distances, which offers coaches the means to rate their athletes' speed test performances. However, from a specificity viewpoint it is important when undertaking speed assessment that the selection of total test distance (and distances for split times) should reflect what occurs during competition in order to evaluate speed abilities that are relevant to the sport.

The importance of assessing sprint performance over a variety of distances is illustrated by the differences observed between athletes' speed performance at different intervals within the overall sprint test distance (Brown *et al.*, 2004). This can be achieved by performing repeated tests over different distances or alternatively recording split times within a speed test over a designated distance.

It is important that electronic timing devices are used when possible when attempting to objectively evaluate athletes' speed performance (Brown *et al.*, 2004). These devices allow measurement of split times so that speed performance over a range of distances can be assessed in a single test. Equally these devices are preferable in view of the lack of accuracy that is reported when sprint times are recorded using a hand-held stopwatch. Although sprint times assessed using a hand-held stopwatch are typically faster, the differences between stopwatch times and those recorded using timing gates are not consistent (Hetzler *et al.*, 2008). Consequently, a 'correction factor' cannot be applied in order to convert or correct stopwatch recorded times.

Typically, the speed measure recorded is the total time to cover the designated distance. Although not widely used, an alternative method that has been employed is to evaluate the fastest split time, for example the best 5-m or 10-m split within the overall sprint trial.

Assessing agility performance

By definition, 'agility' comprises change of direction or speed initiated in response to a stimulus (Sheppard and Young, 2006). This definition stipulates that any true assessment of agility must feature an element of reaction and/or decision-making in addition to the particular change of direction task employed. It is important therefore to clearly define and distinguish tests that incorporate a stimulus–response component and hence attempt to evaluate agility from the more prevalent assessments of change of direction movement abilities. Many of the test protocols described in the literature continue to be referred to as 'agility' tests when they in fact only assess athletes' change of direction. The respective change of direction assessments and 'reactive agility' tests will each be detailed in the following sections.

Tests of change of direction ability

A wide variety of tests of change of direction performance exist that differ in terms of both test duration and complexity – that is, number and direction of changes in direction demanded by the test protocol (Brughelli *et al.*, 2008). The various test measures employed to assess change of direction performance often show varying degrees of statistical relationship to each other (Sporis *et al.*, 2010). This appears to depend in part upon the degree of commonality (number/length of sprints, degrees of changes in direction) between the respective protocols. For example, scores on the Illinois test show no significant relationship to the shorter and simpler 5–0–5 test, which differs considerably in terms of both test duration and number of changes in direction (Brughelli *et al.*, 2008). Athletes' scoring on different change of direction tests therefore appears to depend upon the particular movement demands of the test protocol. In addition, if the test protocol exceeds a certain duration the test outcome may also be influence by the athletes' (anaerobic) fitness (Brughelli *et al.*, 2008).

Similarly, change of direction tests have been reported to show varying degrees of statistical relationship with measures of straight-line speed performance, depending to a large extent on the number and degree of changes in direction involved (Brughelli *et al.*, 2008). It has also been demonstrated that the limb used to execute the changes of direction in the test also influences athletes' performance on the change of direction test (Meylan *et al.*, 2009). Performance on a change of direction test may therefore differ depending on whether cutting movements are executed with the dominant or non-dominant leg. These findings illustrate not only the difficulty in obtaining a comprehensive assessment of athletes' change of direction abilities, but also the influence that test selection can have on athletes' scoring with respect to change of direction performance.

A selection of change of direction test protocols, separated into different movement categories, is presented in the following sections.

Simple 180-degree turns

- 5–0–5 test (Jones *et al.*, 2009):
  The 5–0–5 test features just one 180-degree pivot and turn. The player sprints forward 5 m, pivots and turns to sprint 5 m back to the start line (Sheppard and Young, 2006).
- Pro Agility shuttle test (Sierer *et al.*, 2008):
  This is a test that features in the NFL Combine and is essentially an extended version of the 5–0–5 test protocol. The player sprints 5 yards, pivots 180 degrees to sprint 10 yards in the opposite direction before executing a final 180-degree turn to sprint 5 yards back to the start line.
- 9–3–6–3–9 test (Sporis *et al.* 2010):
  An extended form of the 5–0–5 test run on a straight-line course that extends over a total distance of 18 m and comprises a total of five sprints of varying distances and four 180-degree turns. The protocol consists of an initial sprint of 9 m before executing a 180-degree turn to sprint 3 m in the opposite direction followed by another 180-degree turn and sprint of 6 m in the original direction, then another 180-degree

turn and 3 m sprint before a final 180-degree turn and 9 m sprint to the finish line.
- 9–3–6–3–9 test with backwards and forwards running (Sporis *et al.*, 2010):
    This modification to the above test covers the same course, and involves changing direction at the same points, but features only forwards and backwards running so that the athlete faces in the same direction (i.e. towards the finish line) throughout the test. This version of the test was found to differentiate the particular change of direction abilities of defenders and midfield players versus attackers in soccer.

A number of shuttle change of direction tests also exist in the literature that involve running a prescribed number of shuttle sprints over varying distances. Examples include the 10-yard (9-m) shuttle, 6 × 5-m shuttle and 4 × 5.8-m shuttle tests (Brughelli *et al.*, 2008).

Combination 90-degree and 180-degree turns

- 'L-run' or the 'three-cone drill' featured in the NFL Combine (Sierer *et al.*, 2008):
    Of all the change of direction tests employed in the NFL Combine, performance on the L-run test was found to have the greatest correlation with draft pick ranking of American football players selected for professional teams (Sierer *et al.*, 2008). The course that players run features a cone placed 5 yards in front of the start/finish cone, with a third cone placed 5 yards to the right of the second cone. The course thus features a 90-degree cut to the right, a 180-degree pivot and turn, and a 90-degree cut to the left before the player returns to the start/finish cone.
- 4 × 5-m sprint test described by Sporis and colleagues (2010):
    Set up similar to the L-run course, with the addition of another cone. The protocol is identical to the one described above with an additional 90-degree turn before a final 180-degree turn and 5-m sprint to the finish line.
- The T-test is widely employed as a standard test of change of direction performance:
    This consists of a 10-m sprint forwards to a cone placed at the centre of the 'T', followed by 90-degree lateral cuts to reach cones placed 5 m away to the left and right of the centre cone before sprinting 10 m back from the centre cone to the start/finish cone. Different versions of this test also exist with modifications to the distances between cones and the movement constraints imposed during the test.

Multiple cuts of varying degrees

- Zigzag run test (e.g. Mirkov *et al.*, 2008):
    There are a variety of zigzag run protocols, usually involving cutting change of direction movements around three cones placed between the start and finish cones. The usual cutting angle between successive cones is 100 degrees, and cones are typically placed 5 m apart.
- Slalom test (Sporis *et al.*, 2010):
    Slalom course through six cones placed on a straight line at 2-m intervals – the distance between the start line and the final cone is 11 m so the athlete covers a total

distance of 22 m. The athlete begins on the start line with the first cone of the six-cone slalom course 1 m away; the athlete completes a slalom course past each cone in a forwards direction then performs a 180-degree turn after the final cone to complete the slalom course in the opposite direction to finish back at the start line.
- The Illinois agility test (Sheppard and Young, 2006):
    A well-established protocol that features multiple slalom cuts through cones and 180-degree turns (Figure 3.1). Of all of the standard change of direction tests the Illinois test has possibly the greatest complexity of movement, and the time required to complete the test is also among the longest.

Assessments of 'reactive agility'

Change of direction tests have been modified to incorporate a simple reaction component to the movement task, so that the movement is executed in response to an external cue. The time recorded by the athlete on tests of this type therefore represents a combination

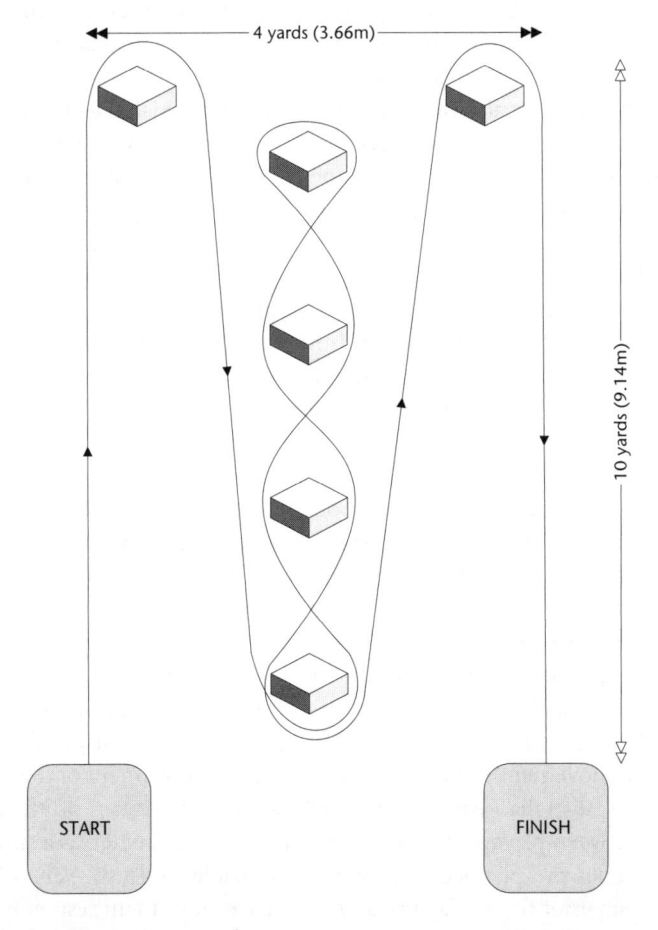

FIGURE 3.1 Illinois agility test protocol.

of both reaction time and the time taken to subsequently complete the movement task. Therefore, in addition to assessing the required movement competencies for the particular change of direction task, this approach also evaluates athletes' perceptual abilities; hence, this form of assessment attempts to account for each of the respective elements that make up sports agility. Proponents of reactive agility tests therefore propose that this form of assessment will also provide additional information allowing the specific area(s) (e.g. physical versus perceptual abilities) requiring development to be identified for each athlete (Gabbett and Benton, 2009).

Some authors have questioned whether using a light or similar to cue the movement response as is often employed in these tests will provide a valid measure of the specific information-processing and decision-making factors that contribute to agility performance in sport (Sheppard and Young, 2006). In response to such concerns some investigators have attempted to account for perceptual factors in the selection of the movement trigger presented to the athlete in order to enhance the ecological validity of these tests (Farrow *et al.*, 2005). In one example the tester initiates the movement response by performing a sidestep motion in the direction that the athlete is required to move (Sheppard *et al.*, 2006). More technologically advanced protocols of this type employ a video display so that the athlete is required to initiate the movement response in response to the movement of players on the screen (Farrow *et al.*, 2005).

Certain study protocols also film the athlete during the trial in order to further analyse reaction time (i.e. time elapsed between presentation of movement cue and initiation of movement response) and movement time (from initiation of movement response to arrival at the finish gate). However, these methods are unlikely to be employed for routine testing of athletes in the field, given the time and specialised recording and analysis equipment involved.

Different reactive agility protocols have been investigated with various groups of field team sports athletes. One study compared the same test protocol, which involved a cut and sprint to gates positioned either side of the athlete, under both pre-planned conditions (the athlete was told which gate to sprint to before the trial) and reactive conditions cued by a video projection of a player passing the ball in the direction of the gate the athlete was to sprint to (Farrow *et al.*, 2005). Movement times are on average slower in the reactive condition because of the perceptual component. However, the difference between split times for pre-planned and for reactive conditions was less for both highly skilled (national institute) and moderately skilled (state-level) netball players, resulting in faster reactive agility times than lesser skilled players (B-grade club players) (Farrow *et al.*, 2005). As a result, test measures recorded under reactive conditions also appear to be superior in differentiating elite competitors from sub-elite players in these sports.

An investigation of the 'reactive agility test' ('RAT') protocol originally described by Sheppard and colleagues (2006), which involves the athlete starting from a stationary position and the movement response being triggered by movement of the tester, reported similar results in Australian Rules football players. Players' scores on the RAT protocol differentiated between players of different playing standards, whereas a similar change of direction test under pre-planned conditions was unable to do so. Very similar findings with respect to superior reactive agility times as well as movement response accuracy have also been reported for elite versus sub-elite rugby league players using the same RAT protocol (Gabbett and Benton, 2009).

Balance and stability testing

The athlete's ability to retain their balance as well as postural and lower limb stability when moving and changing direction at speed would appear to be important factors determining their ability to perform these actions safely, efficiently and quickly. Postural stability when the athlete is relatively stationary and dynamic stabilisation involving the transition from movement to a stationary position will be considered separately on the basis that these appear to be independent and discrete abilities as the respective measures of these abilities are not strongly related to each other (Brown and Mynark, 2007).

Postural balance

The majority of balance measurement protocols have been developed for clinical populations and as such may not be sufficiently challenging to be relevant or useful for the purposes of assessing non-injured athlete subjects (Emery, 2003). Standard assessments of balance ability commonly take the form of unipedal (single-leg support) static balance tests. These protocols challenge the subject to maintain equilibrium (i.e. retain centre of mass over their base of support) under a given set of conditions (e.g. stable/labile surface, eyes closed/open, head movement in various directions) (Emery, 2003).

Some apparatuses are built with contact sensors incorporated into the device in order to detect loss of equilibrium and thereby provide a quantitative measure when scoring the test (Hrysomallis, 2007). Force platforms (both laboratory based and portable systems for field testing) are commercially available that allow postural sway to be measured by recording movement of the subject's centre of pressure. Alternatively, more practical field-based assessments employ qualitative measurement criteria, such as total duration that the athlete is able to retain balance or the number of attempts taken to balance for a specified time period (Hrysomallis, 2007).

One popular mode of assessment of balance or dynamic joint stability for active populations is the Star Excursion Balance Test. In this test the athlete is challenged to maintain their balance during single-limb support while reaching the opposite leg for maximum distance in various directions (Bressel *et al.*, 2007). This test measure appears to involve different abilities from those assessed by tests that are performed in a stationary posture without any contralateral limb movement task. It has been reported that subjects' scores on this test differ markedly from their respective scores on a standard standing single-leg balance test (Bressel *et al.*, 2007).

Dynamic stabilisation

Tests of dynamic stabilisation typically assess the capacity of the athlete to execute the transition from movement to a stationary position. This parameter is typically assessed by jumping or hopping onto either a stable or labile surface; upon landing the athlete attempts to maintain their equilibrium, that is, 'stick' the landing without taking a step or losing balance. Testing conducted in a laboratory or clinical setting commonly involves hopping or landing from a box onto a force plate. Standard measures recorded include postural sway, ground reaction force and time to stabilisation. Some assessments even employ surface electromyography electrodes to detect muscle recruitment and activity during preparatory and reactive phases (Wikstrom *et al.*, 2006). Given the cost, time and access to specialised staff and equipment involved, these forms of dynamic stabilisation assessment are likely to be impractical for routine testing for athletes.

The abilities assessed by dynamic stabilisation tests particularly would appear to be relevant to athletes' capacities for change of direction and deceleration movement, and therefore agility performance. However, to date, investigations of both postural stability and dynamic stabilisation measures have focused only on clinical applications, such as evaluation of injury prevention interventions. Consequently, possible relationships between these measures and athletes' speed and change of direction performance have yet to be explored fully.

Lumbopelvic 'core' stability

Given the complex and multidimensional nature of lumbopelvic stability described, no standard test for core stability currently exists. Standard endurance tests for the trunk muscles measure the time an athlete is able to maintain a given position or posture. Examples of such tests include the side bridge, flexor endurance test and static back extension Biering–Sørensen endurance test (Carter *et al.*, 2006). Normative data have been published for these tests with healthy non-athlete subjects as a reference for comparison from the perspective of identifying low back injury risk (McGill, 2007a). Ratios of flexor versus extensor scores, and comparisons between sides in the case of the side bridge, are suggested to be most useful in identifying low back pain and injury risk. Data for these tests for athlete subjects have also recently been published (Evans *et al.*, 2007). In contrast to the data for non-athletes, the female and male athletes studied had comparable flexor and extensor endurance times. However, side bridge endurance times were significantly lower among the female athletes than male athletes (Evans *et al.*, 2007).

Field-based clinical tests of torsional stability also exist that are becoming routinely employed in functional screening protocols (see next section). Two examples are the 'push-up test' (of which there are two variations) and the 'back bridge test' (McGill, 2007a). These tests are qualitative in that they are subjectively scored by the assessor based upon set criteria (Cook, 2003). However, what is currently lacking are validated assessments of core strength. One of the few existing tests in the literature, which involves projecting a medicine ball from a seated posture, has been used as a measure of the concentric 'power' of the core stabiliser muscles (Cowley and Swensen, 2008).

The data accompanying many of the tests described, which predominantly assess endurance and stability, indicate that they satisfy reliability criteria. Injury prevention studies have identified measures of lumbopelvic stability as a factor determining the ability of female athletes to perform change of direction movements effectively and without risk of injury. Measures of trunk strength indicative of the capacity to control lateral lean of the trunk in particular are strongly associated with incidence of knee ligament injury among female athletes (Zazulak *et al.*, 2007). However, only weak to moderate statistical relationships have typically been reported between measures of trunk endurance and speed or change of direction performance (Nesser *et al.*, 2008; Okada *et al.*, 2011). That said, preliminary data indicating the greater effectiveness of more intensive core strength training modes in improving measures of sports performance (Saeterbakken *et al.*, 2011) suggest that an appropriate assessment of lumbopelvic 'core' strength may elucidate a stronger positive statistical relationship with speed and change of direction performance.

Evaluating endurance capacity

The relevance of assessing anaerobic and aerobic capacities with reference to speed and agility performance is supported by studies which report that these qualities are strongly related to both high-speed running performance (Bundle *et al.*, 2003) and repeated sprint ability (Bishop *et al.*, 2004; Edge *et al.*, 2006a). A wide variety of assessment methods exist for both aerobic and anaerobic endurance parameters. A summary is presented in the following sections.

Direct assessment of maximal oxygen uptake (VO$_2$max)

A variety of progressive tests performed to failure or volitional exhaustion exist, all of which typically involve continuous monitoring of respiratory parameters and/or heart rate; the main outcome measure of these tests is maximal oxygen uptake (VO$_2$max or VO$_2$peak). These tests are commonly conducted in the laboratory, using a motorised or non-motorised treadmill, or even a cycle ergometer. Portable gas analyser apparatus does exist, which can allow this form of assessment to be performed for protocols that involve over-ground running; however, this approach is not widely used.

Aside from issues relating to cost and access to specialised equipment and trained staff that tend to preclude routine use of laboratory testing of this type (Gamble, 2009a) there is preliminary evidence that peripheral rather than central aspects of aerobic capacity are most relevant for repeated sprint performance. Data from high-intensity training studies indicate that it is the peripheral metabolic adaptations supporting oxidative capacity of the muscle that are the critical outcomes resulting in improvements in muscle buffering capacity and repeated sprint ability rather than improvements in central cardiorespiratory factors. In accordance with this, a study examining ice hockey players' VO$_2$peak scores recorded in a laboratory treadmill test in relation to their performance measured with an on-ice repeated (skating) sprint protocol concluded that there was no significant relationship between the two parameters (Carey *et al.*, 2007). This might also explain the relatively modest VO$_2$max values reported for team sports and racquet sports players (Wilmore and Costill, 1999). Given these considerations the merits of including a laboratory assessment of VO$_2$max in a test battery to assess physical parameters of speed and agility performance would appear questionable.

Field-based maximal tests of aerobic capacity

Assessment of maximal aerobic speed

Maximal aerobic speed (MAS) is defined as the minimum threshold work intensity (e.g. running speed) at which VO$_2$max is attained (also known as vVO$_2$max). This parameter has traditionally been assessed using laboratory protocols that involve direct measurement of oxygen uptake. Field tests of MAS have, however, also been developed that have greater ease of application. The 20-m multi-stage shuttle run and 'Yo-Yo' tests described in the following sections can be employed in this way to identify maximum aerobic running speed for 20-m shuttle runs specifically.

The 30–15 Intermittent Fitness Test (30–15IFT) is another protocol that has been developed specifically for the purpose of identifying (shuttle) running speed at VO_2max in the field, in order to prescribe individualised interval conditioning (Buchheit, 2008). This protocol is intermittent in nature: subjects run shuttles for 30 seconds at a given speed interspersed with 15-second active recovery bouts; running speed for the work bouts is progressively increased and the athlete performs the test to failure. The 30–15IFT has been validated against other vVO_2max directly measured in the laboratory and standard field tests that provide a measure of MAS, and scores on this test were also reported to correlate with speed performance (10-m sprint times) in a sample of young team sports players (Buchheit, 2008).

Twenty-metre multi-stage shuttle test

Perhaps the most widely recognised of all field-based tests of aerobic endurance is the 20-m multi-stage shuttle test. This form of assessment does not typically involve directly monitoring physiological parameters, although heart rate can easily be recorded if the relevant apparatus is available, and regression tables predicting VO_2max values from the final test level attained are available.

However, based upon similar grounds to the issues regarding laboratory assessments of VO_2max, some authors have also questioned the relevance of this form of assessment with respect to endurance performance in most sports and athletic events. One such study found no correlation between VO_2peak scores obtained during a 20-m multi-stage shuttle test and a test of repeated sprint ability in a group of basketball players (Castagna *et al.*, 2007).

Modifications to the standard 20-m multi-stage shuttle test have been proposed and studies assessing their reliability and validity appear in the literature. One such modified incremental 20-m shuttle test increases running speed after each shuttle (Wilkinson *et al.*, 1999), as opposed to increasing speed at 1-minute intervals as in the original version of the test. The authors of this study argue that such an approach avoids the tendency for athletes to drop out at the start of a given level as is observed with the original test protocol (Wilkinson *et al.*, 1999).

Yo-Yo intermittent test

The Yo-Yo intermittent fitness test requires subjects to perform repeated bouts of running consisting of two sets of 20-m shuttle runs at increasing intensity, interspersed with 10-second rest periods (Bangsbo *et al.*, 2008). Although the two measures are correlated, this intermittent test protocol is reported to evaluate additional physiological qualities to the continuous 20-m multi-stage shuttle test (Castagna *et al.*, 2006). The Yo-Yo intermittent test protocol would also appear to more closely resemble the intermittent nature of high-intensity running activity that athletes engage in during competition. In support of this, a study of Australian Rules football found that, whereas VO_2max scores showed no difference between starting players and substitutes, Yo-Yo (intermittent recovery level 2,

IR2) test scores did differentiate between starting and non-starting players (Young et al., 2005). A second study found that Yo-Yo (level 1, IR1) test scores recorded by soccer players were shown to correlate with their on-field performance (quantity of high-intensity running undertaken during games), whereas their treadmill VO_2max scores did not (Krustrup et al., 2003).

Two versions of the Yo-Yo intermittent test protocol exist: Yo-Yo IR1 begins at a slower running speed and so features more progressive increases in running speed; IR2 starts at a faster speed so that subjects engage in high-intensity exertion much sooner (Bangsbo et al., 2008). The Yo-Yo IR2 protocol is intended for use specifically by trained athletes: it is run at faster cadence – hence test duration is shorter – and is considered to have a larger anaerobic component, based upon lactate profiles and muscle biopsy samples (Bangsbo et al., 2008). Both IR1 and IR2 tests appear sensitive to training-induced changes in fitness, and performance on these tests is also reported to reflect time spent engaged in high-intensity running during competition (Bangsbo et al., 2008).

Assessment of anaerobic capacity

The standard laboratory measure of anaerobic capacity evaluates the measured difference, described as maximally accumulated oxygen deficit (MAOD), between estimated oxygen demand and measured oxygen uptake during an exhaustive exercise test at an intensity exceeding VO_2peak (Moore and Murphy, 2003). As a consequence of the reliance upon access to a laboratory and trained staff, as well as the complexity of the protocol involved to derive MAOD, this form of assessment is very rarely employed with athletes (Legaz-Arrese et al., 2011).

The Wingate test performed on a cycle ergometer has also been employed widely to evaluate anaerobic capacity; this test is usually conducted in the laboratory but this mode of testing can also be undertaken in the field. Mean power output recorded during the 30-second maximal effort required to complete the test is typically the variable used to quantify anaerobic capacity, often expressed relative to body mass (Popadic Gacesa et al., 2009). However, there is some question about whether this form of assessment is valid for running-based sports, particularly when dealing with elite performers. When expressed relative to body mass, mean and peak power measures derived from the Wingate test reportedly failed to differentiate between trained runners competing in different events with considerably different demands for anaerobic capacity (Legaz-Arrese et al., 2011). Wingate test performance per kilogram of body mass did not differ significantly between the groups of elite-level sprint athletes (100 m, 400 m) and middle-distance runners (800 m, 1500 m, 3000 m) studied.

A running-based field protocol that has been reported to correlate with MAOD measured in the laboratory involves a maximal 20-m shuttle running test over a total distance of 300 m, that is, 15 × 20-m shuttle sprints performed without pause (Moore and Murphy, 2003). The time taken to cover this distance is the outcome measure taken to indicate anaerobic capacity – the typical reported duration is in the range of 62–70 seconds. Although this appears to be a promising and reportedly reliable measure (Moore and Murphy, 2003), further investigation of this type of running-based field assessment of anaerobic capacity is required. Furthermore, any relationships between these measures and the capacity for speed and agility performance are yet to be elucidated.

Tests of repeated sprint ability

Repeated sprint ability is typically assessed as the athlete's ability to sustain repeated high-intensity bouts of exertion within a brief period (Oliver *et al.*, 2009). That these tests assess a specific ability is reflected in the low statistical relationships between these measures and standard field tests of aerobic capacity (Castagna *et al.*, 2007; Pyne *et al.*, 2008). A 'fatigue index' score has often been used when testing repeated sprint ability, expressed as percentage drop-off in sprint times or power output across the prescribed number of intervals (Hoffman *et al.*, 1999; Quarrie *et al.*, 1995). Total distance covered (if work bouts are of a set duration) or sum of sprint times (if sprints of a set distance are used) is also frequently employed as the criterion measure for repeated sprint testing. Of the two indices, the latter (sum of times or distances) appears to provide the more robust (Pyne *et al.*, 2008) and reliable (Oliver, 2009; Spencer *et al.*, 2006) measure of repeated sprint ability, based upon studies of field sports athletes.

Different repeated sprint ability (RSA) test protocols employ a variety of exercise modes (cycling, treadmill and over-ground running) (Oliver *et al.*, 2009). These tests also vary on other parameters including the total number of sprint repetitions, distance or duration of sprints, and the duration and type of recovery (e.g. passive or active) (Spencer *et al.*, 2005). The majority of RSA test protocols employ sprint durations of 5–6 seconds (if cycle or treadmill is used in the test mode), which equates to approximately 30–40 m for over-ground running, interspersed with recovery period durations in the range of 24–30 seconds (work–rest ratio 1:4 or 1:5). The total number of sprint bouts, however, varies between protocols (Spencer *et al.*, 2005). A representative selection of RSA test protocols that are commonly used, and their main outcome measures, are presented in Table 3.1.

TABLE 3.1 Selected repeated sprint ability protocols

Test mode	Distance/ duration	Protocol	Outcome measure	Reference
Cycle ergometer	6-second bouts	Repeated every 30 seconds (i.e. 6 seconds' work, 24 seconds' rest)	Work output scores	Bishop *et al.*, 2001
			Power output values expressed relative to body mass	Bishop *et al.*, 2004
Non-motorised treadmill	5-second sprints	7 × 5-second sprints with 20 seconds' recovery between		Oliver *et al.*, 2009
Over-ground running	30-m sprints	6 × 30-m sprints departing every 20 seconds	Sum of sprint times	Pyne *et al.*, 2008
Over-ground running	30-m sprints	6 × 30-m sprints departing every 25 seconds	Sum of sprint times	Spencer *et al.*, 2006
Shuttle sprints	30-second shuttles	Shuttle sprints over 5 m and 10 m alternately	Sum of distances covered during each 30-second bout	Boddington *et al.*, 2001

The duration or distance selected for the sprint repetitions in a RSA test protocol strongly influences the energy system contribution to work bouts during the test (Spencer *et al.*, 2005). The duration of the rest intervals allowed between sprints also strongly influences physiological responses and performance during consecutive work bouts (Balsom *et al.*, 1992). For example, the capacity for repeated 5-second bouts of sprint running exercise with brief (20-second) rest periods is identified as being a quality that is relatively distinct from the ability to perform repeated 5-second sprints when extended (2-minute) rest periods are provided (Oliver *et al.*, 2009).

Performance effects manifested in the repeated sprint test do, however, appear to depend upon the sprint distance examined. A study investigating fifteen sets of 40-m sprints with different recovery intervals (30 seconds, 1 minute or 2 minutes) found that the 30- to 40-m split times were most consistently affected in the latter sprints whatever the work–rest protocol (Balsom *et al.*, 1992). In contrast, sprint performances over shorter distances appear less affected; in fact, changes in 0- to 15-m split times were seen only with the shortest 30-second rest interval protocol, and even then the changes were minor (Balsom *et al.*, 1992). Similarly, a study that employed a simulated hockey game protocol observed that players' scores on a 5 × 6-second sprint cycle test were positively related to their ability to maintain 15-m sprint times during the game simulation but did not reflect changes in their 10-m and 5-m sprint performance (Bishop *et al.*, 2001).

To be most relevant, it would follow that selection of the distance/duration of sprint bouts and length of recovery periods should be reflective of the particular sport (Bishop *et al.*, 2001). A review of relevant studies identified that sprint distances and durations most commonly observed in field-based team sports were 10–20 m and 2–3 seconds, respectively, which differs from the majority of RSA test protocols currently used (Spencer *et al.*, 2005). The corresponding values are likely to be considerably less for racquet sports and combat sports. Equally, over-ground running would appear to be the exercise mode most specific to sports performance, although some investigators have also employed non-motorised treadmills, which allow force and work output to be concurrently recorded (Spencer *et al.*, 2005).

4
ATHLETICISM AND MOVEMENT SKILLS DEVELOPMENT

Introduction

Whether the term 'athleticism' or 'movement dexterity' is applied, there would appear to be a need for the athlete to possess fundamental movement abilities in order to be able to fully develop the necessary qualities for speed and agility expression. It is possible to identify basic competencies such as mobility, stability, movement skills and strength qualities that would seem to be prerequisites for undertaking dedicated training to develop speed and agility.

Essentially the athlete should demonstrate the requisite neuromuscular capabilities in order to be able to execute fundamental movements efficiently. Fundamental movements identified to be common to most sports include variations of squatting/lifting movements, pushing/pulling, lunging, gait (e.g. running), twisting movements and balance activities (McGill, 2006a). Efficiency with respect to movement concerns both muscle recruitment and motor patterns as well as the degree of effort associated with performing the movement. These fundamental movement capabilities in turn represent a determining factor in the athlete's proficiency in performing the specific movement skills required by the sport (Gamble, 2009b).

Growth, maturation and development of fundamental movement skills

The motor learning and skill acquisition literature highlights the importance of the early developmental years as a key phase for developing mastery in movement skills (Hardy *et al.*, 2010). The enhanced aptitude for movement skill learning during this critical period appears to apply to a wide variety of motor skills, from fine motor skills and musical aptitude to more gross motor skills and locomotor skills in particular. Recent studies of preschool and primary school children in Australia have reported that the level of mastery of the locomotor skills assessed (e.g. running, sprinting, hopping, jumping) varies widely (van Beurden *et al.*, 2002; Hardy *et al.*, 2010).

Proficiency in these fundamental movement and locomotor skills appears to be linked to children's habitual levels of physical activity and active play. This interaction between motor skill development and growth and maturation continues until late adolescence (Naughton et al., 2000). In accordance with these observations, the importance of specific neuromuscular and movement skill training has been emphasised during critical phases before, during and after puberty (Barber-Westin et al., 2005; Philippaerts et al., 2006).

There are characteristic changes observed in functional strength and lower limb neuromuscular control associated with normal growth and maturation, independent of any training intervention. Young males exhibit improvements in a variety of athletic performance tests around the period that their plotted growth curves attain peak height velocity (Philippaerts et al., 2006). Other studies report similar improvements in strength scores and measures of lower limb alignment in young males during this period (Schmitz et al., 2009), and the ability to dissipate landing forces (Quatman et al., 2006). These naturally occurring changes observed with young males during maturation are attributed to a phenomenon known as the 'neuromuscular spurt', which is associated with concomitant hormonal changes (Quatman et al., 2006).

In the absence of these specific hormonal changes, female athletes do not benefit from such a phenomenon. Consequently, the same growth- and maturation-related improvements in strength and motor performance reported for males are not observed with young female athletes. One example which is relevant to speed and agility performance is that following puberty males exhibit increases in active stiffness measured at the hip and ankle joints during a drop jump task (Ford et al., 2010). This is not the case for female athletes, who show no such changes. As a result, post puberty significant differences in neuromuscular performance are evident between males and females, which are not present among prepubescent boys and girls (Ford et al., 2010). These differences in active lower limb stiffness between genders are likely to have implications for speed performance. The apparent differences in activation levels of the muscles of the hip girdle are similarly notable with respect to change of direction performance, given the importance of these muscles during such activity.

Not only do young females not benefit from maturation-related improvements in motor performance, trends are observed for measures of neuromuscular control (dynamic lower limb alignment) to become progressively worse with each stage of maturation into adolescence (Schmitz et al., 2009). Similarly, in the absence of training intervention, young females often exhibit decreased performance on lower limb strength and power measures, when expressed relative to body mass (Barber-Westin et al., 2006).

Interaction between growth, maturation and measures of speed performance

Studies investigating performance changes resulting from speed-training programmes during childhood and adolescence are somewhat lacking. Data examining speed performance of untrained young subjects at different stages of maturation have, however, been published (Papaiakovou et al., 2009). In a sample of schoolchildren who were not involved in any formal programme of physical preparation the expected improvement in 30-m sprint times with increasing chronological age was observed in both boys and girls. The observed changes in sprint times with increasing age were largely uniform for each phase (i.e. 0- to 10-m, 10- to 20-m and 20- to 30-m split times) within the overall 30-m sprint (Papaiakovou et al., 2009).

There appears to be a trend for boys to show superior sprint performance in relation to girls of the same chronological age. The observed differences between genders in this study became more marked from around age 15 onwards, so that from ages 15 to 18 boys showed statistically superior sprint performance to age-matched girls (Papaiakovou et al., 2009). This would appear to reflect the developmental changes and associated improvements in physiological and physical performance that occur with puberty in young males, and the absence of an equivalent 'neuromuscular spurt' for females, as discussed earlier. As a consequence, any increase in sprint performance with age was reported to plateau at age 16 for the girls studied (Papaiakovou et al., 2009).

Importance of movement skill training for female athletes

The implications of the lack of 'natural' improvement in lower limb neuromuscular control with growth and maturation, and the resulting deficits exhibited by female athletes, are self-evident in terms of athletic performance. However, more important is the impact that this has upon lower limb injury risk. It is reported that female athletes suffer a significantly greater rate of lower limb injury than male athletes competing in the same sports (Agel et al., 2005); this trend is apparent from adolescence and continues into adulthood (Hewett et al., 2006b; Murphy et al., 2003).

The importance of specific neuromuscular training to develop landing and change of direction 'cutting' movement skills in particular has therefore been highlighted for adolescent female athletes (Hewett et al., 2006a). As mentioned previously, deficits in measures of lower limb control are not corrected during growth and maturation, and these deficits even appear to become more pronounced as female athletes reach adolescence (Schmitz et al., 2009). Consequently, when compared with males, adolescent and adult female athletes are shown to demonstrate significantly different lower limb kinematics and kinetics during drop jump (Quatman et al., 2006) and stop jump (Chappell et al., 2002) tasks, and sidestep cutting movements under planned (Hanson et al., 2008) and unanticipated (Landry et al., 2007) conditions. Such deficits in neuromuscular control and coordination (Ford et al., 2003; Hewett et al., 2005; Landry et al., 2007) and aberrant muscle recruitment and activation (Silvers and Mandelbaum, 2007) during landing and cutting movements have been identified as factors contributing to the increased incidence of lower limb injury observed with female athletes.

Neuromuscular training interventions that include instruction and deliberate practice of landing, jumping and change of direction movement have proven effective in correcting deficits in dynamic lower limb control in female athletes (Lim et al., 2009; Noyes et al., 2005). Other training studies have similarly reported improved scores on a variety of lower limb injury risk factors (Lim et al., 2009; Myer et al., 2005). Crucially, these improvements have also been reflected in decreased injury rates post training (Hewett et al., 1999).

Importantly, the modifications to movement mechanics imposed by neuromuscular training interventions do not appear to have any detrimental effect on measures of performance. For example, a neuromuscular training intervention for high school and collegiate female basketball players achieved alterations in movement mechanics during a stop jump movement that resulted in a 50 per cent reduction in measured shear forces at the knee, and players' jump height performance was maintained or improved with the altered technique (Myers and Hawkins, 2010). Indeed, a number of studies have reported improvements in speed and change of direction performance alongside the changes in movement mechanics elicited by this form of training with female athletes (Hewett et al., 2006a). It therefore appears that in many cases the 'safer' movement strategy is in fact also the most beneficial in terms of performance.

Screening for fundamental movement skill competencies

As a starting point, a number of movement screens exist in the literature that can be applied to assess the athlete's competence on various aspects of 'functional movement' using set criteria. The most commercially successful of these movement screens is the 'Functional Movement Screen' popularised by Gray Cook. It must be noted that individuals' scores on the functional movement screen have only weak statistical relationships to selected measures of athletic performance (Okada et al., 2011). This underlines two important points: first, where possible each of the movement-based screens selected in the test battery should have been validated in the literature; and, second, the ability to perform these functional movements in isolation will not in itself confer optimal performance on athletic performance measures.

That said, identifying and addressing deficits in mobility and stability or other aspects that may restrict the athlete's ability to perform fundamental movements would still appear to be a prudent approach in the preliminary stages of training. Such an assessment might best be undertaken alongside a comprehensive musculoskeletal assessment in collaboration with sports medicine practitioners to evaluate the structural integrity of the athlete. This will also help to identify any musculoskeletal or postural aspects that may impact upon the athlete's ability to perform speed and change of direction movement efficiently.

The validity of a number of tests has been investigated in the literature. For example, the drop jump test protocol has been employed in order to assess athletes' dynamic control of lower limb alignment during the landing and take-off phase (Noyes et al., 2005; Schmitz et al., 2009). Another protocol in the literature with more direct relevance to change of direction movements that might have similar application for evaluating dynamic lower limb control involves the subject jumping across a line before performing a reactive 45-degree or 90-degree sidestep cutting movement (Imwalle et al., 2009).

Finally, this screening process should be undertaken in the understanding that, in order for improvements in performance to ultimately be realised, training must progress to more performance-focused physical preparation once any identified deficits and restrictions have been addressed.

Fundamental movement skills and specific movement abilities for the sport

In Chapter 2 fundamental movement capabilities were identified as a factor in the expression of speed and agility. Depending on the characteristic demands of the sport there may be further specific requirements with respect to mobility and stability as a result of the particular movement capabilities required. For example, certain racquet sports or evasion sports can demand extremes of movement in certain game situations, for example when lunging at full stretch to intercept a ball at the limits of the player's reach. In this case it will be necessary for the athlete to possess considerable mobility but also the requisite stability to execute these movements safely and effectively; and the latter will in turn require both postural control and dynamic joint stability.

Balance and dynamic stabilisation

Balance can be defined as the ability to maintain equilibrium under a given set of conditions or in response to a particular challenge (DiStefano et al., 2009). The sensorimotor capacities involved comprise input from visual, vestibular and somatosensory systems (Bressel et al., 2007). As discussed in Chapter 8, postural control also involves the various elements that comprise lumbopelvic stability. Discrete abilities within the global term 'balance' can be identified, depending on the nature of the sensorimotor challenge involved:

1. static balance – ability to maintain centre of mass over a static base of support and stationary supporting surface (Bressel et al., 2007);
2. dynamic balance – capacity to maintain centre of mass over a static base of support under a movement challenge: specifically, motion of other limbs and body segments, or unanticipated disturbance to the supporting surface (DiStefano et al., 2009);
3. dynamic stabilisation – ability to maintain equilibrium during the transition from motion to a stationary position, such as a landing movement (Myer et al., 2006a).

In accordance with the complex nature of balance discussed previously, training to develop balance is conceptualised as 'sensorimotor training' (Taube et al., 2007) and takes a variety of forms. Although there is consensus that balance training interventions are effective and worthwhile for those with impaired balance because of illness or injury, there has been some suggestion that this form of training might be redundant for healthy individuals without such issues. This is largely refuted by recent studies which have demonstrated that a variety of balance training interventions are effective in improving dynamic measures of balance ability in particular, among both healthy non-athletes and also athletes (DiStefano et al., 2009). The consensus, therefore, is that even among athletes these abilities remain areas that can be developed through appropriate training.

The effectiveness of training to develop components of balance is observed in studies investigating risk factors for injury (Hrysomallis, 2007; Myer et al., 2006a; Yaggie and Campbell, 2006). Different forms of balance training are therefore recognised as a key component of successful injury prevention strategies to address lower limb injury risk (Hewett et al., 2006a). Observed effects following appropriate interventions include enhanced lower limb neuromuscular control and dissipation of landing forces, and improved fundamental movement abilities (Myer et al., 2006b). Appropriate balance training interventions employed either alone (Yaggie and Campbell, 2006), or in combination with movement skills instruction and training (Myer et al., 2005), have been shown to elicit improvements in measures of athletic performance.

Training to develop balance abilities

Static balance training

There is some suggestion that static balance training on a stable supporting surface is relatively ineffectual in developing static balance abilities for healthy athlete subjects (DiStefano et al., 2009). However, this may just be a consequence of the static balance training employed in this study being insufficiently challenging for athlete subjects. Equally, shortcomings have been identified with the methods employed to assess static balance abilities for healthy subjects (Emery, 2003), which may also be a factor in the lack of reported effects.

In any case it would appear prudent to include some form of static balance training in athletic preparation, particularly when an athlete's screening has identified a deficiency in their static balance abilities. Likewise, this form of balance training would appear beneficial for young athletes at critical stages in their growth and development. This would also appear relevant to female athletes of all ages, given the prevalence of lower limb injury and associated neuromuscular control issues in this group.

Various constraints can be employed during static balance training tasks in order to isolate or emphasise a particular component. For example, performing the balance task with eyes closed eliminates visual input. Conversely, tilting or turning the head modifies the challenge with respect to vestibular system input. Finally, performing the balance task without shoes eliminates the stabilisation provided by the athlete's footwear, thereby accentuating proprioceptive afferent input from cutaneous and joint mechanoreceptors. All of these constraints may be manipulated individually or in combination in order to progress the challenge posed by the balance task

Dynamic balance training

There are essentially two approaches to developing dynamic balance abilities. The first method is typically performed on a stable supporting surface with the athlete challenged to maintain equilibrium whilst performing predetermined movements with the other limbs and body segments from a fixed base of support. One example of this form of dynamic balance training task is the Star Excursion Balance Test (Bressel et al., 2007). This is a single-leg balance task that requires the athlete to reach out with the contralateral (opposite) leg away from the supporting foot in a variety of directions, aiming for maximum distance.

The alternative form of dynamic balance training involves balance tasks performed on unstable supporting surfaces. This form of training employs labile surfaces (e.g. foam pads, inflatable cushions) or training devices such as 'wobble-boards' or 'tilt-boards' (DiStefano et al., 2009). In contrast to the former approach, these training modes require the athlete to minimise motion of limbs and body segments whilst balancing on a movable base of support. Training adaptations following this form of dynamic balance training appear to be mediated predominantly by changes in central or 'supraspinal' input (Taube et al., 2007).

A variety of training regimens employing unstable training modes have reported improvements in dynamic balance measures with athlete subjects, and some carry-over of these training effects to static balance abilities is also evident (DiStefano *et al.*, 2009). Progression can be achieved with the particular dynamic balance training device by manipulating the same constraints as described for static balance training, for example employing head movements or visual tracking tasks and/or introducing an eyes-closed variation of the task.

Dynamic stabilisation

Feedforward control of ankle stabilisers during the preparatory phase prior to touchdown is suggested to be the most important factor in improving active stabilisation during landing or stopping movements (Holmes and Delahunt, 2009). This is a learned effect and thus amenable to development through repeated exposure to relevant movements in conjunction with appropriate coaching (Zuur *et al.*, 2010). A variety of landing tasks can be employed, depending upon what is demanded by the characteristic athletic movements employed in the sport. For example, in the sport of netball players are observed to employ a variety of landing strategies in the act of catching the ball, depending upon factors such as the preceding movement of the player and the height and trajectory of the ball (Otago, 2004). Variations of these dynamic stabilisation training tasks landing onto an unstable surface can also be performed by employing labile surfaces and unstable training devices, as described for dynamic balance.

PART II
Developing physical capabilities for speed and agility

5
STRENGTH TRAINING FOR SPEED AND AGILITY DEVELOPMENT

Introduction

The magnitude and direction of forces generated during running movements are described in relation to the ground. Fundamentally, running and change of direction performance is dependent upon the ability to impart forces to the ground during each foot contact (Randell *et al.*, 2010). Ground reaction force generation is similarly a definitive aspect of closed kinetic chain strength training exercises. Thus, an athlete's maximal strength (one repetition maximum) score for a closed-chain free weight exercise (e.g. barbell squat) is often reported to show a statistical relationship with running performance (McBride *et al.*, 2009).

Production of ground reaction forces serves dual aims during running. The first is to oppose forces acting in a negative direction due to the effects of gravity and the athlete's own inertia (Randell *et al.*, 2010). The second is to generate propulsion in a positive (particularly horizontal) direction. The former demands both isometric and eccentric strength qualities; the latter requires concentric force-generating capacity (Randell *et al.*, 2010).

The particular strength qualities that predominate are also reported to differ for phases within a straight-line sprint (Young *et al.*, 1995). This would appear to reflect the corresponding differences in kinetics and kinematics of starting, initial acceleration, transition and maximal speed phases of sprint running. For example, the capacity to generate horizontal propulsion has been identified as the critical factor throughout the acceleration phases of a straight-line sprint or when increasing speed (Hunter *et al.*, 2005). The determining strength qualities for change of direction performance further appear to differ markedly from those reported for straight-line speed performance. Many of the strength measures identified for straight-line acceleration and speed performance do not consistently report any relation with change of direction performance (Hori *et al.*, 2008).

In addition to determining which strength qualities are important for different aspects of speed and change of direction expression, there is also ongoing debate as to the most effective training methodology to develop the required strength components for speed performance (Sleivert and Taingahue, 2004; Bennett *et al.*, 2009). The situation for agility performance is even more confused in light of the fact that strength training studies reporting improvements in straight-line acceleration or speed performance have typically failed to demonstrate any improvement in change of direction performance (Brughelli *et al.*, 2008).

Strength training requirements of straight-line running or sprinting

Ground reaction forces registered when running at constant velocity, and the corresponding demands placed upon force-generating capacities, are shown to increase at higher running speeds. The magnitude of these increases is, however, markedly different when comparing the forces in vertical and horizontal directions (Randell *et al.*, 2010). Vertical ground reaction forces are shown to increase only moderately, whereas the corresponding relative increase in horizontal ground reaction forces is much more considerable. Furthermore, horizontal ground reaction forces are of particular relevance to acceleration performance. Horizontal ground reaction forces during the acceleration phase of a sprint are reportedly approximately 50 per cent higher than those recorded during maximal sprinting at constant velocity (Randell *et al.*, 2010).

Irrespective of running speed, the role of the extensor muscles of the knee and ankle preceding and during each foot contact is to generate a high degree of joint stiffness. During locomotion the kinetic chain of lower limb joints operates much like a spring with the athlete's centre of mass on top (Brughelli and Cronin, 2008). It is important, therefore, to modulate the stiffness of this lower limb 'spring' prior to and during each foot contact in order to optimise the storage and utilisation of elastic energy during each stride. Conversely, it is the hip extensor muscles that are the primary source of propulsion during ground contact (Belli *et al.*, 2002). During the latter part of the swing phase the hip extensor and knee flexor musculature are required to work in an eccentric fashion in order to decelerate the lower limb and assist in positioning the foot for touchdown (Higashihara *et al.*, 2010). Based upon this assessment, key areas for development for the stance phase of running would appear to be:

1. isometric strength, eccentric strength and reactive speed–strength of the knee extensors and ankle plantarflexors;
2. concentric strength and speed–strength development for the hip extensors and ankle plantarflexors.

Key areas for development for the flight phase would appear to be:

1. concentric speed–strength of the hip flexors;
2. eccentric strength of the hip extensors and knee flexors.

It is important that any downwards displacement of the athlete's centre of mass or collapse at any point in the lower limb kinetic chain be avoided at each foot strike. However, it is also equally important for the athlete to avoid excessive vertical displacement or 'bouncing' upwards when sprinting. Essentially the athlete requires only sufficient vertical displacement to allow repositioning of the lower limb during the swing phase prior to the next ground contact. Elite sprinters are observed to modulate vertical ground reaction force when sprinting so that only moderate relative vertical ground reaction forces are registered even at maximal velocities (Hunter et al., 2005).

These observations would appear to have certain implications for strength training for speed development. On the one hand it is critical that appropriate development of vertical force-generating capabilities is undertaken so that the athlete is able to maintain the requisite vertical stiffness to optimise running mechanics at the upper range of velocities encountered in competition. Conversely, once these minima in terms of vertical force development capabilities have been achieved it would appear prudent to shift the emphasis of strength training to focus more on horizontal ground reaction force development so that further improvements in speed performance may be achieved (Randell et al., 2010). This would appear logical, particularly given that propulsion and therefore acceleration are heavily dependent upon horizontal ground reaction forces.

Strength training requirements for change of direction performance

The strength qualities that are necessary for change of direction and agility performance are much less well defined than is the case for straight-line sprinting (Brughelli et al., 2008). The specific demands will depend upon the kinetics and kinematics of the particular movement, and the characteristic agility tasks will also tend to differ according to the constraints and specific demands of each sport. In general, relative to straight-line sprinting, the specific ability to generate propulsion in a variety of directions would appear to be a critical factor.

To prepare the athlete for change of direction movement it would therefore appear necessary to include strength training modes that provide the requisite strength development and morphological adaptation of the muscle groups involved in executing these multi-planar movements. Specifically, there is a greater demand on the musculature both medial and lateral to the hip when generating medial-lateral ground reaction forces and twisting torques (Kovacs, 2009). It follows that this should be reflected in a greater emphasis upon strength development for the abductor and adductor muscles and the internal and external rotators specifically. This is important not only for enhancing performance but also to guard against injury given the association between specific weakness of the adductors and internal rotators and the prevalence of groin pain in team sports players (Hanna et al., 2010; Tyler et al., 2001). These assertions are reinforced by studies demonstrating the effectiveness of specific adductor muscle strengthening in reducing the incidence of groin pain in these athletes (Tyler et al., 2002).

Agility movements also place a particular emphasis upon eccentric strength qualities (Brughelli et al., 2008; Jones et al., 2009). For example, 'cutting' change of direction movements often require the athlete to decelerate their own momentum prior to accelerating in a new direction of movement. Likewise, agility movements are often initiated with a countermovement such as a 'split step' that acts to preload the locomotor muscles. In accordance with this, one of the rare examples of a strength training study that successfully improved change of direction performance featured a training mode that imposed considerable eccentric loading, that is, (heavy) barbell jump squats performed with loads of 80 per cent barbell squat one repetition maximum (1-RM) (McBride et al., 2002).

Transfer of conventional strength training to agility performance

The majority of studies that have employed a strength training intervention characterised by conventional strength (and speed–strength) training modes have consistently failed to produce corresponding improvements in measures of change of direction performance (Brughelli *et al.*, 2008). It therefore seems apparent that these conventional training modes have very little direct carry-over to change of direction performance and in turn agility.

Reasons proposed for this observed failure to transfer include the lack of correspondence between general strength training modes and change of direction movements with respect to the kinetics and kinematics involved (Brughelli *et al.*, 2008). Specifically, conventional heavy resistance training modes employed are predominantly bilateral exercises that involve primarily vertical force production. This differs considerably from the concentric force production in horizontal and lateral directions characteristic of change of direction movements, as well as the requirement for eccentric strength during the deceleration phase that precedes many 'cutting'-type change of direction movements.

Approaching strength training: conventional or functional training modes?

Neuromuscular adaptations elicited by strength training are largely specific to the nature of the training mode employed (Reilly *et al.*, 2009). The context of the training mode, such as the kinetic and kinematic constraints involved, is therefore a defining factor in terms of what acute training responses are elicited and the degree of immediate transfer to performance. This is the case particularly with elite athletes who have extensive strength training experience.

Strength training modes with the greatest dynamic correspondence (i.e. closest resemblance to the target movement with respect to movement kinetics, kinematics, etc.) can therefore be expected to result in the greatest direct transfer of strength training effects (Gamble, 2006a). However, the paradox of strength training design is that the most task-specific training modes may not necessarily provide the best development of contractile properties and morphological aspects that have been identified as determinants of both speed and change of direction performance.

The high mobility and stability challenge which characterises highly task-specific training modes is identified as limiting the amount of load that can be handled with these exercises (Santana *et al.*, 2007). As a result, these training modes are not generally amenable to imposing significant overload. Taking the example of an upper-body strength training exercise, it has been identified that the standing cable press is limited to a maximal loading that is only in the region of 40.8 per cent of the athlete's body mass (Santana *et al.*, 2007). For an athlete with a bench press 1-RM of 1.5 times their body mass the maximal loading provided by the standing cable press would represent a relative loading of less than 30 per cent of maximum for their upper-body pressing musculature.

Although the upper-body pressing strength in this example is not limiting for athletic performance such as running it remains illustrative in terms of the limitations of functional training modes with respect to imposing maximal loading. The consequences of this will be a failure to recruit the higher threshold type II motor units that produce the greatest power output. Strength training modes must develop maximal or near maximal forces in order to activate these higher threshold type II motor units (Harris *et al.*, 2007b).

As force is a product of mass and acceleration, force development may be maximised by employing maximal loads or maximal acceleration during training – or some combination of the two. Speed–strength training modes that allow acceleration to be maximised will be discussed in Chapter 6. Of the strength training modes, heavy resistance training exercises remain the sole means available for imposing maximal loading for both muscle and connective tissues. Heavy resistance training has been consistently shown to produce the mechanical and morphological adaptations that underpin gross development of strength qualities. In accordance with this, heavy resistance training alone is reported to improve acceleration performance in particular (Delecluse et al., 1995).

On this basis it is unlikely that highly task-specific or 'functional training' modes alone will provide the level of gross development of contractile properties or elicit the morphological adaptation offered by more conventional heavy resistance training modes. These movement-specific training modes might therefore be categorised as 'transfer training' modes. Fundamentally the athlete must, however, first possess the gross strength qualities so that they have something to transfer, and to do so will require training approaches that provide the best development of the underlying contractile and morphological elements. As observed in the previous section, conventional training modes typically employed with heavy resistance training may not directly transfer to certain aspects of speed and agility performance when employed in isolation. However, these training modes still appear to have a critical role to play in the athlete's overall strength development to ultimately improve speed and agility performance capabilities.

The scheduling and structure of the overall strength training plan therefore assumes great importance from the point of view of both ensuring requisite development of gross strength qualities and assuring transfer of training effects to sports speed and agility performance. Specifically, this would appear to require a sequential shift in selection of training modes throughout successive phases of the athlete's training year or macrocycle. Heavy resistance training modes might therefore feature in the general preparation phase of the annual plan, followed by a progressive shift in exercise selection during subsequent training cycles, ultimately culminating in the introduction of transfer training modes that do carry over more readily to performance in later training cycles.

General strength development

As mentioned, heavy resistance training will tend to offer the best development of gross strength qualities that underpin speed and agility performance. Conventional free weights training modes (i.e. barbell and dumbbell exercises) will provide a means to develop the underlying contractile properties and elicit morphological adaptation of the locomotor musculature and associated connective tissues. Variations of a bilateral free weight squat have typically been employed in studies examining the relationship between strength training and speed performance (Cronin et al., 2007). However, issues of dynamic correspondence do still apply with respect to exercise selection even at this early phase in the athlete's strength training plan. It follows that free weights exercises involving unilateral (single-leg) support should form an integral part of general strength development, alongside bilateral lower-body strength training modes.

Exercise selection should also take account of the direction of force production (Randell et al., 2010). Strength training modes can be categorised into those that feature predominantly vertical force production and those that comprise a combination of vertical and horizontal forces. Hence, in addition to exercises executed with both feet planted and involving generation of vertical ground reaction forces, exercise selection should also include alternative strength training modes that involve horizontal as well as vertical force production.

In view of the importance of the hip extensor and knee flexor musculature in generating propulsion during the stance phase of running and conversely the high eccentric force demands placed on these muscles during the mid–late swing phase (Higashihara *et al.*, 2010) it follows that they should be afforded particular emphasis during all phases of strength training. Specifically there is a need for dedicated strength development for the hamstring muscles and this should comprise both concentric and eccentric force production (Figure 5.1). Unilateral versions of conventional strength training modes for the hip extensors avoid the level of lumbar spine loading documented with bilateral lifts of

FIGURE 5.1 Single-leg barbell straight-legged deadlift.

this type, such as the 'barbell good morning' (McGill, 2006b). Performing these exercises from a unilateral base of support also incorporates activation of stabiliser and synergist muscles of the hip.

When considering change of direction performance, one identified limitation of conventional strength training modes is that they do not comprise production of lateral ground reaction forces to any great extent. However, selecting strength training modes that feature horizontal force production remains critical with respect to the component sagittal plane deceleration and propulsion movements involved in various change of direction movements. Furthermore, the requirement for stabilisation in frontal and transverse planes should be accounted for in exercise selection when undertaking general strength development. Both of these considerations again point to the importance of unilateral strength training modes – particularly lunge and step-up movements.

Given the role of arm and shoulder mechanics with respect to the arm drive and counter-rotation that occurs during running and change of direction movements it is important that upper-body strength training modes also remain an integral part of each phase throughout the training year. During the general strength development phase, exercise selection will feature predominantly bilateral upper-body pressing and pulling exercises in a variety of planes of motion. On the basis that upper-body strength development is being undertaken for the purposes of enhancing (lower-body) locomotion performance it follows that where possible upper-body strength training modes should feature some coordination or co-contraction of the trunk and lower-body musculature. One way of ensuring this is to employ upper-body strength training modes that are performed in a partial or fully weight-bearing posture (Figures 5.2 and 5.3). Similarly, bilateral upper-body strength training modes reported to feature significant trunk and lower-body co-contraction will be favoured. Relevant examples in the literature include the inverted row exercise performed partially weight-bearing (Fenwick *et al.*, 2009). However, in view of the technique flaws identified when performing the inverted row a modified version of this exercise in which the athlete's feet are supported on a stability ball has been proposed in a previous publication (Gamble, 2009b). The modifications aim to encourage greater anterior trunk stabiliser recruitment and also help avoid hiking the hips and extending the lumbar spine as observed with the inverted row exercise (Fenwick *et al.*, 2009).

Aside from exercise selection, the other parameters of training prescription will in general follow those typically recommended for general strength training. Training frequencies of two to three times (per body part) per week have been concluded to optimise strength gains in advanced lifters and athletes alike (Peterson *et al.*, 2004; Rhea *et al.*, 2003). Typical intensity or load ranges for the general preparation phase are in the range of 5- to 12-RM loads. However, when training primarily to develop speed and agility capabilities, hypertrophy is not a primary programme goal. It has been reported previously that performing a hypertrophy-oriented strength training workout can have a negative short-term effect on power output (Baker, 2003). On this basis the upper limit is likely to be around 8-RM, and average intensity will tend towards 6-RM. Similarly, as well as avoiding excessive strength training volume, the very brief rest intervals characteristic of hypertrophy-oriented training are likewise not appropriate; rest intervals that allow more complete recovery are more beneficial. Finally, there should be appropriate emphasis on the acceleration/deceleration profile of each repetition as this can influence force output as well as the eccentric phase of the lift (Harris *et al.*, 2007b). A previous study reported

FIGURE 5.2 Split stance bilateral cable press.

that greater gains in strength resulted when subjects were specifically instructed to focus on maximally accelerating the barbell for every repetition, as opposed to lifting without specific focus or instruction (Jones et al., 1999).

'Special preparation phase' strength development

It has been common in track athletics for sprinters' strength training to progress directly from heavy resistance training (e.g. barbell squats) to highly specialised training modes such as bounding and sprinting whilst towing weighted sleds. These highly contrasting training approaches can be viewed as two extremes at either end of a continuum of strength training modes. Logically, it would seem vital that intermediate steps feature in the progression of exercise selection from the conventional heavy resistance training modes employed during athletes' general strength development to the highly task-specific training modes that will ultimately characterise 'transfer training' cycles. Such an approach would be analogous to the staged model described by Bondarchuk (2007). Following the initial *general preparatory* training block this model depicts a progression through intermediate training blocks (*specialised preparatory* and *specialised developmental* cycles), ultimately culminating with a *competitive* training block (Bondarchuk, 2007). Bondarchuk also highlights that it is crucial that there is a 'succession' in the training methods employed during the respective stages in this model, to ensure transfer of training effects when the athlete arrives at the competition phase.

FIGURE 5.3 Split stance dumbbell row.

What training modes might be employed with each training block in order to provide a coherent shift in exercise selection from conventional heavy resistance training to the highly task-specific training modes is not an area that has been explored to any great extent in the literature to date. In the absence of published studies upon which to base training prescription during the intermediate stages of strength development it is necessary to speculate on what modifications to conventional strength training modes might be employed to provide the requisite progression towards task-specific transfer training modes (Figures 5.4–5.7).

With reference to change of direction performance there is a need to develop the lateral and medial muscles of the hip and lower limb. These muscles act as stabilisers and synergists during straight-line running and so are also important from this perspective. The importance of the adductor, abductor and internal and external rotator muscles is greater still during change of direction activities, as they are employed directly in lateral propulsion, twisting and turning movements that comprise agility movements in the

FIGURE 5.4 Front-racked barbell alternate knee raise.

FIGURE 5.5 Loaded overhead single-leg good morning.

FIGURE 5.6 Front-racked barbell backward lunge.

FIGURE 5.7 Barbell overhead forward lunge.

particular sport. It would appear critical that the development of internal/external rotators and abductor/adductor muscles is approached in combination, in much the same way as the flexor and extensor lower limb muscles are treated as a pair. The function of the anterior-posterior and medial-lateral lower limb muscles during locomotion emphasises the need for coordinated action and agonist and antagonist muscle co-contraction in particular when generating lower limb stiffness.

The training studies that have successfully elicited improvements in measures of change of direction performance have employed bilateral and unilateral jumping and bounding exercises (performed without external resistance) in horizontal and lateral directions (Brughelli *et al.*, 2008). Although speculative, strength training modes that employ similar movements performed with external resistance might prove more effective in improving change of direction performance measures than has been reported for conventional strength training modes. There are some examples of specialised versions of conventional strength training exercises performed with barbell or dumbbells that are employed for athletic development in certain sports, notably ice hockey (Figures 5.8–5.11).

The selection of upper-body strength training modes should once more cater for pressing and pulling movements in a variety of planes (Figure 5.12). However, in general there will also be a progression towards variations of these exercises that pose a greater neuromuscular challenge, particularly with respect to torsional strength and stability. Imposing a torsional challenge requires the athlete to generate axial 'twisting' stiffness in order to resist any twisting motion of the trunk occurring during the exercise (Fenwick *et al.*,

FIGURE 5.8 Front-racked barbell lateral step-up.

2009). This type of stability challenge, and the specific capabilities developed, is analogous to what is encountered during twisting and pivoting change of direction movements in particular.

The torsional strength/stability challenge described above can be achieved by employing alternate arm and single-arm variations (Figure 5.12) of conventional strength training exercises (Behm *et al.*, 2005). Exercises performed in a weight-bearing posture can further serve to combine both a torsional stability challenge as well as trunk and lower-body

FIGURE 5.9 Front-racked barbell cross-over lateral step-up.

FIGURE 5.10 Front-racked barbell diagonal single-leg squat.

FIGURE 5.11 Barbell diagonal lunge.

co-contraction; hence they are favourable from both viewpoints (Figures 5.13–5.16). One example of a single-arm pressing exercise performed in standing displayed significant activation of the muscles of the back and trunk, particularly those on the contralateral

FIGURE 5.12 One-arm incline dumbbell bench press.

(opposite) side (Santana *et al.*, 2007). Another example in the literature, this time a pulling exercise performed in standing (one-armed cable row), reported similar findings with respect to contralateral trunk muscle activation (obliques) (Fenwick *et al.*, 2009).

Training frequency of twice (per body part) per week and an average intensity of 6-RM should be employed in this phase of training, in keeping with what is identified to be optimal for strength gains in athlete subjects (Peterson *et al.*, 2004). The order of exercises in the workout is also shown to influence both the quality and number of repetitions that an individual is able to perform with a particular exercise (Spreuwenberg *et al.*, 2006). Accordingly, it has been recommended that exercise modes deemed most important for a specific training goal should be performed early in the workout, regardless of the relative loading involved or amount of muscle mass recruited in the exercise (Simao *et al.*, 2010). It follows that exercise order should prioritise the more challenging exercises in terms of stability and neuromuscular control demands.

'Transfer' strength training

As implied in the title, strength training modes employed in this phase of the athlete's preparation will be highly task-specific, and as such many will bear clear resemblance to the component actions involved in sprinting and change of direction movements (Figures 5.17–5.20). One such example is the hip flexor training mode described in the study by Deane and colleagues (2005), which essentially involved performing the knee drive action

FIGURE 5.13 Single-arm cable press.

FIGURE 5.14 Single-arm cable row.

FIGURE 5.15 Single-leg cable straight-arm pull-down.

FIGURE 5.16 Front-racked B-drill.

under resistance (Figure 5.18). Another example is the cable lateral walkout investigated by McGill and colleagues (2009).

By their nature these exercises are not amenable to producing maximal levels of muscle activation. Studies that have investigated muscle activity during 'functional' exercises of this type consistently report submaximal activation of the agonist muscles involved – typically in the range of 30–70 per cent of maximal voluntary contraction, depending on the muscle and movement featured (Fenwick *et al.*, 2009; Santana *et al.*, 2007; McGill *et al.*, 2009). This is attributed to the high stabilisation requirement of these tasks, which demands co-contraction of a wide variety of muscles working in unison to stabilise the supporting lower limb and stiffen the athlete's spine and torso. This delicate balance means that a higher level of activity of any one single muscle would effectively destabilise the athlete (McGill *et al.*, 2009).

These 'transfer' training modes can therefore be conceptualised as motor control/coordination training. Despite their limitations for strengthening the limb muscles, exercises of this type do place a considerable emphasis upon the muscles that brace the torso and stiffen the spine and lumbopelvic region. In this way, these training modes represent a potent tool for developing the core strength required for stabilising the torso and stiffening the spine to transmit force during speed and agility tasks (McGill, 2010).

Summary

An approach to designing a strength training plan to develop speed and change of direction capabilities has been described that attempts to provide systematic development of foundation strength qualities with a coherent and progressive shift in exercise selection which culminates in highly specific training in order to transfer strength qualities developed

FIGURE 5.17 Cable-resisted leg drive.

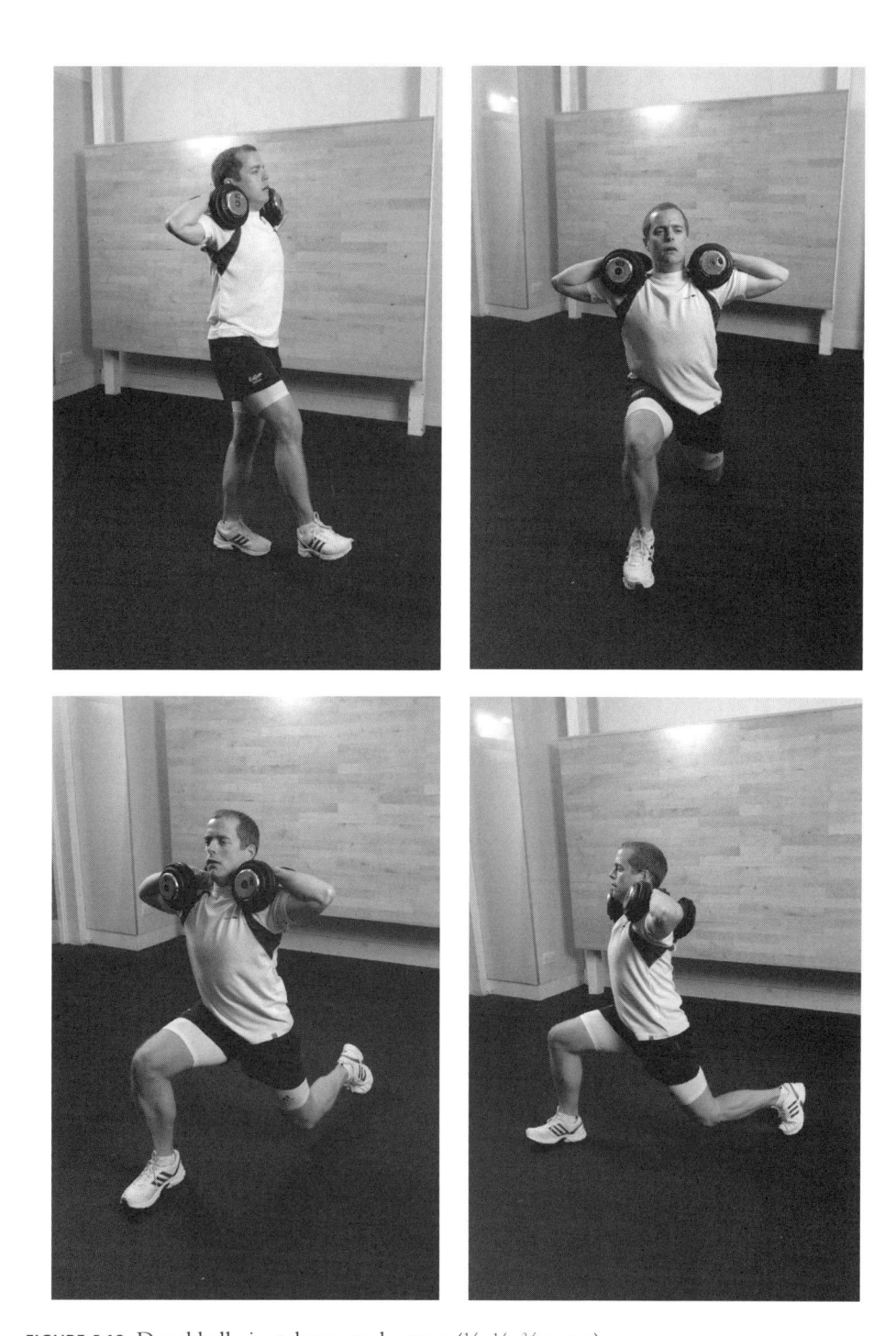

FIGURE 5.18 Dumbbell pivot, lunge and return (¼, ½, ¾ turns).

FIGURE 5.19 Cable-assisted lateral pivot, lunge and return.

FIGURE 5.20 Single-leg cable arm drive.

into speed and agility performance. Such a 'mixed methods' approach to strength training for speed development has been advocated previously (Cronin *et al.*, 2007). The relative length of each phase will vary according to the training history and corresponding level of strength development already undertaken. Broadly, for a younger athlete with limited strength training history the general strength development phase will be more lengthy and extensive than would be the case for another athlete who has completed years of systematic training and thus already developed a foundation of strength qualities.

6
SPEED–STRENGTH DEVELOPMENT AND PLYOMETRIC TRAINING

Introduction

Power can be viewed as a neuromuscular phenomenon that comprises various contractile and neural aspects, as well as the interaction between tendon and muscle (Reilly *et al.*, 2009). Factors that influence power expression include both intramuscular and intermuscular coordination, a variety of strength qualities including maximal strength, and the various structural and neural elements that comprise the 'stretch-shortening cycle' (SSC) (Gamble, 2009c). In view of the multidimensional nature of power expression it follows that speed–strength training to develop power will necessarily feature multiple elements (Newton and Kraemer, 1994).

Previous authors have therefore advocated a 'mixed methods' approach to developing power (Newton and Kraemer, 1994). Such approaches advocate that, in addition to conventional heavy resistance training, athletes should also undertake a variety of specialised speed–strength and plyometric training methods designed to develop each of a number of factors identified as contributing to increases in power. The relevant literature also shows that undertaking dedicated speed–strength or plyometric training in combination with strength training can help to produce superior strength gains (Sáez-Sáez de Villarreal *et al.*, 2010).

Training adaptations elicited by speed–strength and plyometric training modes include neuromuscular effects, such as changes in intramuscular and intermuscular coordination, as well as changes in structural and mechanical properties of the muscle–tendon complex. A key aspect of the interaction between tendon and muscle for ballistic movements, particularly those that involve short ground contact times, is the phenomenon known as the SSC.

Applications of speed–strength training to sports speed and agility

Dedicated speed–strength and plyometric training modes have become an established part of physical preparation in sports that are characterised by jumping, throwing and sprinting activities, which rely heavily upon speed–strength, reactive speed–strength and

SSC capabilities. Furthermore, it has been observed that these training modes have the potential to improve the efficiency and economy of locomotion. Accordingly, the benefits of speed–strength and plyometric training modes are increasingly becoming realised not only for sports requiring speed but also for athletes in endurance events.

With specific reference to speed and agility activities, speed–strength and plyometric training modes serve the following functions:

- developing initial acceleration during sprinting and change of direction activities;
- maximising horizontal propulsion forces developed in the brief period of ground contact during sprinting and agility locomotion movements (Weyand *et al.*, 2010);
- potential decrease in duration of ground contact when sprinting (Rimmer and Sleivert, 2000);
- contribution of 'slow' SSC and reactive speed–strength during the transition from deceleration to acceleration movement when changing direction (Jones *et al.*, 2009);
- optimising elastic energy return and 'fast' SSC performance during each foot contact when sprinting (Wilson and Flanagan, 2008);
- enhancing economy and efficiency of locomotion when executing speed and agility movements (Berryman *et al.*, 2010).

Thus, it is apparent that speed–strength development and plyometric training have a number of potential roles to play in the development of speed and agility capabilities.

Approaching training for power development

Slow velocity strength is required when initiating athletic movements in order to overcome the athlete's own inertia (Stone, 1993). Maximum strength therefore has a major influence on the initial rate at which force is developed early in athletic movements (Stone *et al.*, 2003). High positive correlations are observed between one repetition maximum (1-RM) strength and power output during jumping movements even when performed without any external resistance. In particular, maximum strength relative to body mass is a key element in expression of power for gross motor actions involved in a variety of athletic movements (Peterson *et al.*, 2006).

Maximal strength (developed by means of heavy resistance training) also improves the athlete's capacity to tolerate stretch loads during the eccentric portion of rapid eccentric–concentric muscular actions (Cormie *et al.*, 2010a), such as those involved in change of direction movements. The athlete's enhanced capacity to regulate the stiffness of the musculotendinous unit following heavy resistance training is reflected in observed changes in the movement kinematics that they employ during rapid eccentric–concentric athletic movements.

Strength therefore appears to be a key prerequisite in the expression of power. Accordingly, there is some evidence that strength development is to some extent a necessary precursor for dedicated power development. The initial strength level of those who undertake specific speed–strength training is shown to be related to the magnitude of the training response to this form of training (Cormie *et al.*, 2008). Specifically, subjects who had greater baseline strength scores exhibited more pronounced training adaptation following the speed–strength training intervention (Cormie et al., 2010b). That said, an equally important finding of this study is that weaker subjects did also respond to speed–strength training in the form of jump squats.

Heavy resistance training therefore has a key role in athletes' general preparation to provide the necessary foundations for the specific development of explosive power expression that will follow in later training cycles. Following this initial foundation strength development it is, however, apparent that there is a need for dedicated speed–strength training in order for the athlete to fully develop the ability to express their explosive power capabilities. The importance of dedicated speed–strength training is demonstrated by the finding that speed–strength training modes are consistently shown to produce gains in power beyond those elicited by heavy resistance training alone (Newton et al., 1999; Baker, 1996; Delecluse et al., 1995). That speed–strength training interventions are observed to increase power output independently of any change in measures of maximum strength or morphological changes to the muscle is similarly testimony to the efficacy of dedicated speed–strength training (Newton et al., 1999; Winchester et al., 2008).

The importance of the eccentric phase and the neuromuscular capacities involved when performing rapid eccentric–concentric movements such as those seen in change of direction and running activities has been underlined with respect to concentric power expression (Cormie et al., 2010a). Reactive (speed–)strength has been identified as a discrete property of the neuromuscular system, which is defined as the ability to rapidly make the transition from eccentric to concentric movement (Young and Farrow, 2006). Measures of reactive strength performance also typically show a greater statistical relationship with change of direction performance (Sheppard and Young, 2006), which reflects the considerable eccentric and deceleration component that is common to many change of direction activities (Gamble, 2009d). It therefore appears that the eccentric phase of power activities is equally important and these qualities should receive appropriate emphasis during speed–strength training.

Developing the various components that contribute to power expression in combination appears to have a cumulative impact upon the athlete's ability to develop explosive power. Combining training modes has been shown to not only yield the benefits associated with both single training modes, but also produce specific improvements on some measures that were not seen with either high-force or high-velocity training alone (Harris et al., 2000). Combined methods have similarly been found to be most effective in improving vertical jump height (Baker, 1996), the standard measure of vertical lower-body power performance. It follows that the same should hold true for the horizontal power production required by sprinting and change of direction activities.

Speed–strength training modes

Intramuscular coordination aspects as well as the constraints associated with the training mode (such as the ability to unload the resistance at the termination of the concentric phase) are key factors that differentiate specialised speed–strength training modes from similar conventional strength training modes that fail to elicit the same improvements (Young, 2006). Dedicated speed–strength training modes that are employed to develop power expression can be broadly divided into two categories:

- speed–strength training modes that emphasise predominantly concentric power expression;
- training that comprises rapid transition between eccentric and concentric action in a way that harnesses the properties of the SSC.

There exists a variety of training modes within these broad categories. Speed–strength training modes include ballistic resistance training, derivations of Olympic-style weightlifting exercises, and concentric variations of numerous bounding activities. Similarly, there are numerous training modes that fulfil the criteria of SSC training. The most recognised of these SSC training modes is plyometrics, although rapid eccentric–concentric ballistic resistance training exercises also meet the criteria. Plyometric exercises can also be further subdivided into 'slow' SSC and 'fast' SSC training modes, based upon the duration of ground contact.

A key factor common to all forms of speed–strength and plyometric training is the issue of exercise selection. In much the same way as discussed in the strength training chapter, biomechanical aspects strongly influence the nature of the neuromuscular training stimulus and in turn the training adaptation that results from speed–strength training. The principal factors are whether the exercise is performed from a bilateral or unilateral base of support and the direction of force development during the exercise.

Although this is an area of investigation that has yet to receive much attention in the literature, a common theme for all the speed-training modes discussed is the potential for adapting training modes to more closely resemble speed and change of direction activities. Different authors have highlighted that there is a lack of emphasis on lateral movement with the majority of conventional strength, speed–strength and plyometric training exercises (Hedrick, 1999; Kovacs, 2009; Young, 2006). This is despite the fact that lateral movement comprises the majority of movement observed in some sports, particularly racquet sports (Kovacs, 2009). The principle modifications suggested are therefore to employ unilateral variations of conventional exercises and also to modify exercises to emphasise force production in horizontal and lateral directions (Hedrick, 1999; Twist and Benicky, 1996). The strength and conditioning specialist may also be creative in designing novel training exercises that reflect movements which are characteristic of the sport (Kovacs, 2009).

Olympic-style weightlifting exercises

Mechanisms

Olympic-style weightlifting exercises are unique in that the external load is propelled up the natural line of the athlete's body (Kraemer, 1997), which enables relatively high external resistance to be handled in an explosive manner. As a result, very high power outputs can be registered, which far exceed those recorded when performing conventional heavy resistance training exercises such as the barbell squat or deadlift (Garhammer, 1993; Stone, 1993). Another consequence of the unique nature of this form of speed–strength training is that power output is maximised at much greater relative external loads than is the case for ballistic resistance training modes (Kawamori et al., 2005).

Intramuscular firing patterns during rapid muscle contractions are in part pre-programmed by higher motor centres in anticipation of how the movement is expected to occur (Behm, 1995). Thus, power output for an explosive action exhibits learning effects with repeated exposure to the specific training movement (Ives and Shelley, 2003). Repeated exposure to ballistic resistance training thus develops this rapid firing of motor units during the short interval for force development allowed by the ballistic action. Changes in intramuscular coordination with explosive resistance training exercises, such as Olympic weightlifting movements, include improved recruitment and firing of high-threshold motor units at the high contraction velocities associated with the ballistic training movement (Stone, 1993; Hedrick, 1993). These adaptations in intramuscular coordination are reflected in both enhanced rate of force development and high-velocity strength.

With the exception of press and jerk variations of these lifts, Olympic-style weightlifting exercises feature primarily concentric force development. The behaviour of the musculotendinous unit in the plantarflexor muscles particularly differs markedly between concentric-only movements and eccentric–concentric muscular actions (Kawakami *et al.*, 2002). Specific differences relate to the degree of shortening between the contractile elements (muscle fascicle) and connective tissue structures (tendon). In the case of concentric-only movements fascicle length decreases throughout the concentric action, so that the majority of the shortening of the musculotendinous unit occurs at the muscle fascicle (Kawakami *et al.*, 2002). This is reflected in the training adaptations that result from Olympic-style weightlifting exercises, which are largely restricted to measures of concentric power output (Hakkinen *et al.*, 1987).

Application

Characteristically, the classical weightlifting movements are bilateral in nature and feature predominantly vertical force production. Split variations or even single-leg versions of these lifts are possible, which may improve the transfer to single-leg athletic tasks (Gamble, 2009c). However, even with these modifications force production with these lifts remains primarily in the vertical plane. Olympic lift training appears to transfer best to the initial acceleration phase (5-m and 10-m split times) of a straight-line sprint. No improvements are typically reported in measures of change of direction performance following Olympic-style weightlifting training (Young, 2006; Hoffman *et al.*, 2004; Tricoli *et al.*, 2005).

As discussed with respect to heavy resistance training, in spite of the lack of direct transfer observed, the ability to train power expression against heavier resistance offered by this form of speed–strength training will provide foundation development of contractile elements and morphological and neural adaptations. The improved capacity for concentric power development conferred by this form of training will ultimately be favourable for speed development. For these benefits to be realised the transfer of these training effects to speed and change of direction expression might subsequently be achieved by way of more specific training modes in successive training cycles.

Ballistic resistance training

Mechanisms

The advantages of ballistic resistance training modes derive from the fact that the external resistance is unloaded (projected or released) at the termination of the concentric movement (Cronin *et al.*, 2001, 2003). As a result, the load can be accelerated for longer (as the athlete is not required to bring it to a halt at the end of the range of motion), allowing higher peak velocities to be achieved later in the movement (Newton *et al.*, 1996) and appreciably higher motor unit firing rates than those observed with conventional strength training (Behm, 1995; Hedrick, 1993).

Intermuscular coordination during rapid ballistic movements is to a large extent pre-programmed (Behm, 1995). For example, co-contraction of antagonist muscles is in part pre-programmed based upon the anticipated forces and limb accelerations as a protective mechanism to maintain joint integrity. With repeated exposure ballistic resistance training, antagonist muscle activation can be fine-tuned, which can reduce co-contraction and thereby increase net concentric force output for the movement employed during training (Behm, 1995).

Both eccentric–concentric and concentric-only variations of ballistic resistance exercises can be performed. The mechanisms of, and adaptations to, concentric-only ballistic resistance training will be similar to those described previously for Olympic-style weightlifting. It should be stated, however, that much of the improvement in concentric power production following ballistic resistance training derives from improvements during the eccentric phase, which confer increased power output during the subsequent concentric portion of the movement (Cormie *et al.*, 2010a). The rapid coupling of eccentric and concentric phases would therefore appear to be a key feature that underpins much of the training effect elicited by particular ballistic resistance training modes, such as the barbell jump squat exercise. On this basis, eccentric–concentric ballistic resistance exercises appear superior for developing power expression during speed and change of direction movements.

When the concentric phase is executed immediately following an eccentric phase (performed rapidly) the plantarflexor muscles are observed to contract almost isometrically with relatively little change in muscle fascicle length (Kawakami *et al.*, 2002). As a result, the majority of the change in length of the musculotendinous unit occurs at the tendon. This interaction between contractile elements and connective tissues has the effect of increasing both the storage of elastic energy within the tendon and the degree of elastic recoil that follows (Kawakami *et al.*, 2002).

Another consequence of this behaviour of the contractile and elastic elements during rapid eccentric–concentric actions is that both the length–tension relationship and the force–velocity relationship will also then contribute to the augmented force development during these actions (Cormie *et al.*, 2010a). Specifically, the muscle is able to operate close to its optimal length throughout, and the shortening velocity is slow because of the small change in length, which in turn allows high levels of force to be produced (Kawakami *et al.*, 2002). Although speculative, the considerable involvement of tendon recoil during these activities is also likely to elicit morphological and mechanical adaptation in tendon structures in the same way as is seen with plyometric training (Fouré *et al.*, 2010).

Application

One of the major benefits associated with ballistic resistance training exercises such as the jump squat is the coupling of eccentric and concentric muscular actions performed with augmented load. As stated in the previous section, much of the improvement in power expression during the concentric portion of the movement originates from developing the ability to execute this rapid coupling of eccentric and concentric phases (Cormie *et al.*, 2010a). When performed in this way, this mode of training is analogous to a slow SSC plyometric exercise (see later section) performed with added resistance.

Previously it was widely advocated that, to optimise training, practitioners should first identify the resistance that purportedly maximises power output and then undertake training at this specific 'P_{max}' resistance. Contrary to these suggestions, not only have recent data highlighted flaws in the way that this P_{max} resistance is evaluated, but also it has been identified that for many of the ballistic exercises commonly employed (e.g. barbell jump squat) the load that optimised power output actually equates to is body mass resistance (Cormie *et al.*, 2007b; Dayne *et al.*, 2011). Irrespective of what constitutes the P_{max} load, studies have also indicated that training at a range of loads is in fact likely to produce superior results (Cronin and Sleivert, 2005).

The majority of investigations of ballistic resistance training have featured bilateral movements, in particular the barbell jump squat (Figure 6.1). However, split and single-leg variations of these movements that feature unilateral force production are possible (Figures 6.2 and 6.3). That said, the majority of these exercises will still feature predominantly vertical force production, which may limit the direct transfer to the propulsion movements involved in speed and change of direction activities (Randell *et al.*, 2010; Young, 2006).

Plyometrics

Mechanisms

Authors increasingly distinguish between 'fast SSC' (100–200 ms) and 'slow SSC' (300–500 ms) movements based upon the duration of ground contact or force application. The mechanisms and training adaptations associated with slow SSC movements are similar to what has been described for rapid eccentric–concentric ballistic resistance training exercises in the previous section. In addition to the briefer time window for force application that is characteristic of fast SSC plyometric training, a greater level of neural activation both before and during ground contact is also observed with fast SSC exercises (McBride *et al.*, 2008).

Aside from these neural aspects, intensive plyometric training is also found to produce morphological and mechanical changes at the level of the muscle and tendon, in part because of the degree of eccentric and stretch loading involved. Both shortening velocity and peak power output of single type II muscle fibres were shown to be increased in response to a plyometric training intervention that comprised predominantly fast SSC exercises (Malisoux *et al.*, 2006). Although no detectable changes in tendon cross-sectional area are typically evident following short-term plyometric training featuring fast SSC exercises, qualitative changes in the tendon structure have been reported (Fouré *et al.*, 2010). These structural adaptations are reflected in changes in the mechanical properties of the Achilles tendon observed post training. These adaptations include changes in stiffness and dissipative properties (Fouré *et al.*, 2010). In accordance with this, athletes who participate in sports characterised by intensive SSC movements (long jump and triple jump) exhibit increased plantarflexor musculotendinous stiffness when performing SSC activity (Rabita *et al.*, 2008).

FIGURE 6.1 Barbell jump squat.

FIGURE 6.2 Barbell bound step-up.

Changes in intramuscular coordination following exposure to plyometric training include alterations in descending neural input from the motor cortex. Pre-activation of agonist muscles serves to modify the stiffness of the muscle–tendon complex during SSC activities (McBride *et al.*, 2008). The stiffness of contractile tissues in turn modulates the spring-like properties of the lower limb kinetic chain, in particular the capacity to store and return elastic energy during the activity (Wilson *et al.*, 1996).

As described previously for loaded slow SSC movements (rapid eccentric–concentric ballistic resistance training exercises), a major adaptation following training is an improved capacity to regulate stiffness of the musculotendinous unit (Cormie *et al.*, 2010a). The result of this adaptation is that relatively minimal shortening occurs at the muscle fascicle so that the majority of shortening occurs at the tendon, which ultimately allows for augmented power output during the concentric portion of the movement. The muscle and tendon complex behaves in a similar way during fast SSC activities; however, the eccentric phase is much briefer so that pre-activation of motor units prior to touchdown or the landing phase assumes greater importance in terms of regulating stiffness and optimising tendon recoil. In accordance with this, a greater level of neural activation both prior to touchdown and during the eccentric phase is reported during fast SSC exercises (drop jump) in comparison with slow SSC exercises (countermovement jump) (McBride *et al.*, 2008).

Neural control during fast SSC activities includes not only central neural drive but also modulation of local spinal reflexes (Taube *et al.*, 2008; Zuur *et al.*, 2010). Part of the neuromuscular adaptation to fast SSC plyometric training essentially involves over-riding protective neural mechanisms. Intramuscular and intermuscular neural inhibition may be observed prior to exposure to SSC training (Schmidtbleicher, 2008), which is of both central and local origin. Control of neural input during fast SSC movements is in part

FIGURE 6.3 Loaded split bound.

pre-programmed (Taube et al., 2008) but sensory input does also play a role (Zuur et al., 2010). Protective neural mechanisms act upon the descending central input to agonist muscles prior to and during the eccentric phase as well as stretch reflex-mediated activation of agonist motor units, and antagonist muscle co-contraction may also occur (Newton and Kraemer, 1994).

Following a period of fast SCC training this protective neural mechanism is modified (Schmidtbleicher, 2008). Neural adaptations elicited by plyometric training therefore have the combined effect of increasing direct central neural activation as well as acting to reduce presynaptic inhibition at local spinal level on stretch reflex-mediated excitatory input to the agonist muscles (Taube et al., 2008). However, the protective neural mechanism remains in the event that the athlete's stretch or eccentric loading capabilities are exceeded. For example, pre-activation of agonist muscles is withdrawn when the athlete attempts depth jumps above a certain threshold height (Schmidtbleicher, 2008), reflected in a decrease in measured muscle activity (EMG) at the higher drop jump height (Ebben et al., 2008).

Application

Despite the popularity and reported effectiveness of plyometric training there is very little information in the literature upon which to base plyometric training prescription (Ebben et al., 2008). Classically, arbitrary textbook guidelines are provided with respect to athletes' readiness to undertake plyometric training – the most common being that the athlete should first be able to lift twice their body weight for the barbell squat so that they are able to tolerate the stresses associated with plyometric training. Although a minimum level of strength development makes intuitive sense there are no data in the literature upon which to base these specific recommendations. In fact, the ground reaction forces reported for a number of bilateral plyometric exercises are only at a level comparable to those reported for running activities (Wallace et al., 2010). It should also be considered that studies do report improvements following speed–strength training that featured SSC activities even among 'weaker' subjects (barbell squat 1-RM scores less than 1.55 times subject's body mass) (Cormie et al., 2010b).

Ultimately, in the absence of evidence-based guidelines, the strength and conditioning specialist must use their judgement on a case-by-case basis when deciding on the athlete's readiness for plyometric training. Clearly this will also depend on the form of plyometric training being considered, that is, slow SSC versus fast SSC exercises, and care must also be taken with the intensity of plyometric exercises prescribed. Other important considerations are the stage of development of the athlete and their training history, which will include their level of strength development but also more specifically their previous exposure to eccentric loading activities.

The available data with regard to plyometric training prescription indicate that moderate frequency and volumes appear to be most beneficial. One study identified that one or two sessions per week were superior in eliciting improvements in jumping and sprinting performance in comparison with a higher weekly training frequency (four sessions per week) (Sáez-Sáez de Villarreal et al., 2008). It should be noted that the plyometric training employed consisted solely of fast SSC drop jump training and the subjects in this study were only recreationally active.

An analysis of the literature similarly suggests that the dose–response relationship with respect to the volume of plyometric training also shows a ceiling effect, and this appears to be the case for both untrained and athlete subjects. Increases in volume beyond this threshold level appear to produce no further benefit in terms of training effects observed (Sáez-Sáez de Villarreal *et al.*, 2010). Additional volume may carry an added risk of injury and will also lead to impaired performance during the latter part of the session. Peripheral fatigue is evident following a single session of high-volume plyometric exercise, based upon decrements observed on a number of indices of muscle twitch properties and neuromuscular function (Drinkwater *et al.*, 2009).

The most sensible approach, therefore, might be for the strength and conditioning specialist to monitor the athlete's performance during each set and repetition, and terminate the session once fatigue begins to impair performance (Drinkwater *et al.*, 2009). For similar reasons, plyometric training should not be undertaken following fatiguing endurance activity so that the athlete's ability to perform high-intensity plyometric exercise is not compromised (Moran *et al.*, 2009). It follows that plyometric training should be performed first thing in the training day when the athlete is fresh; and in terms of exercise order, plyometric exercises should likewise be placed early on in the workout. A brief rest (approximately 6–8 seconds) is recommended before each repetition, and extensive rest (approximately 8–10 minutes) is advocated between each set of plyometric exercises (Schmidtbleicher, 2008).

There is some suggestion that the conventional intensity guidelines provided by many textbooks may in fact be misleading and incorrect in some instances (Ebben *et al.*, 2008). To resolve this lack of a reliable standard index for plyometric training modes, recent investigations have attempted to assess relative intensity for typical plyometric exercises based upon quantitative data. One such study evaluated a range of slow SSC and fast SSC plyometric exercises by recording activity (EMG) of locomotor muscles during the movement (Ebben *et al.*, 2008). Although this may provide some worthwhile information, employing EMG as the sole measure of intensity risks underestimating the degree of stretch loading and contribution of elastic elements during the movement, particularly for fast SSC exercises. This is reflected in the low relative level of motor unit recruitment (and therefore 'intensity') reported for the drop jump exercise in this study (Ebben *et al.*, 2008). In fact, based upon these criteria a drop jump performed from a height of 61 cm rated lower in terms of relative intensity in this study than a drop jump performed from a lower height (30.48 cm).

Another study quantified intensity in terms of measured peak vertical ground reaction forces, albeit this study assessed only bilateral jumping exercises (Wallace *et al.*, 2010). This study assessed not only the forces exerted during the jumping exercise itself but also the landing forces when the subject touched back down onto the ground following the jump. Unsurprisingly, fast SSC exercises in the form of drop jumps performed from drop heights exceeding 30 cm (i.e. 60 cm and 90 cm) involved greater impact forces upon initial touchdown and landing than the landing forces seen with a countermovement vertical jump (slow SSC exercises) (Wallace *et al.*, 2010). That said, the impact forces when landing from a standing horizontal jump, which is classed as a slow SSC exercise, were also found to be considerable. In the latter instance, coaching of correct landing mechanics in order to more efficiently dissipate impact forces may help to reduce the stresses involved.

Employing plyometric training alone has been shown to improve 10-m and 40-m sprint times of national-level team sports players (Rimmer and Sleivert, 2000). In addition to the documented effects of plyometric training on speed performance, a plyometric training intervention that featured lateral and diagonal jumping and bounding exercises likewise reported improvements in two separate measures of change of direction performance (Miller et al., 2006). Fast SSC plyometric training in the form of drop jumps is also shown to be highly effective in eliciting improvements in endurance athletes' running economy (i.e. reducing energy cost of running at a given speed) (Berryman et al., 2010).

In terms of exercise selection, it follows that in order to improve speed and agility performance there should be appropriate emphasis on multidirectional movements that feature in change of direction activities (Miller et al., 2006), as well as plyometric exercises that are specific to sprinting (Rimmer and Sleivert, 2000). The benefits of employing different forms of plyometric training – that is, slow SSC and fast SSC training modes – in combination has also been advocated, based upon analysis of the relevant research literature (Sáez-Sáez de Villarreal et al., 2010).

Slow SSC training

Athletes will often perform a preload movement such as a split step (Kovacs, 2009) or a 'false step' (Frost et al., 2008) when accelerating from a stationary position. A range of horizontal bounding movements in various directions, executed from a stationary position but initiated with a countermovement, might be employed in this way (Figure 6.4).

Fast SSC training

Careful selection and progression should be employed regarding the intensity of fast SSC exercises, in terms of the stretch loading imposed during the touchdown or landing phase. In terms of progression, using the drop jump example the athlete should be progressively exposed to increasing drop heights over time to allow the necessary adaptation to take place. Monitoring vertical jump height achieved with different drop heights over time can help to guide this process. In this instance, identifying the threshold drop height at which vertical jump height becomes compromised can serve to guide the upper limit of the athlete's present eccentric loading capabilities (McBride et al., 2008).

In addition to developing the athlete's capacity to handle (vertical) eccentric loading, exercise selection should also reflect the need to develop the ability to generate horizontal propulsion during the subsequent concentric phase. The single-leg drop horizontal jump exercise in particular has been identified as being reflective of the unilateral eccentric loading and horizontal propulsion featured in running (Meylan et al., 2009). A similar approach to progressing drop height by monitoring horizontal jump distance might also be employed with horizontal drop jump training.

Horizontal bounding fast SSC exercises with initial contact through the midfoot have been identified as featuring kinetic parameters that are favourable for developing sprinting performance (Mero and Komi, 1994). Short-term plyometric training that featured unilateral and horizontal bounding exercises was reported to be successful in improving 10-m (acceleration) and 100-m (maximum speed) sprint times in non-athlete subjects (Delecluse et al., 1995). Although not widely studied to date, a similar approach to fast SSC training can also be applied to change of direction movements (Figure 6.5).

FIGURE 6.4 ¼, ½ and ¾ counter-movement pivot and bound into lunge.

FIGURE 6.5 ¼, ½ and ¾ drop pivot and bound into lunge.

Coordination training: resisted sprint training methods

Mechanisms

Coordination training is an approach to speed–strength training that involves applying resistance directly to sports and motor skill movements (Gamble, 2009c). Typically, ballistic movements such as throwing and jumping activities are most amenable to this approach, as they allow the resistance to be projected at the termination of the concentric action. Numerous methods have been employed to impose resistance during the sprinting action. These include uphill running, towing a weighted sled, running with a parachute to impose added wind resistance, running with weighted vests and running with weight added to lower limb joints (Bennett et al., 2009).

The rationale for resisted sprint training modes is that they are highly specific to the sprinting action and on this basis should favour direct transfer to sprinting performance. One implication of this is that the resistance imposed should not dramatically alter the kinetics and in particular the kinematics of the sprinting motion – as doing so would appear to violate the biomechanical specificity ascribed to these training modes. Changes to sprint kinetics and kinematics are observed with resisted sprint training modes. These changes include increased ground contact time, decreased stride length and decreased stride frequency, although to a lesser extent (Cronin and Hansen, 2006). The degrees of forwards lean and hip flexion are also increased when towing a weighted sled, as is the degree of upper-body motion, and these changes appear to become more marked with greater towing loads (Lockie et al., 2003). Exposure to resisted sprinting conditions might therefore be detrimental to sprinting technique over time if these training modes are used excessively or if the level of resistance imposed is inappropriate.

Application

The characteristic changes to running kinetics and kinematics associated with sled towing make this form of training most appropriate for developing sprint acceleration (Cronin and Hansen, 2006; Gamble, 2009c). The increased forwards lean and hip flexion observed with sled towing replicate the kinematics of the acceleration phase of sprinting quite closely (Lockie et al., 2003). These changes become more marked with greater loads, so one issue with this form of training is that the towing load should not be excessive to the extent that the disruption to running mechanics becomes too great. In addition to the quantity of load on the sled the amount of friction between the sled and the running surface must also be considered (Cronin and Hansen, 2006).

One approach suggested by a number of authors that takes account of both of these factors is to monitor the athlete's running speed when towing the sled (Alcaraz et al., 2009; Cronin and Hansen, 2006). It is proposed that running speed should be maintained at or above 90 per cent of the athlete's sprint times under unloaded conditions; if the decrease in normal running speed exceeds this value then the amount of loading should be reduced (Lockie et al., 2003). For trained athletes running on an outdoor synthetic athletics track this threshold load value equates to around 10 per cent of the athlete's body mass (Alcaraz et al., 2009).

Of all the resisted sprint training methods described, adding mass directly to the lower limb (10 per cent of respective segment mass to both lower leg and thigh) appears to be the training mode that reportedly imposes the least interference to sprinting kinematics. Although sprint times were slowed under the resisted condition, sprint kinematics were maintained so that stride variables (stride frequency, flight time, contact time) did not differ significantly from normal conditions in the group of trained sprinters studied (Bennett et al., 2009). Further study is, however, required to ascertain whether these apparent advantages translate into improvements in speed performance following a period of training with this training modality.

Although not explored in the literature to date, resistance could be applied to the acceleration movements that feature during change of direction activities in much the same way as the resisted sprint training modes described. This form of training might therefore comprise resisted acceleration movements in a variety of directions, incorporating various forms of resistance (towing sleds, bungee cords, added mass to lower limbs).

Postactivation potentiation: complex training

Mechanisms

Preceding muscle activity is shown to influence the contractile performance of a muscle when another muscle contraction is subsequently performed. One of these residual effects is fatigue; however, another effect that can be observed is for twitch contraction force to be enhanced above normal levels (Hamada et al., 2000). This latter effect has been termed postactivation potentiation (PAP). These effects are transient and reportedly dissipate approximately 20 minutes after the initial muscle contraction (Kilduff et al., 2007). The net result of these opposing fatigue and potentiation effects ultimately determines any observed changes in athletic performance.

One of the underlying biochemical processes responsible for these changes is phosphorylation of regulatory myosin light chains, which occurs as a result of the calcium release during the initial muscle contraction (Chiu et al., 2003). This process renders the contractile elements (actin and myosin) within the muscle fibre more sensitive to further calcium release during subsequent muscle contraction (Paasuke et al., 2007). Postactivation potentiation effects are also attributed to other neural mechanisms, in particular acute changes in both central and local regulatory inputs to motor units involved in the movement (Kilduff et al., 2007).

Both isometric and dynamic heavy resistance modes have been successfully used to elicit PAP effects (Paasuke et al., 2007). Studies have shown, however, that maximal voluntary contractions are superior in eliciting PAP effects than submaximal muscle contractions (Hamada et al., 2000), regardless of the contraction type employed (e.g. isometric versus eccentric/concentric). When performing complex training it would also appear critical to minimise fatigue whilst optimising any transient potentiation effect (Kilduff et al., 2007). The rest interval between the preceding 'primer' exercise and the target activity is therefore a key factor. Studies assessing complex training for the lower limb extensor muscles have typically employed 4- and 5-minute rest periods; however, the results have been equivocal. One study failed to produce any significant PAP effect using rest intervals up to 4 minutes between performing a 5-RM barbell squat and five repetitions of a countermovement jump (Jensen and Ebben, 2003). However, a 4-minute rest interval was reported effective in eliciting PAP effects in another study, albeit only in a subgroup of subjects (McCann and Flanagan, 2010).

Aside from the rest interval employed, other variables that might influence relative fatigue versus potentiation effects are the load and volume employed with the preceding primer activity (Kilduff *et al.*, 2007). Finally, the resistance exercise mode would appear to be another key variable that might conceivably influence the nature and respective time frames of fatigue and PAP effects (McCann and Flanagan, 2010). Although maximal voluntary activation is a key factor, how this is achieved in terms of the load (i.e. mass) versus acceleration demands of the exercise mode employed may influence fatigue versus PAP effects differently. For example, one possible alternative to a heavy resistance training mode for the primer activity is to employ a speed–strength training mode (Gamble, 2009c). One study employed a ballistic resistance exercise (barbell jump squat) in this way (Baker, 2001) whereas another more recent study employed an Olympic-style weightlifting exercise (barbell hang clean) (McCann and Flanagan, 2010). Both of these studies reported that the speed–strength exercise mode employed was successful in producing PAP effects.

There is considerable variability between individuals with respect to the degree of PAP or even whether any effect is observed (McCann and Flanagan, 2010). The presence of PAP effects appears to be linked to the relative proportion of type II fast twitch fibres and the cross-sectional area of type II fibre subtypes in individuals tested (Hamada *et al.*, 2000). This appears to be reflected by the finding that power athletes seem to exhibit different responses from endurance athletes with respect to PAP (Paasuke *et al.*, 2007). Both the magnitude and the time course of PAP may therefore differ according to the athlete's training background. The degree of potentiation is likewise suggested to be related to the lower-body strength scores of the subject (Young *et al.*, 1998). This is supported by a study which reported that PAP effects were demonstrated by athlete subjects whereas the recreationally trained subjects did not show such a response (Chiu *et al.*, 2003).

Application

As mentioned above, the characteristics of the individual, which include muscle fibre composition, strength level and training history, strongly influence the presence of and nature of any PAP effect observed (Chiu *et al.*, 2003; Hamada *et al.*, 2000; Paasuke *et al.*, 2007; Young *et al.*, 1998). What adds further complexity to the issue is that there also appears to be an interaction between these individual factors and the variables relating to the 'primer' exercise (mode, load, volume and rest). Specifically, preliminary data suggest that the 'optimal' resistance exercise mode and rest interval for eliciting PAP may vary according to the individual athlete (McCann and Flanagan, 2010). This study reported that, for some of the college team sports athletes studied, a heavy resistance exercise (5-RM barbell squat) elicited the greater PAP response in terms of vertical jump performance assessed before and after the 'primer' exercise. In contrast, for other athletes in this study the 'power' exercise (5-RM hang power clean) proved more effective. Similarly, within the subjects studied one subgroup exhibited greater PAP effects when vertical jump height was assessed after a 5-minute rest interval than after a 4-minute interval, whereas the converse was found in another subgroup of subjects, that is, the improvement was observed after the 4-minute rest interval (McCann and Flanagan, 2010).

From the available evidence it would appear that complex training prescription might best be approached on a case-by-case basis. Essentially, a trial and error approach has been advocated to establish what parameters (exercise mode, rest interval) are found to produce the maximum PAP effect for the individual athlete (McCann and Flanagan, 2010). Pilot testing with each athlete might therefore be the best way to determine what is optimal for each individual. Given the lack of clear guidelines and time commitment involved in undertaking preliminary testing for each athlete, the strength and conditioning specialist must ultimately decide whether this form of training is appropriate or justified. Furthermore, there is currently a lack of data to support the longitudinal benefits of this advanced form of speed–strength training.

7
METABOLIC CONDITIONING FOR SPEED AND AGILITY PERFORMANCE

Introduction

During competition in intermittent sports the athlete is required to perform numerous bouts of high-speed running activity. Therefore, the athlete's capacity to recover sufficiently to perform such successive bouts of high-intensity activity is therefore a critical factor in these sports (Spencer *et al.*, 2005). Ultimately, the ability to perform maximally for one sprint or bout of high-intensity agility movement is of limited value if the athlete is not capable of doing so again when the match situation next demands it.

Characteristic fatigue-related changes are observed to occur when performing repeated bouts of sprint running, which alter the athlete's 'spring–mass' characteristics when running (Girard *et al.*, 2011). Specifically, vertical stiffness is shown to decrease over the course of successive sprint bouts so that there is greater vertical displacement of the athlete's centre of mass during ground contact. These changes are accompanied by reductions in propulsion forces during ground contact and a lengthening of both stance and flight phases, with associated reductions in stride frequency in particular (Girard *et al.*, 2011). The athlete's capacity to resist these negative changes in running mechanics when performing repeated bouts of high-intensity activity will be key to maintaining speed and agility performance during the course of a contest.

Two major determining factors with respect to energy metabolism for speed and agility performance are the *power* [i.e. rate of adenosine triphosphate (ATP) production] of the metabolic pathways involved and the overall *capacity* of these metabolic systems (Bundle *et al.*, 2003; Weyand and Bundle, 2005). In a single bout of running the relative rate of anaerobic energy production decreases at an exponential rate with time elapsed. Conversely, the rate of aerobic energy production shows an exponential increase from an initially very low rate. As the duration of a single bout of running increases, the relative contribution from anaerobic sources thus decreases whilst the aerobic contribution increases. The maximal rate of energy (ATP) production from aerobic metabolism is far less than that from anaerobic pathways. For example, an athlete's maximum running speed when working at maximal oxygen uptake (vVO$_2$max) is reported to be around 60 per cent of the maximal anaerobic running speed they can sustain for a brief (approximately 3-second) period (Bundle et al., 2003). Consequently, this relative shift from anaerobic towards aerobic metabolism as run time increases is reflected in a considerable decrease in average running speed (Weyand and Bundle, 2005).

This situation is altered when dealing with repeated bouts of running. Even if lengthy periods of recovery are allowed following the initial bout of sprinting, subsequent efforts are characterised by an increased contribution from aerobic sources, which appears to offset a decreased relative contribution from anaerobic metabolism (Bogdanis et al., 1996). Thus, there are additional factors that come into play with repeated bouts of high-intensity running compared with the relatively simple equation for single efforts. Specific areas requiring consideration are the capacity to perform at high intensity under conditions of residual fatigue, and developing fatigue resistance in order to offset changes in mechanical and contractile properties of the lower limb musculature that occur as a result of peripheral and/or central fatigue (Wilson and Flanagan, 2008).

Metabolic bases of high-intensity effort

Anaerobic energy pathways

Anaerobic metabolism comprises the phosphagen system and glycolytic metabolic pathway, with the biochemical processes involved all taking place outside the mitochondria within the cytoplasm of the muscle cell. The phosphagen system consists of high-energy phosphates within the muscle fibre – specifically, intramuscular stores of ATP and phosphocreatine (PCr) (Maughan and Gleeson, 2004b). This is the most immediate source of ATP and provides the highest rate of energy production (predominantly by means of very rapid ATP resynthesis) of all metabolic systems. The glycolytic system consists of non-oxygen-dependent energy production from carbohydrate within the muscle fibre by way of the glycolytic metabolic pathway (Maughan and Gleeson, 2004b). Glycolytic metabolism contributes a considerable portion of the total energy production during sprint exercise lasting approximately 10 seconds. Glycolysis is associated with lactate production and correspondingly the release of hydrogen ions, which alters the pH level (i.e. acidity) within the muscle (Maughan and Gleeson, 2004b).

Anaerobic capacity

This parameter involves both the capacity for energy production by way of glycolytic metabolism and the capacity to sustain this form of metabolism for the duration required (Maughan and Gleeson, 2004c). In turn, this involves the following components:

1. muscle fibre composition – type II fibres have a higher glycolytic capacity;
2. content and activity of glycolytic enzymes within the muscle cell;
3. lactate handling and muscle buffering capacity – to offset acidosis within the muscle cell and inhibition of glycolytic metabolism (see section on muscle buffering capacity).

Aerobic metabolism

Aerobic sources of energy production all involve oxidative metabolism within the mitochondria in the muscle cell (Maughan and Gleeson, 2004d). Carbohydrate and fat are both used as substrates for oxidative metabolism (as is protein under certain conditions). The contribution of aerobic metabolism to energy production for single high-intensity efforts of brief duration is relatively small (Spencer *et al.*, 2005). However, the aerobic contribution to longer-duration efforts and repeated bouts of high-intensity running (particularly with incomplete recovery) can become considerable (Bogdanis *et al.*, 1996; Ross and Leveritt, 2001).

Peripheral adaptations supporting enhanced muscle oxidative capacity appear to be most influential with respect to sprint and repeated sprint performance (Bishop *et al.*, 2004). That said, faster oxygen uptake kinetics measured during recovery bouts (also termed VO_2 off-kinetics) has also been identified as a factor that correlates to repeated sprint ability (Dupont *et al.*, 2010). Central adaptations that support oxygen delivery to the muscle therefore also appear to play a role when performing repeated high-intensity efforts.

Muscle buffering capacity

Glycolysis is one of the major sources of energy production (ATP resynthesis) for bouts of high-intensity running. The hydrogen ions released simultaneous to glycolytic lactate production require buffering to prevent acidity levels within the muscle cell falling into ranges that inhibit biochemical pathways and interfere with contractile processes (Maughan and Gleeson, 2004b). Lactate transporters work to clear lactate and hydrogen ions from the muscle cell (Kubukeli *et al.*, 2002). Additionally, muscle buffering mechanisms serve to handle hydrogen ions to minimise the impact on muscle pH. In this way the net effect of acidosis resulting from glycolytic metabolism is minimised – up until the point when hydrogen ion accumulation overwhelms the buffering capacity of the muscle cell (Ross and Leveritt, 2001). Accordingly, increasing the content of buffering substances or enhancing the capacity of the various processes that clear lactate or buffer hydrogen ions within the cell can improve hydrogen ion handling, which in turn can allow the athlete to operate at high intensity for longer.

Repeated sprint ability

The majority of intermittent sports (team sports, racquet sports, combat sports) feature brief bouts of high-intensity activity (sprints or agility movements) interspersed with periods of varying length during which the athlete operates at lower intensity (Bishop *et al.*, 2004). The requirement for repeated high-intensity performance impacts considerably upon the bioenergetics of repeated sprint activity in relation to what is described for single bouts of maximal sprint exercise (Spencer *et al.*, 2005). The metabolic demands of repeated sprint activity effectively alternate between energy production (i.e. generating ATP) during sprint bouts and recovery processes (ATP and PCr resynthesis and handling/clearing metabolites) during the rest periods in between (Balsom *et al.*, 1992). In addition, when more than one sprint is performed the proportional contributions from different metabolic systems to energy production also shift in each successive bout of high-intensity running. The major differences between a single bout of sprint exercise and repeated sprints involve an increased oxidative contribution to energy production accompanied by a decreasing direct contribution from glycolysis in successive sprints (Bogdanis et al., 1996).

The precise energy system contribution to repeated sprint work is dependent upon a variety of factors, such as the distance or duration of sprint bouts (Spencer et al., 2005). The length of recovery periods between work bouts is another decisive factor that impacts upon not only the bioenergetics (energy system contribution) but also the performance changes between successive sprints (Balsom et al., 1992). Intermittent field sports typically feature sprints over distances of 10–20 m or of an average duration of 2–3 seconds; however, the duration of recovery periods between bouts of high-intensity running is highly variable – even within a particular sport a wide range of work–rest ratios are reported (Glaister, 2005).

These considerations necessitate an increase in the direct contribution from aerobic metabolism to energy production during work bouts (Bogdanis et al., 1996). Repeated sprint activity also involves a greater requirement for oxidative capacity of the muscle to facilitate restoration of PCr between work bouts (Spencer et al., 2005). During rest periods between work bouts the athlete's oxygen uptake and heart rate therefore remain elevated to support oxygen-dependent processes involved with restoring energy substrates and also clearing metabolites (Glaister, 2005).

Another decisive factor in the athlete's ability to maintain levels of sprint or agility performance when undertaking repeated bouts of high-intensity activity is their capacity to operate under conditions of residual fatigue, incomplete restoration of energy sources and accumulation of metabolites from preceding work bouts (Edge et al., 2006a). The ability to clear and buffer metabolites – in particular hydrogen ions – is identified as a determining factor in repeated sprint ability (Bishop et al., 2004; Edge et al., 2006a). For example, this is a key factor in offsetting the inhibition of glycolytic pathways, thereby maintaining the contribution of glycolytic metabolism to ATP production in successive high-intensity efforts (Glaister, 2005).

The specific performance and fatigue effects associated with repeated sprint activity will be dictated by the duration and intensity of high-intensity running, the distribution of work bouts in relation to periods of active recovery and, finally, the duration and intensity of activities performed during these periods of active recovery (Billaut and Basset, 2007). Each of the factors described will clearly have implications for the design of metabolic conditioning. This point will be explored further in later sections of this chapter.

Relevant training adaptations for speed and repeated sprint performance

Studies typically focus on peripheral adaptations that occur in and around the trained muscle – although concurrent developments in aerobic capacity are also likely to include central adaptations. The primary peripheral adaptations with respect to metabolic processes fall into three broad categories (Ross and Leveritt, 2001):

1. enzyme adaptation;
2. energy substrate availability or restoration;
3. capacity to clear and buffer metabolites.

Enzyme adaptation

Adaptations with respect to enzyme content and activity characteristically observed with sprint training predominantly involve glycolytic enzymes in the cytoplasm as well as those associated with glycogenolysis (Kubukeli *et al.*, 2002). Increases in oxidative enzyme activity have also been reported by some sprint training studies; however, this appears to be dependent upon the structure of the training employed, in particular the duration of sprints and length of recovery bouts employed (Ross and Leveritt, 2001). Repeated sprint training protocols that are characterised by short sprint intervals interspersed with relatively brief rest periods have more consistently been shown to elicit improvements in oxidative enzyme capacity (Gibala *et al.*, 2006) and aerobic performance (Hazell *et al.*, 2010).

Energy substrate availability and restoration

Resynthesis of ATP and in particular restoration of PCr stores are key factors if the athlete is required to perform more than one bout of high-intensity running in isolation, which by definition is inevitably the case for intermittent sports (Spencer *et al.*, 2005). The duration of recovery prior to the next bout of high-intensity effort is often too brief to allow for complete recovery of PCr stores within the working muscle. The initial fast phase of PCr resynthesis is identified as being dependent upon oxygen availability (Bogdanis *et al.*, 1996). Accordingly, peripheral adaptations that improve the oxidative capacity of the muscle will serve to enhance the athlete's capacity to restore PCr levels between work bouts (Spencer *et al.*, 2005).

Another key factor with respect to the resynthesis of ATP is the progressive loss of the adenine nucleotides (required for reconversion back to ATP) that can occur with repeated sprint exercise (Spencer *et al.*, 2005). Specifically, as the rate of breakdown of ATP exceeds the rate of ATP resynthesis, the by-products of the ATP hydrolysis are further broken down to their constituent parts [adenosine monophosphate (AMP) and inorganic phosphate (Pi)] in order to produce more ATP – and these substrates may then diffuse out of the muscle (Glaister, 2005). This process can conceivably reduce the adenine nucleotide pool (ADP, AMP) that is available for subsequent ATP resynthesis (Maughan and Gleeson, 2004c). Adaptations that serve to reduce this further breakdown and diffusion of substrates for ATP resynthesis are reported with high-intensity conditioning and repeated sprint training (Spencer *et al.*, 2004).

Glycogen stores within the muscle required to fuel glycolysis are likewise finite and have been shown to be depleted during the course of a contest in some sports, which in turn has been reported to impact upon the number of high-intensity bouts that athletes attempt during the latter stages of a contest when in a depleted state (Spencer *et al.*, 2005). This is similarly a factor for events that require multiple contests within a short period of time, for example tournaments in racquet sports and team sports that involve competing on consecutive days or even multiple matches on the same day. This will obviously restrict the time available for taking on nutrients to replenish depleted muscle glycogen stores. In the case of aerobic metabolism the availability of substrates (which for oxidative metabolism includes carbohydrate, lipid and protein) is very unlikely to be a limiting factor – aside from ultra-endurance sports, which are obviously beyond the scope of this text. However, one highly relevant adaptation that occurs following a period of training (including high-intensity interval training) is increased mobilisation of lipid stores within the muscle to fuel aerobic metabolism (Iaia and Bangsbo, 2010). The importance of this is that it serves to spare the finite muscle glycogen stores required for non-oxidative metabolism (i.e. glycolysis).

Capacity to clear and buffer metabolites

The capacity of buffering and lactate transport mechanisms within the muscle has been shown to improve following a period of training involving long sprints or repeated sprint training. Short-term high-intensity interval training is shown to elicit superior improvements in muscle buffering capacity compared with moderate intensity continuous training matched for total training volume, despite similar improvements in VO_2peak and lactate threshold (LT) (Edge et al., 2006b). In accordance with this, repeated sprint-trained athletes demonstrate a capacity to tolerate a higher relative lactate level within the working muscle without a corresponding change in muscle pH (Edge et al., 2006a).

Accumulation of other metabolites produced from high-intensity energy metabolism – specifically P_i – has also been implicated in the mechanism of fatigue associated with repeated sprint activity (Glaister, 2005). The removal of P_i within the muscle cell is another oxygen-dependent process. It is therefore postulated that improvements in oxidative capacity elicited by appropriate training will benefit the capacity to perform repeated high-intensity efforts by this mechanism.

The loss of potassium (K^+) ions from the muscle cell as a consequence of the repeated activation of the sodium/potassium pump during muscle contractions is also identified as a fatigue mechanism during high-intensity running exercise (Iaia and Bangsbo, 2010). Higher levels of sodium/potassium pump activity are associated with a reduced net loss of K^+ ions from contracting muscle. One of the major adaptations identified with a high- and maximal-intensity interval training is an increased expression of sodium/potassium pump subunits with a concurrent reduction in K^+ ion accumulation measured in venous blood (Iaia and Bangsbo, 2010). Much of the improvement in performance associated with this form of training is attributed to this specific training adaptation.

Running economy and movement efficiency

Aside from metabolic aspects, there is also a neuromuscular component to endurance performance, typically termed running economy or movement efficiency depending on the mode of locomotion involved (Jones and Carter, 2000). Studies examining the effects of different modes of training with respect to running, cycling and swimming performance identify that neuromuscular training adaptations that relate to work economy are specific to the training mode employed (Foster et al., 1997; Millet et al., 2002). Improvements in running economy are likewise closely related to the running velocities employed in training – so that runners are observed to exhibit superior running economy at the speed at which they habitually train (Jones and Carter, 2000).

From a repeated sprint activity viewpoint, the capacity to recruit and activate motor units under conditions of fatigue is a trainable quality (Paavolainen et al., 1999). This is a critical point in view of the adverse changes in lower limb stiffness and mechanical properties and the associated alterations in sprinting mechanics that are observed under conditions of fatigue (Wilson and Flanagan, 2008). However, the findings observed in relation to running economy show that the underlying neuromuscular adaptations observe the same rules of specificity as other aspects of training adaptation.

One of the implications for metabolic conditioning is that the unorthodox forms of locomotion and agility movements that occur during high-intensity efforts in the sport should feature in order to provide appropriate development of movement economy and efficiency (Gamble, 2009e). Similarly, these activities should be executed at the velocities that occur in competition to facilitate these improvements.

Approaching metabolic conditioning for sports speed and agility

'High-intensity' aerobic conditioning

Despite the advantages of high oxidative capacity in supporting single and repeated sprint efforts, the training outcomes associated with conventional aerobic endurance training are contrary to those required for sprint performance. There is necessarily a trade-off between training to optimise speed performance and training to optimise aerobic endurance performance. Fundamentally, it is unlikely that any athlete will achieve maximal aerobic and anaerobic power values that are both in the upper physiological range for elite athletes (Weyand and Bundle, 2005).

Despite the association identified between oxidative capacity or oxygen availability and the capacity for repeated sprint activity, there is currently a lack of training studies reporting a direct causal relationship between aerobic conditioning and improvements in repeated sprint ability (Glaister, 2005). Inconsistent findings reported by studies assessing the impact of aerobic conditioning on various indices relevant to repeated sprint ability may be a consequence of the form of endurance training employed. The format and intensity of conditioning has been reported to strongly influence training responses, for example with respect to adaptations in lactate threshold (Tabata *et al.*, 1996) or muscle buffering capacity (Edge *et al.*, 2006b), both of which are relevant to repeated sprint ability.

It follows that the approach to developing oxidative capacity for predominantly sprint or repeated sprint athletes will necessarily be different from the more conventional endurance training methods that might be undertaken with endurance athletes (Gamble, 2009e; Stone and Kilding, 2009). The objectives of aerobic conditioning might rather focus on the peripheral adaptations that support energy metabolism and oxidative recovery processes for repeated sprint activity, as opposed to solely aiming to improve aerobic capacity or maximal oxygen uptake (VO_2max). Similarly, the design of aerobic conditioning to support repeated sprint ability should be reflective of the intermittent nature of this activity.

There is an increasing body of published data that support the potency of high-intensity metabolic conditioning (Laursen, 2010). For example, it has been shown that brief maximal sprint interval training can elicit comparable short-term changes in oxidative capacity and endurance performance to conventional moderate-intensity endurance training (Burgomaster *et al.*, 2008; Gibala *et al.*, 2006; Macpherson *et al.*, 2011). Authors do, however, acknowledge that improvements in performance are greatest when this form of training is employed in combination with other forms of high-intensity aerobic conditioning (Iaia and Bangsbo, 2010).

'Aerobic' interval training

Aerobic interval training describes conditioning protocols that feature relatively brief periods working at velocities at or above maximum lactate steady state intensity, interspersed with active or passive rest intervals (Billat, 2001a). Both long aerobic interval training (1- to 8-minute work bouts) and short aerobic interval training (10- to 30-second work/rest bouts working at or around VO_2max velocity) methods have been described. In both cases the defining characteristic of these conditioning modes is that aerobic metabolism remains the dominant energy source as a result of the combination of work intensities and work–rest durations employed (Billat, 2001a).

In the case of long aerobic training modes the intensity of work bouts is effectively self-limited in a way that ensures that aerobic metabolism predominates. It is evident that the majority of the energy for work durations exceeding approximately 75 seconds is supplied by oxidative metabolism (Laursen, 2010). Hence, high-intensity conditioning modes that employ work bouts that exceed this duration can be classified as fuelled predominantly by aerobic metabolism. One protocol that employed 4-minute bouts of hill running reported significant improvements in measures of endurance performance in junior elite soccer players that were reflected in performance measures (including number of sprints) observed during competitive matches (Helgerud et al., 2001).

'Anaerobic' interval training

What differentiates anaerobic interval training from the aerobic interval conditioning approaches described is that the intensity of work bouts is 'supramaximal' (i.e. above the velocity that elicits VO_2max) and the combination of work–rest durations employed results in anaerobic metabolism predominating (Billat, 2001b). Commonly used anaerobic interval training methods employ 10- to 15-second work bouts at intensities of 130–170 per cent VO_2max, with relatively brief rest intervals ranging from 15 to 120 seconds.

In between these two broad classifications, combinations of exercise intensities and work–rest ratios have been identified that elicit close to maximal rates of both aerobic and anaerobic energy production (Tabata et al., 1997). In the varsity athletes studied by Tabata and colleagues (1997) a cycling interval training protocol consisting of six sets of 20-second work bouts at 170 per cent VO_2max interspersed with 10-second recovery intervals was effective as a maximal stimulus for both aerobic and anaerobic metabolism.

Instead of employing a set recovery time between work intervals, another approach to regulating rest periods between intervals for long aerobic interval training and anaerobic interval training particularly is to use a set criterion heart rate value – that is, once heart rate has dropped to a target value during the recovery following a work bout the athlete then initiates the next interval. This is suggested to be a superior approach to using a set recovery time. Specifically, this will help to avoid a scenario whereby the athlete takes either too long between intervals so that the overall physiological stimulus is compromised or conversely too short a recovery between bouts, which can impair performance in later intervals (Vuorimaa and Karvonen, 1988). This approach is also sensitive to changes in fitness over time and acute effects of environmental conditions or daily fluctuations in the athlete's performance capacities. Target recovery heart rates of 120 beats/minute and 130 beats/minute are commonly reported in the literature (Billat, 2001a,b). Another perhaps more individualised approach is to use a set percentage of the athlete's heart rate maximum (e.g. 60 per cent HR_{max}) (Vuorimaa and Karvonen, 1988).

It is apparent that there is a continuum in terms of interval training protocols, whereby running speed and the relative duration of work and rest intervals may be manipulated to elicit varying relative contributions from aerobic versus anaerobic metabolic pathways. Within a periodised scheme, the metabolic conditioning employed to develop an athlete's capacity for repeated high-intensity exertion might therefore follow a progression so that the initial part of the training year begins with training akin to the aerobic interval conditioning methods described, with a relative shift over time to anaerobic interval training, prior to undertaking repeated sprint conditioning.

Repeated sprint or speed-endurance conditioning

Repeated sprint conditioning or 'sprint interval training' can be seen to differ from the anaerobic interval conditioning methods described previously in that work bouts are characterised by all-out efforts or sprints at maximal speed (Burgomaster et al., 2008). Other differences are that relatively longer recovery durations (approximately 2–4 minutes) are used to help maintain performance in successive sprints and the duration of work bouts may also be shorter (approximately 5–10 seconds) – although this is not always the case (Hazell et al., 2010). The fact that this form of conditioning consists of sprints or all-out running efforts facilitates specific adaptations associated with 'speed endurance' – that is, developing fatigue resistance for high-intensity running performance (Wilson and Flanagan, 2008). Repeated sprint conditioning provides a specific training stimulus in that it challenges the athlete to maintain maximal levels of muscle activation and force output under conditions of residual fatigue (Paavolainen et al., 1999).

A range of repeated sprint protocols have been reported to improve parameters of both anaerobic and aerobic performance (Hazell et al., 2010). Sprint interval training protocols that have attracted recent attention involve 30-second all-out efforts separated by 4-minute recovery periods (Gibala et al., 2006). Training interventions employing this sprint interval training format have reported significant gains in muscle oxidative capacity and endurance performance that are comparable to those from conventional high-volume endurance training. These studies to date have mostly featured untrained (Burgomaster et al., 2008) or recreationally active (Macpherson et al., 2011) subjects. However, there are also examples in the literature of studies that have successfully employed a similar protocol (30-second sprint bouts with 3 minutes' recovery) with trained athletes (Iaia and Bangsbo, 2010).

A notable finding of one study that reported comparable gains in endurance running performance (2000-m time trial) and VO_2max following sprint interval training (Macpherson et al., 2011) was that whereas the conventional endurance training group showed improvements in maximal cardiac output this was not the case with the repeated sprint training group. The authors of this study concluded that repeated sprint conditioning elicits predominantly peripheral adaptations that support high-intensity endurance performance, as opposed to the central adaptations elicited by conventional moderate-intensity high-volume endurance training (Macpherson et al., 2011). It is, however, notable that this form of training is effective in maintaining oxidative capacity despite drastic reductions in weekly training volume (Iaia and Bangsbo, 2010).

Another recent study identified that a modified protocol employing shorter 10-second work bouts with either 2-minute or 4-minute recovery periods appears to be equally effective in improving both aerobic and anaerobic performance parameters (Hazell *et al.*, 2010). From a specificity viewpoint, the more brief 10-second all-out efforts are somewhat closer to how athletes in intermittent sports work under competitive conditions. That said, even when 10-second work intervals are employed for repeated sprint conditioning this remains considerably longer than the average sprint duration or distance associated with intermittent sports. The range of durations reported are ≤ 6 seconds for team and racquet sports in general (Glaister, 2005) and 2–3 seconds or 10–20 m for field-based team sports (Spencer *et al.*, 2005). When such work bouts of shorter distance or duration are examined the performance and fatigue patterns change accordingly. Performance over shorter distances (0- to 15-m split times) can be maintained over fifteen sets of 40-m sprints with either 1-minute or 2-minute rest intervals (Balsom *et al.*, 1992). An investigation comparing different work–rest ratios with either 15-m or 40-m sprint intervals reported that, in the professional soccer players studied, sprint times for the repeated 15-m sprints were well maintained up until the thirteenth sprint interval with only approximately 15-second rest periods (work–rest ratio of 1:6) (Little and Williams, 2007).

Sport- and movement-specific conditioning modes

From a work economy viewpoint it follows that the characteristic modes of locomotion or high-intensity game-related activities that occur in the particular sport should be identified and then incorporated during repeated sprint conditioning (Spencer *et al.*, 2005). This is necessary to elicit the relevant neuromuscular adaptations involved in developing the capacity to activate locomotor muscles under the conditions of residual fatigue that are characteristic of repeated sprint ability. Therefore, as well as the distance/duration of work bouts and relative length of recovery intervals, the modes of activity employed during repeated sprint conditioning is another key parameter when prescribing metabolic conditioning to develop repeated sprint ability for a particular sport.

One approach to metabolic conditioning that employs relevant movements for the sport involves the use of skill-based conditioning games (Gamble, 2009e). The efficacy of skill-based conditioning games in eliciting physiological responses in the upper ranges necessary to produce significant improvements in measures of endurance has been supported by a number of studies (Gamble, 2004; Hoff *et al.*, 2002). This approach has accordingly been widely employed with team sports players particularly.

Both the format of the particular conditioning game employed and the rules that are imposed are shown to influence training intensity (Hill-Haas *et al.*, 2010), and there are a number of other parameters that can be altered to manipulate overall intensity. For example, modifying the playing area, changing the number of players on each team, minimising the time that the ball is out of play and having coaches present are all shown to elicit greater physiological responses (Hoff *et al.*, 2002; Rampinini *et al.*, 2007).

Given the inherently unstructured nature of this form of conditioning there is a need for some form of monitoring (typically heart rate) to evaluate each athlete's work output during sessions (Gamble, 2004). If these conditions are met, this approach might be employed as a training mode for aerobic/anaerobic interval conditioning that offers a high degree of movement specificity and potential concurrent development of movement efficiency and economy (Gamble, 2009e).

A similar approach, sometimes termed tactical metabolic training, comprises conditioning drills modelled upon sports skill activities and work–rest ratios observed from competition in the sport. This competition-specific form of metabolic conditioning has likewise been demonstrated to elicit physiological responses in excess of 90 per cent of players' maximum heart rate and VO_2max values (Hoff *et al.*, 2002). Accordingly, these conditioning modes have been reported to elicit improvements in endurance fitness in team sports players (McMillan *et al.*, 2005). This approach can also be applied to racquet sports. For example, skill-based pattern work can be modified to elicit the greater physiological responses necessary to serve as aerobic interval training.

Finally, high-intensity movement-based conditioning drills may be adapted for use as a repeated sprint conditioning mode. This approach differs from the tactical metabolic training approach described above in that it does not feature the same sports skill element, which would necessarily limit work intensity. One such high-intensity conditioning protocol that was designed to simulate movement patterns for badminton and conducted on court was investigated in a recent study (Walklate *et al.*, 2009). The high-intensity conditioning bouts consisted of 20-second work bouts comprising a sequence of rehearsed movements covering the area of the court, interspersed with 10-second recovery periods – the number of repetitions completed was progressively increased over the course of the 5-week training period. The 'badminton-specific' repeated sprint conditioning protocol employed in this study reported improvements in measures of anaerobic capacity and repeated sprint ability in highly trained national-level badminton players (Walklate *et al.*, 2009). On the available evidence, this approach therefore has the potential to serve as a highly movement-specific mode of repeated sprint conditioning or speed-endurance training.

8
LUMBOPELVIC 'CORE' STABILITY

Introduction

Athletic movement demands the capacity to stabilise the lumbopelvic region in all three planes of motion, as the athlete must resist internal loads and external forces to maintain postural integrity and joint stability throughout the lower limb kinetic chain during movement (Leetun et al., 2004). The lumbopelvic–hip complex also represents a critical link from the point of view of transmitting forces generated during foot contact through the kinetic chain of lower limb joints and body segments to generate movement of the body as a whole (Gamble, 2009f). The 'core' muscles are described as functioning collectively as synergists for athletic activity (McGill, 2010). For such reasons the lumbopelvic complex has been described as the 'anatomical basis for motion' (Kibler et al., 2006).

The fact that the athlete's centre of mass resides in this region of the body means that lumbopelvic control is similarly implicated in the athlete's efforts to overcome their own inertia and thereby translate propulsion forces generated through the ground into resultant motion of the body. This is pertinent not only to straight-line motion in the case of sprinting, but also during change of direction movements. Applying the spring–mass model of running locomotion to change of direction movement illustrates the importance of the 'core'. Specifically, the capacity to control the position and orientation of the trunk with respect to the athlete's base of support and controlling the tension of the lumbopelvic hip complex are key factors when executing change of direction movement.

In addition to playing a decisive role in the transmission of forces from the ground up, the ability to control the orientation and motion of the trunk is conversely shown to impact upon loading on joints further down the lower limb kinetic chain during change of direction movements (Zazulak et al., 2007). This is particularly relevant to female athletes as the interaction between trunk stability and lower limb joint kinetics has been identified as a key factor underlying the increased intrinsic risk of lower limb injury during change of direction movements observed with female team sports athletes (Hewett et al., 2009).

Appropriate training for the lumbopelvic region is a critical adjunct when undertaking other aspects of training to develop speed and agility. It has been identified that a lack of sufficient emphasis on 'core training', or conversely inappropriate training, is a potential major risk factor for lower limb injury (Waryasz, 2010). Furthermore, in accordance with the variety of functions served by the respective subsystems that provide lumbopelvic stability, there is also a need to develop endurance, strength and power for these muscles (Willardson, 2007). These diverse training goals will require a variety of approaches to 'core training' to be employed during the course of an athlete's physical preparation (Gamble, 2009f).

Components of lumbopelvic stability

Investigations of muscle activity during different exercises has identified that a wide variety of different muscles contribute to providing lumbopelvic stability to differing degrees, depending on both the athlete's posture and the magnitude and direction of forces imposed by a given activity (Juker et al., 1998). Furthermore, these studies report that no single muscle contributes more than 30 per cent of the total spinal stabilisation (Cholewicki and Van Vliet, 2002). These findings have a number of implications:

1. an integrated approach to developing lumbopelvic stability is required;
2. a broad range of training modes and loading conditions will be necessary to recruit the various combinations of muscles that operate during speed and agility activities;
3. no single muscle group or subsystem should be emphasised above any other;
4. training techniques that compromise the capacity of other stabilising subsystems to function should be avoided.

Broadly, the diverse array of muscles that can contribute to stabilising the lumbo-pelvic–hip complex can be divided into three subsystems (Gamble, 2009f), as detailed in the following sections.

Deep local stabiliser muscles

The deep lumbar spine stabiliser muscles have attachments at the level of the lumbar vertebrae and so are uniquely placed to provide stability at the segmental level (Anderson and Behm, 2005; Barr et al., 2005). These muscles are small, which limits their torque-generating capacity, and are therefore mainly concerned with providing local support (McGill, 2007b). Their role as postural muscles is reflected in the observation that these muscles fire at a low level (approximately 10–30 per cent of maximum) in a tonic fashion for prolonged periods (Barr et al., 2005). These muscles are also shown to contain a high density of receptors, and they collectively serve to provide proprioceptive sense of the position and orientation of the pelvis and lumbar spine segments (McGill, 2007b).

The capacity to control lumbar spine posture and the positioning and orientation of the pelvis in particular serves a critical role in determining the ability of other muscles that stabilise the lumbo-pelvic–hip complex to function (Workman et al., 2008). As the site through which compressive and shear forces are transmitted, segmental control of the lumbar vertebrae and the orientation of the pelvis also strongly influence the loading imposed on the lumbar spine, and the activity of these muscles is critical for spine stability (Cholewicki and McGill, 1996).

It has been emphasised that the deep postural muscles that provide local support and stability must not be neglected when training to develop athletes' 'core' strength/stability to avoid a scenario whereby the larger more superficial muscles attempt to compensate at the cost of restricted and impaired movement (Hibbs et al., 2008). Maintaining a neutral lumbar spine posture, and controlling the position and orientation of the pelvis in all three planes/axes of motions, is therefore critical to any activity. Depending on the posture and degree of loading imposed by the task the other two subsystems described below may also be employed; however, engaging the deep local stabiliser muscles must be viewed as fundamental to all activities undertaken in training and competition.

Trunk musculature

Essentially this component functions as a corset formed of the thoracolumbar fascia and the more superficial muscles of the abdomen and back (McGill, 2007b). The larger muscles of the shoulder girdle, specifically those that stabilise the scapula (e.g. latissimus dorsi, trapezius), also contribute to generating tension of this 'corset' when activated (Pool-Goudzwaard et al., 1998). Collectively, these muscles and connective tissues serve to brace the trunk during strenuous activity (McGill, 2007b). The larger trunk muscles, for example the internal and external obliques, can also directly contribute to generating movement (Hibbs et al., 2008). This is of direct relevance to the twisting and pivoting movements that occur in change of direction tasks.

Muscles of the hip girdle

In standing postures and during locomotion the various muscles of the hip girdle act to stabilise the pelvis from the supporting lower limb (Nadler et al., 2000). For example, the hip abductors of the supporting leg help to prevent the pelvis dropping on the opposite side. Although often forgotten, the adductor muscles and internal rotators likewise co-contract with the larger gluteal muscles (abductors and external rotators) to stabilise the pelvis and hip of the supporting leg (McGill, 2007b). The hips and pelvis are described as the anatomical base of support for the trunk (Kibler et al., 2006). The muscles of the hip girdle act to brace the pelvis and trunk during high force movements (McGill, 2010).

Lumbopelvic stability demands of speed and agility movement

The importance ascribed to trunk stability is underlined by a study that examined the views of expert sprint coaches with regard to aspects of technique. Posture was one of the four critical elements of sound sprinting technique identified by the seven international-level sprint coaches interviewed (Thompson et al, 2009). Indeed, for five out of the seven coaches 'posture' was in fact their first given response to the question 'what are the technical characteristics of good sprinting technique?' Further questioning on what constituted correct posture with respect to sound sprinting technique elucidated responses characterised by 'total body control' and specifically the ability to control the muscles of the trunk to maintain a stable and fixed trunk position from which to propel the limbs in the sprinting action (Thompson et al., 2009).

The specific stability demands placed on the lumbo-pelvic–hip complex during straight-line running are mainly concerned with stabilisation in the frontal, sagittal and transverse planes. There is some axial rotation of the pelvis and hips during sprinting, whereby the hip of the lead leg rotates inwards as the leg is propelled forwards during the flight phase before returning to a neutral position at foot strike (Schale et al., 2001). There is some rotation of the hips during sprinting, which is accompanied by counter-rotation at the shoulder girdle (Fujii et al., 2010). Although this motion should be allowed to occur naturally during locomotion, expert sprint coaches have identified the importance of maintaining an extended and relatively stationary trunk posture (Thompson et al., 2009).

In addition to this stabilisation function, the muscles of the lumbo-pelvic–hip complex also appear to have a role in transmitting propulsion forces during each foot contact. These muscles are identified as acting collectively to stiffen the spine and torso during high force movements (McGill, 2010). Returning to the spring–mass model of sprinting, in much the same way as the extensor muscles of the lower limb contribute to lower limb stiffness (and therefore propulsion), these muscles that stiffen the spine can be viewed as fulfilling a similar function. In this way, the action of the 'core' muscles assists the athlete's torso by allowing it to function as a continuation of the 'spring' formed by the lower limb in order to maintain vertical stiffness and prevent collapse when running.

In contrast to straight-line running, change of direction movements also involve considerable shifts in momentum. Bracing the trunk to avoid unwanted movement during deceleration and change of direction movements involves a considerably different stabilisation challenge. For example, 'cutting' change of direction movements are identified as having a particular requirement for lateral trunk strength and stability (Leetun et al., 2004). In turn, this demands a high level of eccentric and isometric strength for the muscles involved, because of the magnitude of the forces imposed as a result of the body's own inertia.

In addition to their role in providing stability and helping to maintain whole body equilibrium, muscles of the lumbo-pelvic–hip complex are directly involved in producing torque to generate motion when performing the twisting and pivoting movements that feature in change of direction activities (Kibler et al., 2006). In accordance with this, some authors have characterised the larger more superficial or 'global' muscles as 'mobiliser muscles', as opposed to the local 'stabiliser' muscles (Hibbs et al., 2008).

Relationship between lumbopelvic stability training and speed and agility performance

In accordance with the theorised role of lumbopelvic strength and stability when performing speed and agility movement, 'core' training in some form is routinely employed in athletes' physical preparation. The potential benefits of appropriate 'core' training are likewise widely promoted as a means to safeguard against injury and enhance performance. The role of lumbopelvic stability training modes in addressing known risk factors for a variety of injuries and its efficacy as an integral part of successful injury prevention and rehabilitation programmes is supported by a number of studies (Barr et al., 2005; Carter et al., 2006; Cusi et al., 2001). However, data to substantiate a strong link between lumbopelvic strength/stability training and athletic or functional performance remain elusive (Gamble, 2009f). This is in part owing to a lack of studies investigating this topic (Hibbs et al., 2008).

The limited number of studies that have been published have typically reported limited statistical relationships between measures of lumbopelvic stability and a variety of athletic performance measures. The first of these studies employed trunk muscle endurance tests as measures of lumbopelvic stability and found only weak to moderate correlations with speed and change of direction measures among college American football players (Nesser et al., 2008). Another study employed similar trunk endurance tests and likewise reported weak to moderate correlations with a test of change of direction performance (T-test) (Okada et al., 2011). Both studies concluded that core stability or 'core strength' were not significant predictors of performance. These studies essentially failed to differentiate between core endurance and core strength. It is entirely possible that a measure of core strength (as opposed to endurance) might have shown a stronger statistical relationship. The fact that the trunk endurance tests (in particular side flexion) still showed significant (albeit weak to moderate) positive relationships with speed and change of direction performance is in itself noteworthy.

To date there have been a selection of studies employing 'core' training interventions that have failed to produce significant improvements in measures of running performance, despite reporting improvements in measures of lumbopelvic stability or endurance (Stanton et al., 2004; Tse et al., 2005). These contradictory findings can be explained in part by the lack of clarity regarding both the nature of the training stimulus, and which of the various components providing lumbopelvic stability were employed during training (Gamble, 2009f). In general, the training interventions employed have comprised relatively low-intensity training modes, reflected in the improvements noted in trunk endurance post training (Stanton et al., 2004; Tse et al., 2005). One study that investigated muscle activity of postural and trunk muscles during similar stability ball exercises to those employed in the above studies concluded that the level of trunk muscle activation associated with these exercises was insufficient for producing gains in strength (Nuzzo et al., 2008).

It has been highlighted that it is important to distinguish between lumbopelvic stability training modes designed to develop motor control and endurance and the more intensive and challenging training modes that develop core strength (McGill, 2010). Although both approaches have merit for athlete preparation, the latter would appear to naturally transfer more readily to performance. Therefore, more challenging 'high threshold' training modes might be expected to produce more favourable results in terms of both core strength and measures of athletic performance. In support of this, preliminary evidence from recent studies that have investigated more demanding training modes has shown improvements in performance during high-velocity whole-body rotational sports skill movements (i.e. throwing velocity) (Saeterbakken et al., 2011).

An integrated approach to training the lumbo-pelvic–hip complex

There appear to be differing lumbopelvic demands during the stance phase versus the flight phase when running. There is a need for torsional stability when the hips and shoulders are in alignment during ground contact and the stance leg is acting to propel the athlete forwards, Conversely, there is a need for axial lumbopelvic control and whole-body equilibrium during the flight phase when the rotation of the hips and shoulders in opposing directions takes them out of alignment.

In addition to the stabilising role described, change of direction activities further require the muscles of the hip and the trunk to generate torques to produce twisting and pivoting movement. Hence, there is a requirement for both 'core stability' and 'core strength'. Furthermore, a variety of strength qualities are involved, specifically isometric strength when stiffening the torso and spine, concentric dynamic strength when generating torque from the hips and, finally, eccentric strength when decelerating and opposing unwanted movement (McGill, 2010).

In view of the different subsystems involved in providing lumbopelvic stability, as well as the variety of roles that these muscles are required to fulfil during speed and agility movement, it follows that an array of training modes will be required to develop each of the different aspects required. It is therefore increasingly recognised that the optimal approach to training the 'core' is to train for both lumbopelvic strength and stability, and to employ a range of different training methods (Hibbs *et al.*, 2008).

Postural stability neuromuscular training

A number of authors have emphasised the importance of training 'low threshold' postural movements, in addition to higher load training for core strength/stability (Hibbs *et al.*, 2008). This points to the need for dedicated training to develop the postural muscles and neuromuscular control capacities involved with precise control of lumbopelvic posture and maintaining whole body equilibrium. The aim of these exercises has therefore been conceptualised as 'an endurance and motor control challenge – not a strength challenge' (McGill, 2010: 39).

The cues employed to activate these deep postural muscles are highly influential in terms of the effect this can have when performing more demanding activities that require the bracing support of the more superficial trunk muscles. Specifically, any cue that encourages hollowing of the abdominal wall must be avoided as this can compromise the ability of these superficial muscles to brace the trunk (McGill, 2006c).

'Low threshold' core exercises

These training modes comprise the more basic static trunk exercises, for example bridge and side bridge, and exercises typically employed in corrective training and rehabilitation. Essentially, these exercises can be viewed as a tool to develop the athlete's motor control and recruitment of deep postural muscles and muscles of the hip girdle (Hibbs *et al.*, 2008; McGill, 2010). The key element common to all training modes employed to develop these capabilities is the inclusion of a static hold during the exercise. This static hold element has been found to differentiate rehabilitation training modes that proved successful in developing the deep postural muscles, including the multifidus (Danneels *et al.*, 2001). With respect to repetition schemes, static hold durations of less than 10 seconds are advocated for developing endurance in a way that avoids the adverse effects of oxygen starvation and acidosis (McGill, 2010).

Postural balance training

Some of the exercises involved will have elements in common with the balance training modes in Chapter 4. It is important that these exercises incorporate postures in which the torso is rotated in order to develop postural balance when the hips and torso/shoulders are not aligned (Figure 8.1).

FIGURE 8.1 Single-leg balance with whole-body rotation.

Lumbopelvic strength and higher load stability training modes

During the higher load training modes described in the following sections it is vital that the deep postural muscles are engaged. Conceptually the deep postural muscles represent the core of the 'core', with the larger muscles and connective tissues forming the outer layers on top. Much the same cues to those employed during postural training described above can be used to engage these muscles, and this will help to ensure that pelvis and lumbar spine alignment is maintained so that the larger muscles of the hip girdle and trunk are able to function optimally. Co-contraction of these larger muscles acts to stiffen the torso to help maintain postural integrity under the loading conditions imposed by the particular exercise (McGill, 2010).

The higher load core strength/stability exercises should predominantly be executed with the spine in a neutral position, as opposed to exercises such as abdominal curls or crunches that involve repeated spine flexion. Training in a neutral spine/pelvis position better reflects the posture employed during the majority of speed and change of direction movements (McGill, 2010). Furthermore, this approach also avoids a potential mechanism for low back pain and injury (McGill, 2007c). The cumulative stresses from performing repetitive spine flexion/extension movements over time can exceed the failure limits of these tissues (McGill, 2010). The significant hip flexor (e.g. psoas) involvement that typically occurs with abdominal 'curl' or sit-up exercises (Juker et al., 1998) also imposes considerable compressive loading on the lumbar spine (McGill, 2007c). An investigation into spine loads and trunk muscle activation (i.e. injury risk versus benefit) for a variety of exercises identified the sit-up as having the highest compressive spine load relative to abdominal muscle activation (Axler and McGill, 1997).

Static trunk stability exercises

As discussed in the previous section, exercise selection will effectively comprise progressions and variations of the front plank, bridge and side bridge exercises. There are numerous means to progress the stabilisation and strength stimulus with these exercises, with various permutations. For example, the stability challenge can be increased by incorporating contralateral limb movement to challenge equilibrium, and/or performing the exercises on a labile surface (e.g. stability ball, domed training device). Performing a given exercise on a labile (i.e. unstable) surface increases the stability challenge, which in turn increases the level of trunk muscle activity – activation of external obliques, in particular, has been shown to be enhanced in the exercises studied (Vera-Garcia et al., 2000). Any combination of these progressions can be employed in the design of static core strength/stability exercises (Figure 8.2).

Variations of bridging exercises are widely advocated to develop the capacity to engage the muscles of the hip girdle whilst concurrently activating the stabilisers of the trunk (McGill, 2006d). The efficacy and importance of the side bridge exercise have similarly been advocated previously (Gamble, 2007) based upon EMG data (Behm et al., 2005) and lower back compressive loads recorded during this exercise (Axler and McGill, 1997). Where possible, exercise selection should favour exercises that report a high level of activation of a broad range of trunk muscles and relatively low compressive load penalty

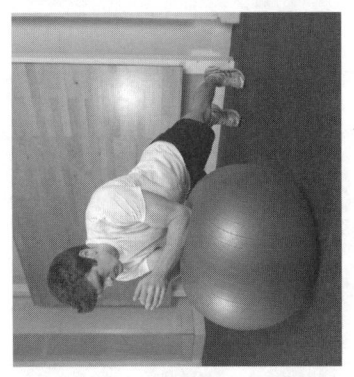

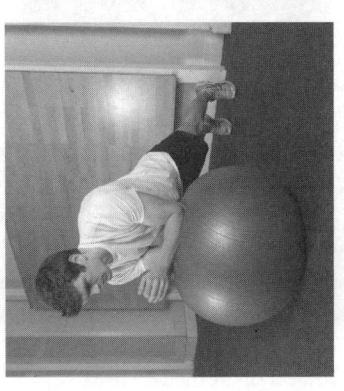

FIGURE 8.2 Swiss ball plank figure-eight exercise.

on the spine, although inevitably there will be some trade-off between these two factors (Figure 8.3).

Studies have identified the importance of lateral trunk strength/stabilisation when performing change of direction movement. Deficits in lateral trunk strength/endurance measures have been found to contribute to instability of lower limb joints, and knee injury risk specifically, in female team sports athletes (Zazulak et al., 2007).

Torsional stability training modes

As with the static trunk stability exercises described, exercise selection for torsional stability training modes will predominantly feature advanced versions of standard exercises

FIGURE 8.3 Side bridge with hip flexion on domed device.

(i.e. plank, bridge, side bridge). The front plank in particular is amenable to challenging torsional stability, which is reflected in its use in movement screens employed with athletes to assess this capacity (McGill, 2006e). The torsional stability challenge with these exercises is mainly achieved by manipulating the points of contact (Figures 8.4–8.6), that is, moving from equal weight-bearing to a unilateral base of support.

Unilateral resisted training modes

This form of lumbopelvic training comprises alternate limb or single-limb resisted movements employing cable resistance or free weights. By this means, the athlete is challenged to maintain postural integrity under conditions of external loading. These exercises

FIGURE 8.4 Extended plank with alternate arm raise on domed device.

FIGURE 8.5 Front plank with alternate arm/leg raise.

FIGURE 8.6 Swiss ball alternate leg jackknife.

specifically challenge the ability to brace the trunk and hip girdle in order to maintain a stationary and stable posture as the athlete performs the resisted movement with upper or lower limb(s) (Figures 8.7–8.9). This form of stabilising challenge therefore features elements of both torsional stability and isometric trunk and hip muscle strength.

The importance of movement specificity has been emphasised for this form of training (Hibbs et al., 2008). Specifically, the recruitment and sequence of activation of trunk muscles should correspond to what occurs during movement in the sport. There is a degree of feedforward control of trunk muscle activation, corresponding to the anticipated stabilisation challenge (Hibbs et al., 2008). Accordingly, to optimise carry-over of neural adaptations following training, the design of core strengthening exercises should aim to reflect the type of loading conditions that the athlete is exposed to during speed and change of direction movements.

FIGURE 8.7 Single-leg alternate arm cable press.

FIGURE 8.8 Front plank with lateral dumbbell raise.

Rotational training

It has been identified that it is important to differentiate between twisting and twisting torque (McGill, 2010). The combination of twisting movements performed under load can be particularly injurious for the spine. In general, the safest and best approach may be to separate twisting exercises from exercises involving rotational torques. Specifically, twisting movements should be performed under limited load, and performed chiefly by generating torque from the hips with a neutral and braced spine (McGill, 2010).

Although it is important to be strong and stable during movements in which the hips and shoulders are aligned, it is equally critical that the athlete is able to retain lumbopelvic stability and posture when the pelvis and shoulders are moving independently of each other. This situation occurs not only during the flight phase when running but also during

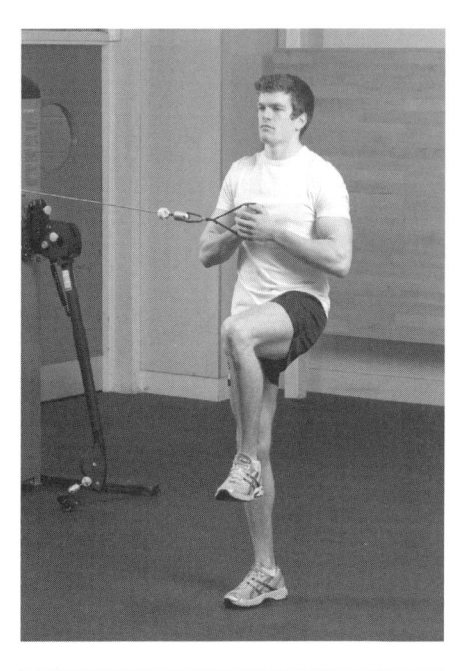

FIGURE 8.9 Side-on single-leg cable push out.

the pivoting and twisting movements involved in change of direction activities. From this point of view, it is vital that exercise selection for stabilisation exercises progresses to movements in which the motion of the shoulders is dissociated from the hips, and vice versa (Figures 8.10–8.12).

FIGURE 8.10 Swiss ball overhead Russian twist.

FIGURE 8.11 Swiss ball hip rotation onto domed device.

FIGURE 8.12 Single-leg cable-resisted rotation.

9
WARM-UP METHODS AND MOBILITY TRAINING

Introduction

The warm-up has become an established part of athletes' preparation for both competition and training. Warm-up protocols vary widely; however, in most intermittent sports the warm-up will tend to comprise an element of low- to moderate-intensity running activity combined with some form of stretching. The stated purposes of the warm-up process are typically:

1. to elevate heart rate and breathing rate;
2. to raise muscle and core temperature; and
3. to increase flexibility of muscles and joints.

One of the main benefits commonly attributed to the warm-up is a reduction in the risk of injury when the athlete subsequently undertakes the training session or competition. The other major benefit that has become associated with a proper warm-up is an increase in muscle function and performance. Other relevant aspects of the warm-up process concern the athlete's mental preparation (Bishop, 2003a). Of particular relevance to speed and agility performance is the potential impact of an appropriate warm-up routine on athletes' level of psychological arousal.

Stretching and flexibility training are similarly undertaken with the aim of improving athletic function and reducing injury risk. Traditionally, stretching has commonly been part of an athlete's warm-up and cool-down routine. In recent times stretching in its conventional form has fallen out of favour as a standard component of athletes' warm-up. Stretching has been removed from the warm-up process in a number of sports because of fears about potential negative effects on performance. Stretching does remain a recognised aspect of the 'cool-down' procedure that follows training and competition; however, given the increasing emphasis placed upon a variety of other passive and active recovery methods that are employed during the cool-down, stretching may increasingly be overlooked.

The rationale and underpinning evidence for the 'warm-up'

In the following sections we will explore each of the functions commonly ascribed to the warm-up, with reference to the underpinning evidence, and discuss the potential impact upon the capacity to perform speed and agility activities.

Initiating metabolic processes

Undertaking preparatory activity serves a role in priming the metabolic and biochemical processes that will be employed during the type of repeated sprint activity that features in training and competition. In particular, initiating oxidative metabolism prior to undertaking high-intensity exercise would appear a potential means to enhance performance. There is a time lag associated with increasing oxygen consumption and fully mobilising this metabolic pathway at the onset of exercise (Maughan and Gleeson, 2004b). Initiating oxygen uptake kinetics and aerobic metabolism and increasing blood flow and thus oxygen delivery in advance of the onset of high-intensity activity would therefore appear beneficial (Bishop, 2003b). The importance of these oxidative processes in the recovery between bouts of sprint activity and the direct contribution of aerobic metabolism to energy production in successive sprints has been discussed in Chapter 7. Accordingly, increased oxygen uptake at the onset of exercise and reduced blood lactate accumulation are observed when high-intensity exercise is performed following an appropriate active warm-up (Gray and Nimmo, 2001). The effect of this increase in oxygen uptake and blunted blood lactate response on repeated sprint performance has yet to be investigated; however, the potential positive effects of an increase in the contribution of oxidative metabolism and improved lactate handling are worthy of consideration.

Improved ventilatory function

In addition to the benefits described for the skeletal muscles that produce movement, there is some evidence that warming up the muscles involved in breathing can serve a similar function (McConnell, 2011). Previous activity that serves to warm up the respiratory muscles has been shown to have a beneficial effect on athletic performance when incorporated into an overall warm-up regime. This has been shown when utilised in combination with a variety of exercise modes, including intermittent running (Tong and Fu, 2006). These performance changes are attributed in part to a reduction in athletes' perception of dyspnoea (sensation of breathlessness) during intensive activity as a result of warming up the respiratory muscles (Tong and Fu, 2006). That said, there is some indication that to fully realise these benefits may require the use of specialised apparatus in order to produce a specific inspiratory muscle warm-up (McConnell, 2011). This contention is primarily based upon the finding that a warm-up involving strenuous whole-body (rowing) activity failed to elicit significant changes in inspiratory muscle function (Voliantis *et al.*, 1999).

Reducing tissue viscosity

One function of warming up the limbs is to decrease the viscosity of contractile and connective tissues. Raising the temperature of the tissues in itself reduces passive joint stiffness (Bishop, 2003a). Warm muscles and connective tissues are also better able to tolerate passive stretching and eccentric loading (Woods *et al.*, 2007). Aside from raising muscle temperature, a key factor with respect to reducing the viscosity of the muscle–tendon complex is the mode of activity and the joint range of motion (ROM) involved in the warm-up. A critical issue that must be considered is the effect of the warm-up activity on the active stiffness of the muscle–tendon complex. Although reducing muscle and connective tissue viscosity can be beneficial, it is critical that active stiffness regulation is not compromised, as this is identified as a key factor in speed performance.

Enhanced neuromuscular function

Increasing muscle temperature by performing general warm-up activities will in itself increase the rate of biochemical processes involved in muscle contraction (Stewart *et al.*, 2003). This is reflected in twitch contraction time parameters, including reduced time to peak tension and relaxation time (Gray and Nimmo, 2001). Essentially, when performing rapid movements a warm muscle will contract at a faster velocity (Bishop, 2003a). Improvements in muscle twitch characteristics (maximal torque and contraction time) may therefore be observed following any activity-based warm-up that increases muscle temperature (Škof and Strojnik, 2007). Similarly, nerve conduction velocity and motor unit activation may also increase as a result of raising muscle temperature. Accordingly, an active warm-up on a stationary cycle that raised muscle surface temperature by 3°C increased a marker of nerve conduction velocity and this was also accompanied by an increase in peak instantaneous power output measured when the subjects performed a squat jump (Stewart *et al.*, 2003). Indeed, improvements in a variety of measures of dynamic force and peak power output are noted following an active warm-up (Bishop, 2003a). Improved mechanical efficiency at high movement speeds is also observed when muscle temperature is raised (Stewart *et al.*, 2003).

Specific warm-up protocols that comprise more intensive running and bounding activities may confer additional benefits with respect to neuromuscular function (Škof and Strojnik, 2007). Specifically, in addition to the improvements in contractility related to biochemical processes, performing high-intensity sprinting and bounding activity may also yield a postactivation potentiation effect, resulting in enhanced neural activation. As was discussed in Chapter 6, the recent contractile history of a muscle can influence its neuromuscular function and power output when high-intensity activities such as sprinting are subsequently performed within a certain time window following the initial potentiating activity. In support of this, significant increases in both maximal torque and shortening velocity were observed following an active warm-up protocol that incorporated sprinting and bounding activities (Škof and Strojnik, 2007). These effects were not elicited to the same degree following an active warm-up that consisted solely of low-intensity running activity.

Reducing injury incidence

From the available evidence, warming up has been concluded to confer protective effects in terms of reducing the incidence of injuries sustained in the early stages of a game or immediately after a scheduled break between periods in a match (Woods *et al.*, 2007). The trends for a higher incidence of injury apparent among team sports players in the initial stages when substitute players enter the game also provide indirect evidence for the necessity of a comprehensive warm-up (Gamble, 2009f). The protective effect associated with warming up appears to be most evident for muscle strains and ligament sprains.

Acute effects of stretching on performance

Stretching is an integral component of warm-up protocols that are routinely employed across all sports (Woods *et al.*, 2007). However, a number of studies published over recent years have suggested that the use of static stretching might cause short-term impairment of performance. As discussed in the previous section, although reducing muscle and connective tissue viscosity is beneficial, it is important that this is not achieved at the cost of reduced active stiffness of the muscle–tendon complex. Neural effects evoked when prolonged stretch is applied to muscle appear to result in a decrease in motor neurone excitability (McHugh and Cosgrave, 2010) and a reduction in stretch reflex-mediated activation of motor units during stretch-shortening movements (Rubini *et al.*, 2007). Both static stretching and partner-resisted proprioceptive neuromuscular facilitation (PNF) stretching methods have been reported to elicit these inhibition effects (Bradley *et al.*, 2007).

A variety of studies have investigated the acute effects of static or isometric stretching on a number of different measures of neuromuscular performance. Although results are equivocal, a number of studies have reported reduced scores on various measures of explosive performance immediately following isometric stretching protocols. Impaired performance on isokinetic knee extension power output (Yamaguchi *et al.*, 2006), vertical jump height (Bradley *et al.*, 2007), running economy (Wilson *et al.*, 2010) and 20-m (Fletcher and Jones, 2004; Nelson and Bandy, 2005), 50-m (Fletcher and Anness, 2007) and 60- and 100-m (Kistler *et al.*, 2010) sprint times have all been reported in the literature. In the last study, the detrimental effects of static stretching on performance all appeared to occur in the initial 20 m of both sprints (Kistler *et al.*, 2010).

In contrast, other studies have found no such deleterious effects of static stretching (in relation to subjects who performed no stretching) (Chaouachi *et al.*, 2010; Little and Williams, 2006). The reasons for the differences in findings are unclear at present, although there are a number of factors that might play a role in whether any impairment in explosive performance is observed. For example, the duration and intensity of stretches employed could conceivably influence the effects elicited by the static stretching protocol (Chaouachi *et al.*, 2010). Similarly, the muscle groups involved in the selected stretches may also be a decisive factor. Specifically, stretches involving the lower limb extensors will potentially be more critical than those involving other muscle groups not directly involved in providing propulsion during running activities.

The training background and performance level of subjects studied also appear to influence the degree of any performance effects elicited by static stretching (Chaouachi *et al.*, 2010). This was the explanation offered by one study that reported no impairment in running performance among the professional soccer players studied (Little and Williams, 2006). Another important consideration is the length of time between stretching and undertaking the performance test (Chaouachi *et al.*, 2010). A related factor is what (if any) activity is undertaken during this period. A group of subjects in one study that performed bounding and sprinting activity following warm-up and static stretching reported enhanced contractile performance in comparison with another group that underwent the warm-up and stretching protocol in isolation (Škof and Strojnik, 2007). Therefore, it is possible that performing explosive activities following stretching might offset any negative effects.

An alternative to static stretching involves the use of dynamic flexibility or dynamic range of motion exercises. With these exercises the athlete moves through the active range of motion in a controlled fashion; this method should therefore not be confused with ballistic stretching. In contrast to the findings of studies investigating static stretching discussed previously, dynamic flexibility exercises do not appear to produce the neural inhibition associated with static stretching (McHugh and Cosgrave, 2010). Furthermore, dynamic flexibility exercises are reported to exert a positive influence on subsequent sprint performance (Fletcher and Anness, 2007; Fletcher and Jones, 2004). Postactivation potentiation may play a role in the improvement in performance observed following dynamic stretching (Chaouachi *et al.*, 2010). Indeed, even studies that report no detrimental effects of static stretching have still identified that dynamic stretching appears to be the superior method for preparing the athlete to perform (Little and Williams, 2006). The fact that this form of stretching involves active movement also helps to concurrently elevate muscle temperature (Nelson and Bandy, 2005).

An evidence-based approach to warming up for speed and agility activities

Some authors have used the acronym RAMP to describe the different objectives of the warm-up with respect to performance – that is, Raise, Activate, Mobilise, Potentiate (Jeffreys, 2010). The first part (raise) refers to elevating muscle temperature, a variety of other physiological parameters (heart rate, ventilatory rate), and potentially also psychological arousal. Activate and mobilise refer to recruiting the musculature that will be employed in the training or competition activity and working through appropriate joint ranges of motion. The final element – potentiate – refers to the acute effects elicited by the warm-up that can serve to enhance explosive performance.

Active warm-up

Various modes of exercise have been employed successfully to increase muscle temperature and elicit the associated benefits described in the previous section. The range of activities employed in the literature includes stationary cycling and jogging or low-intensity running activity. However, to best prepare the athlete for the high-intensity running and change of direction activity to follow it would appear beneficial if the active warm-up featured relevant movements. Either a closed-skill approach to warm-up (featuring pre-planned and self-paced running and change of direction activities) or an open-skill warm-up involving a ball and reactive movement appears to be equally effective (Gabbett *et al.*, 2008).

The intensity of the warm-up activity and the time elapsed between warming up and performing high-intensity activity are two issues that will determine the effectiveness of the warm-up and in particular the effect on performance. Furthermore, the level of conditioning of the athlete is likely to influence both of these factors (Bishop, 2003b).

Specifically, if the relative intensity of the warm-up is too high and/or insufficient time is allowed before performing the high-intensity activity then performance may be impaired as a result of acute fatigue effects and also depletion of high-energy substrates, in particular phosphocreatine (PCr) (Bishop, 2003b). Conversely, excessive volume or duration of warm-up activity could conceivably deplete finite muscle glycogen stores, which could in turn impair speed performance during the latter stages of a match or extended training session.

Conversely, if the intensity of warm-up activities is insufficient then the physiological ergogenic effects described in the previous section are unlikely to be observed. Likewise if the time elapsed between warm-up and high-intensity activity allows muscle temperature and oxygen uptake to return to resting levels this will nullify any effect on performance (Bishop, 2003b). It therefore appears that there is a trade-off in terms of both the intensity and duration of warm-up activities and the time elapsed between warm-up and high-intensity activity. Essentially the objective is to maximise the elevation in muscle temperature and physiological parameters (oxygen uptake, ventilatory rate, etc.) whilst minimising fatigue and high-energy substrate (PCr and glycogen) depletion. The following recommendations have therefore been published (Bishop, 2003b):

- moderate exercise intensity approximately 70 per cent VO_2max or $HR_{Reserve}$ (for 'moderately trained' athletes);
- warm-up duration approximately 10 minutes;
- interval between warm-up and high-intensity activity $\geq$ 5 minutes, but not in excess of 15–20 minutes.

It is likely that there will be certain constraints imposed by the nature of competition in the sport that will determine the time interval between warm-up and the start of competitive activity. Certain passive warm-up techniques may be used to help maintain the elevation in muscle temperature during this period (Bishop, 2003a). A more difficult challenge is maintaining oxygen uptake at an elevated level, as this will typically return to baseline within 5 minutes of a warm-up of moderate to heavy intensity (Bishop, 2003b).

Stretching or mobilisation exercises

In view of their apparent superiority, and to avoid any potential negative effects on explosive performance, the consensus is that dynamic range of motion methods represent the preferred approach for preparing the athlete for high-intensity running activity (Chaouachi et al., 2010; Little and Williams, 2006; McHugh and Cosgrave, 2010). These methods should therefore be employed to mobilise the relevant musculature through the ranges of motion required by the activity to follow. Practically, this will tend to comprise dynamic variations of standard stretching exercises, which are performed in standing, as well as dynamic squats and walking lunges in various directions.

However, in the event that soft-tissue restrictions are identified then static stretching remains an option, particularly in the case of muscle groups not directly involved in generating propulsion. For example, tightness in the hip flexors may cause an anterior tilt of the pelvis (Waryasz, 2010), thereby altering lumbopelvic posture, which can in turn impair activation of core muscles (Workman et al., 2008). In this case, static stretching and other passive methods to relieve the restriction and enable the athlete to correct their lumbopelvic posture will be necessary to prepare them to perform.

If the strength and conditioning specialist does opt to include static stretches then it appears prudent to allow an interval of ≥5 minutes before competing or undertaking explosive training activities (Chaouachi *et al.*, 2010). As detailed in the following section, specific bounding and sprinting warm-up activities might be undertaken during this period, which will also help to offset any negative effects on explosive power performance (Škof and Strojnik, 2007). The following guidelines with respect to the intensity, duration and volume of static stretching prior to high-intensity activity have likewise been provided (Chaouachi *et al.*, 2010):

- moderate intensity – stretch held should be before the point of discomfort;
- brief duration ≤ 30 seconds;
- low volume.

Specific warm-up for speed and agility movements

Following a general warm-up to raise muscle temperature, heart rate and ventilatory rate and initiate metabolic processes, and flexibility exercises to activate and mobilise the relevant musculature through the relevant range of motion, specific warm-up activities should be undertaken to potentiate sprint and agility movement. Performing a variety of sprints and bounding activities following a general active warm-up has been shown to enhance maximal muscle torque production and twitch contraction time parameters (Škof and Strojnik, 2007). There are similarly preliminary data showing that performing sprints prior to explosive power activities can have a potentiation effect that is reflected in enhanced performance. This specific warm-up should necessarily comprise the same types of movement as those that will be employed during the speed and agility activities to follow.

By definition these activities will be of a high intensity and therefore the duration should be kept very brief to minimise fatigue effects that may compromise subsequent performance. Similarly, the strength and conditioning specialist should employ lengthy rest intervals between bouts of high-intensity activity during this phase of the warm-up. Likewise there should be sufficient time between the completion of the specific warm-up and the high-intensity activity to be performed to enable complete resynthesis of high-energy phosphates and allow for any residual fatigue to dissipate (Bishop, 2003b).

Flexibility and mobility training

Supporting evidence for the benefits of stretching and flexibility

Developing flexibility is commonly cited as a major objective of physical preparation programmes for the majority of sports. The proposed benefits of improving an athlete's flexibility include reduced injury risk and enhanced athletic performance (Nelson and Bandy, 2005). Restricted flexibility or an imbalance in flexibility between limbs has been identified as an intrinsic injury risk factor for a variety of muscle strain injuries (Arnason *et al.*, 2004; Witvrouw *et al.*, 2003) and tendinopathy (Witvrouw *et al.*, 2001). It follows that a more flexible muscle–tendon complex will theoretically be better able to absorb energy, so that trauma to these tissues is less likely to occur (Witvrouw et al., 2004). There are some data to suggest that stretching is associated with a reduced incidence of muscle strain injury (McHugh and Cosgrave, 2010).

However, a number of other studies have not reported any significant reduction in injury incidence among those who perform stretching, so the relationship between flexibility training and injury remains ambiguous (Witvrouw et al., 2004). One reason for this may be that the majority of studies have examined stretching prior to activity (McHugh and Cosgrave, 2010). As has been discussed previously this can lead to transient inhibition of both the motor neurone and stretch reflexes; it could be speculated that this might make the athlete more susceptible to injury following stretching. Therefore, the timing of flexibility training appears to be a critical factor with respect to both injury prevention and performance.

There is similarly some ambiguity regarding the relationship between flexibility training and performance. As has been discussed in previous chapters, lower limb musculotendinous stiffness is recognised as critical for stretch-shortening cycle (SSC) activities such as sprinting. However, a study of fast SSC activity (hopping) identified tendon compliance as a key factor in optimising elastic recoil and therefore propulsion when bounding and sprinting (Rabita et al., 2008). Passive musculoskeletal stiffness (i.e. compliance of tendon and muscle) must therefore be differentiated from the active musculotendinous stiffness observed during SSC activity. Flexibility training comprising static stretching is documented to reduce the viscosity of connective tissues (predominantly tendon) without altering the elasticity of these tissues (Kubo et al., 2002).

The role of flexibility training therefore is to maintain or increase tendon compliance and elasticity alongside SSC training and speed training, which serves to increase active lower limb stiffness. Although controversy surrounds the use of some forms of flexibility training (e.g. static stretching, PNF stretching) prior to high-intensity exercise, based on the available evidence flexibility training should still merit a place in athletes' physical preparation. The timing of flexibility training is the key issue; stretching is commonly employed as part of an athlete's cool-down routine following a match or training session, and flexibility training can likewise be undertaken as a standalone session.

Approaching flexibility training

The athlete's specific requirements with respect to flexibility training can be assessed by a qualitative analysis of the movement demands of the sport and a thorough musculoskeletal assessment and dynamic movement screening to assess their intrinsic levels of flexibility. Some sports require considerable levels of mobility to allow the athlete to operate at quite extreme ranges of motion – for example when lunging at full reach to intercept a ball in racquet sports such as squash. In the event that the athlete exhibits hypermobility during their musculoskeletal assessment then additional flexibility training will not be a priority – indeed, this may even be contraindicated from an injury prevention standpoint (Witvrouw et al., 2004).

Following a bout of stretching an increase in range of motion is observed with a corresponding reduction in resistance to passive stretch, and these effects persist for up to an hour (McHugh and Cosgrave, 2010). The total duration that the stretch is applied appears to be a critical factor with respect to these observed acute effects. Other methods can be employed in combination with stretching to facilitate these changes (McHugh and Cosgrave, 2010). Examples include techniques that incorporate (static) muscle contraction during the stretching protocol.

Essentially the rationale for flexibility training is that if appropriate stretching is performed with sufficient (e.g. daily) frequency then these transient effects will ultimately result in chronic changes in compliance of connective tissues and joint range of motion. The available data from longitudinal studies tend to support this. For example, a 20-day training intervention of daily static stretching of the plantarflexor muscles produced increases in flexibility (passive range of motion with a given external resistance) without any loss of tendon elasticity (active stiffness) (Kubo et al., 2002). These chronic changes are attributed to structural adaptations within the connective tissues that result from repeated exposure to the stretch stimulus.

Flexibility training modes

Ballistic stretching

Ballistic stretching movements typically involve open-chain movements whereby the limb is rapidly propelled through its active range of motion. The stretch is therefore applied only for a brief duration, which is contrary to the identified requirement for prolonged application of stretch to elicit changes in passive resistance to stretching (McHugh and Cosgrave, 2010). Furthermore, the rapid swinging or bouncing motion employed is likely to elicit stretch reflex-mediated muscle activation as a protective response (Nelson and Bandy, 2005). This reflexive muscle contraction is clearly counterproductive when the objective is to allow the muscle to relax to enable greater range of motion to be attained. This form of stretching may even place the muscle at risk of strain injury.

Dynamic range of motion exercises

Although dynamic range of motion exercises are identified as the superior method for mobilising the joints and muscle prior to training and competition, it has yet to be established whether this method is effective for increasing flexibility (McHugh and Cosgrave, 2010). Although the controlled nature of this form of stretching will help to avoid eliciting a stretch reflex, the duration of stretch applied is once more unlikely to be of sufficient duration to alter passive resistance to stretch.

Static stretching

Static stretching is by definition much more conducive to applying stretch to the muscle for the duration required to elicit acute changes in passive resistance to stretch (McHugh and Cosgrave, 2010). Accordingly, flexibility training interventions employing static stretching are documented to successfully elicit both acute and chronic increases in range of motion (Woods et al., 2007). Static stretching protocols found to be effective in increasing flexibility have employed the following parameters (Nelson and Bandy, 2005):

- 30–60 seconds' duration per repetition;
- one to three sets;
- five to seven sessions per week, one or two sessions per day.

Proprioceptive neuromuscular facilitation stretching

What defines PNF stretching methods is that the static stretch is alternated with periodic isometric contraction of the agonist and/or antagonist muscle group (Nelson and Bandy, 2005). The most common PNF stretching technique involves sequentially applying passive stretch to the muscle for a set duration (e.g. 30 seconds) and performing brief (5-second) agonist muscle isometric contractions whilst the muscle is in a lengthened position (Bradley *et al.*, 2007). This technique commonly involves partner-resisted stretching exercises so that another person applies tension to passively stretch the muscle and then provides the resistance when the athlete performs the static muscle contraction whilst the muscle is in a stretched position (Nelson and Bandy, 2005).

Incorporating muscle contraction during the stretching exercise appears to facilitate more rapid reductions in passive resistance to stretching (McHugh and Cosgrave, 2010). There is also some indication that flexibility training employing PNF stretching methods may produce greater gains in flexibility than static stretching (Nelson and Bandy, 2005).

Eccentric flexibility training

Eccentric flexibility training exercises are another option available to the strength and conditioning specialist (Nelson and Bandy, 2005). These exercises involve closed-chain movements (i.e. the supporting limb is planted and weight-bearing) and can be performed with or without external resistance (i.e. body weight resistance only). As the muscle is active whilst stretch is gradually applied this approach has aspects in common with PNF stretching.

PART III
Developing technical and perceptual aspects of sports speed and agility

10
TECHNICAL ASPECTS OF ACCELERATION AND STRAIGHT-LINE SPEED DEVELOPMENT

Introduction

Sprinting is a complex cyclical motion involving multiple joints and comprising various phases that each include a variety of joint motions and types of muscle action (Belli et al., 2002). As such, even when treated as a closed skill, sprinting demands a high degree of intramuscular and intermuscular coordination and timing (Ross et al., 2001). Although the literature is relatively limited there is some consensus among expert sprint coaches, sport scientists and biomechanists regarding the specific elements that constitute sound sprinting technique (Thompson et al., 2009).

The importance of highly specific training to develop the neuromuscular skill and coordination elements of sprinting performance is underlined by a study which found that standard sprint training elicited superior short-term improvement in short-distance speed compared with either supramaximal (assisted running) or resisted running modes following a 6-week training period (Kristensen et al., 2006). Although the subjects employed in the study had no specific sprint training history, it remains clear that to achieve optimal transfer of training, sprinting must remain a fundamental part of the training undertaken by the athlete (Cissik, 2005). Indeed, it has been identified that the degree of neural activation as well as the relative timing and sequencing of muscle actions is modifiable and becomes gradually refined over time with repetition of the sprinting action (Ross et al., 2001).

Mechanics of sprint running

The gait cycle when sprinting can be divided into two distinct parts:

- the *contact* or *stance phase*, which begins at initial foot strike and ends when the foot leaves the ground, that is, 'toe-off' – this can be subdivided into a braking or 'weight-acceptance' phase and a propulsion phase;
- the *flight* or *swing phase*, consisting of the initial recovery during which the initial rearward motion of the lower limb is first slowed then reversed as the leg is brought

forwards to pass under the athlete's centre of mass, after which the leg is then swung forwards before positioning the foot and lower limb for the next foot strike.

In a sample of track athletes the stance phase comprised 26.6 per cent of the overall gait cycle when sprinting, with the remainder (73.4 per cent) consisting of the flight or swing phase (Yu et al., 2008).

As described in Chapter 2, running is characterised as a bouncing motion whereby the lower limb kinetic chain of joints and limb segments collectively functions as a linear spring with the athlete's centre of mass on top (Brughelli and Cronin, 2008). In accordance with this 'spring–mass model' of running locomotion, a critical aspect of neuromuscular coordination when running is the ability to modulate the stiffness of the spring formed of the lower limb kinetic chain. A key consideration is that the athlete is able to maintain vertical stiffness of the body to prevent any collapse with each foot strike (Girard et al., 2011).

Conversely, it would appear beneficial to avoid excessive vertical displacement of the centre of mass or 'bouncing' in an upwards direction. At higher running velocities the centre of mass is observed to follow a flatter trajectory (Brughelli and Cronin, 2008). In accordance with this, elite sprinters are observed to generate only moderate levels of vertical ground reaction forces – sufficient to prevent collapse – with less resultant vertical motion (Hunter et al., 2005).

Foot strike during sprinting

Based upon observation of sprinters versus endurance runners, sprinting is characterised by foot strike occurring at the midfoot or forefoot. Forefoot striking is identified as producing significantly lower rates of loading at foot strike than rearfoot striking (Lieberman et al., 2010). Forefoot striking also reduces the initial spike or 'passive peak' in ground reaction forces observed when foot strike occurs with initial contact through the heel (Divert et al., 2005). For this reason forefoot or midfoot striking is suggested to be more mechanically efficient and also potentially less injurious to lower limb structures.

The spring–mass model described in Chapter 2 can be complemented by the 'L-shaped double pendulum' model, which allows collision forces at the foot and torques at the ankle joint at foot strike to be considered (Lieberman et al., 2010) (Figure 10.1). This model shows forefoot striking to be beneficial in terms of storage and return of elastic energy during ground contact. Specifically, as the ankle joint and associated muscles and connective tissue structures remain under tension during a forefoot strike this allows the elastic energy storage capacities of the Achilles tendon as well as the longitudinal arch of the foot to be harnessed (Jungers, 2010). Conversely, with a rearfoot strike much of the kinetic energy is lost at initial contact (Lieberman et al., 2010) and a lower level of pre-activation of lower limb muscles prior to foot strike may also be observed when running in this way (Divert et al., 2005).

Foot strike when running inevitably involves a trade-off between braking forces and propulsion forces generated during ground contact. In addition to controlling the point of initial contact, superior sprinting performance is also identified to occur with an 'active' foot strike (Hunter et al., 2005), that is, faster sprinters are observed to maximise propulsion and minimise braking forces.

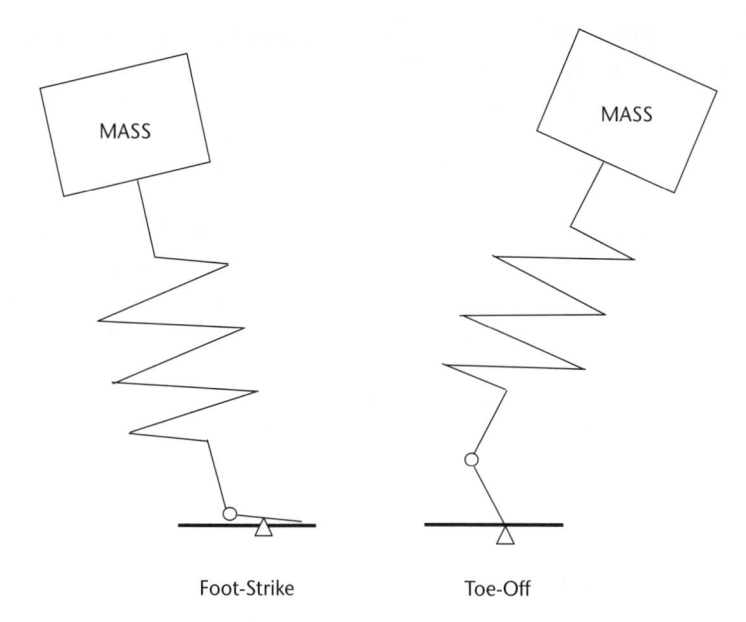

FIGURE 10.1 Spring–mass model applied to the 'L-shaped double pendulum' model at foot strike and toe-off.

Variation in running mechanics during a sprint

Running mechanics vary according to the phase of a sprint, so that the kinematics of acceleration movements over short distances are markedly different from those seen when sprinting at top speed. The mechanical parameters that vary include the degree of forward lean, and the leg angle or the distance between the athlete's centre of mass and initial foot strike, which in turn changes the duration of ground contact time (Kugler and Janshen, 2010).

Specifically, acceleration mechanics are characterised by a pronounced forward lean of the torso, and a greater leg angle or horizontal distance at foot strike – and accordingly longer ground contact times in which to generate propulsion. Conversely, when sprinting at maximal speed athletes exhibit a tall and upright posture, shorter distance between centre of mass and initial foot strike, and much shorter ground contact times. In between these extremes, increases in running speed are effectively achieved by modulating the following mechanical factors in combination (Weyand *et al.*, 2010):

- increasing net horizontal ground reaction forces applied during ground contact;
- employing more brief foot contact to reduce stance time;
- repositioning the limbs more rapidly during the swing phase to reduce flight time.

The importance of 'arm action' to stride mechanics

Although it is yet to be documented by the scientific literature, expert sprint coaches consistently put great emphasis on arm action as being integral to sound sprinting technique

(Thompson *et al.*, 2009). What is described as arm action actually involves the whole of the shoulder girdle; essentially the scapula (shoulder blade) glides around the thorax whilst the arm performs a piston action. The arm action likely has implications for stabilising the trunk in view of the role identified for the proximal musculature of the upper limb in contributing to trunk stability (Kibler *et al.*, 2006; McGill, 2006f).

Arm action (including counter-rotation of the shoulder girdle) also appears to play a key role in counterbalancing the movement of the hip girdle and lower limbs. Arm action has been identified as influencing both knee lift and stride length, and also stride cadence (Thompson *et al.*, 2009). When arm action is forcibly restricted during running, subjects are observed to adapt their running style by shortening their stride to maintain stride frequency (Fujii *et al.*, 2010). Anecdotally, tension in the shoulders and upper arms is recognised as adversely affecting sprinting performance. This is likely to be a result of the identified negative effects on stride length associated with restricting the counter-rotation of the shoulder girdle, and limiting the cadence of the arm swing can also interfere with stride frequency.

Neuromuscular coordination during swing and stance phases

Returning to the spring–mass model it can be seen that modulating the stiffness or compliance of the 'spring' encompassing the lower limb kinetic chain will influence the kinetics of the bouncing motion at each foot strike (Brughelli and Cronin, 2008). Co-activation of hip, knee and ankle extensors and hip and knee flexors in the interval immediately prior to touchdown and during foot contact is crucial for modifying leg stiffness and in turn mechanical and contractile properties (Wilson and Flanagan, 2008). These aspects of neuromuscular coordination do exhibit learning effects. Pre-activation of knee and ankle extensors and regulation of leg stiffness is observed to alter with exposure to appropriate (e.g. plyometric) training (McBride *et al.*, 2008).

Conversely, after the transition into the swing phase following toe-off the lower limb must be compliant so that the swing action and hence stride length are not ultimately impeded. The coordination of muscle activation and (relative) relaxation to coincide with the transitions between stance and swing phases can likewise be instructed and reinforced with repetition and coaching feedback with appropriate sprint technique training.

The placement and orientation of the foot at touchdown, as well as achieving an 'active' foot contact to maximise propulsion forces and minimise braking forces, are key aspects of sprinting technique instruction and practice (Nummela *et al.*, 2007). Less well recognised as a specific coaching point is the importance of lower limb relaxation following the transition into the subsequent swing phase, despite the fact that 'stride length' is a major area of emphasis and a number of training drills exist to develop it.

Another key element of sprinting technique involves the initial part of the recovery phase immediately after the foot leaves the ground at 'toe-off'. Specifically, as the hip simultaneously flexes the athlete also flexes their knee to bring the heel close to the buttocks as the leg is propelled forwards underneath the body. The purpose of this is to minimise the moment of inertia of the lower limb during this phase to avoid unwanted increases in swing time that would ultimately restrict the athlete's stride rate (van Ingen Schenau *et al.*, 1994).

Development of acceleration mechanics

It has been identified that the direction of resultant propulsive forces is strongly related to the athlete's posture when accelerating. The decisive factor is the orientation of the athlete's body at the end of foot strike ('toe-off'), specifically the degree of forward lean (Kugler and Janshen, 2010). This effectively serves to determine the direction of ground reaction forces and in turn the relative amount of horizontal versus vertical propulsion generated. As described previously for sprinting mechanics, the objective is to maximise horizontal propulsion and optimise ground contact time whilst minimising vertical bouncing motion; and it is the degree of forward lean achieved when accelerating that is found to determine these outcomes (Kugler and Janshen, 2010).

The importance of these factors is underlined by research that found the degree of forward lean to have a greater effect on sprint times than the magnitude of propulsion forces recorded – that is, faster subjects achieved superior performance as a result of optimal body orientation in a forward direction, even with relatively modest maximum ground reaction forces (Kugler and Janshen, 2010). The authors of this study identified that the optimal ground reaction force when accelerating depends upon the degree of forward lean of the body; however, if ground reaction forces generated exceed this optimal level it will be counterproductive to the net horizontal acceleration produced.

Acceleration can therefore be conceptualised as a controlled falling motion on the basis that the head and centre of mass of the athlete are positioned in front of their base of support. How this forward lean and falling motion are best achieved is a matter of some debate. One study by Frost and colleagues (2008) that investigated standing start techniques from a stationary position with the feet parallel suggested that there are two options available to the athlete from this position (Frost et al., 2008). The first option is for the athlete to actively lean forward to shift their centre of mass in front of their feet. The second option is to step backwards to position the supporting limb behind their centre of mass; this technique is described as a 'false step'. This study reported that the latter false-step (stepping backwards) technique achieved faster sprint start times over short distance (in comparison with leaning and stepping forward) when starting from this stationary 'parallel foot' position (Frost et al., 2008).

In reality the athlete will rarely execute a forwards acceleration movement from a stationary position with their feet exactly parallel. It is more likely that one foot will be positioned in front of the other – that is, a split stance. In the final condition employed in the study the subjects employed a split stance posture with the left foot positioned in front and stepping forwards with the right (i.e. back) leg. The fastest times of all the conditions employed were recorded (0–2.5 m) with this split stance starting technique (Frost et al., 2008). The alternative starting technique to a split stance position that was not investigated in this study would be for the athlete to execute the first step with their front leg so that their centre of mass would be positioned in front of their supporting (back) leg. Also not investigated in this study were the preparatory movements that the athlete will often adopt in anticipation of executing an acceleration movement – for example the 'split step' preload movement employed in racquet sports.

Importance of competition-specific velocities and high-speed sprint training

It has been identified that although drills may be useful to assist in developing certain aspects of stride mechanics it is critical that training must ultimately progress to actual sprinting (Cissik, 2005). Sprinting involves highly complex neuromuscular coordination that differs even from what occurs during lower-velocity running. Even within the same muscle group the recruitment and activation patterns are shown to differ markedly at different running speeds (Higashihara *et al.*, 2010). Furthermore, the changes observed at different running speeds also vary between each individual hamstring muscle (biceps femoris versus semitendinosis) and at different parts of the swing phase (i.e. mid-swing phase versus late swing phase).

These observations underline the importance of sprinting at the range of speeds encountered during competition and at maximal speed to allow these highly specific neuromuscular coordination patterns to be developed. In addition, high-speed sprint training is also identified to be effective in eliciting improvements in muscle function, including isometric leg extensor strength and measures of both concentric and SSC performance (Markovic *et al.*, 2007).

Practical approach to acceleration and sports speed development

The duration and distances of sprints most commonly recorded for athletes in various team sports are 2–3 seconds and 10–20 m, respectively (Spencer *et al.*, 2005). However, in cases in which the athlete is already in motion when they initiate the sprint, and with the greater occurrence of longer sprints associated with certain playing positions, maximal sprinting ability remains a relevant area of development (Little and Williams, 2005). Conversely, in racquet sports athletes perform within a much more restricted playing area and so the corresponding duration and distances of sprints will be considerably less. Similarly, these sprints will most often be initiated from a relatively stationary starting position. These considerations will dictate that acceleration movements merit the greatest training time in these sports, with little emphasis on maximal sprinting.

As described in the previous sections sprinting is a highly complex motor task involving a high degree of coordination of multiple elements executed at high velocity (Ross *et al.*, 2001). Even when accelerating from a stationary start technical aspects such as orientation of the body during acceleration supersede the importance of generation of maximum levels of ground reaction force (Kugler and Janshen, 2010). Instruction of acceleration and sprinting techniques and deliberate practice of these motor abilities should begin early in the training year and these aspects should be reinforced thereafter. During this phase the acceleration and sprinting techniques can be viewed as closed skills (Young *et al.*, 2001b). This initial development may therefore take the form of technique drills and closed-skill practice involving self-paced repetitions of sprint starts and short-distance sprints with heavy emphasis on coaching and instruction. This approach has been reported to be superior to assisted or resisted sprint training methods during the early development of sprinting abilities (Kristensen *et al.*, 2006).

Once the fundamentals of acceleration and sprinting technique have been developed to a sufficient degree the strength and conditioning specialist must then turn their attention to the other factors involved in expressing these qualities in the context of the sport. One key issue is the eccentricities of the running technique employed during competition in many sports, which differ in many instances from those observed in track athletics (Gamble, 2009d). For example, in general a team sports athlete will adopt a more crouched running style when opposing players are in close proximity so that they are better able to decelerate and change direction as the situation requires. Conversely, when in space they might adopt a sprinting technique that bears closer resemblance to that of a track athlete.

Athletes competing in ball sports must also adapt their running style when in possession of the ball. In fact, the ability of elite players to accommodate holding or dribbling the ball without significantly compromising running technique and movement speed is identified as underpinning the superior running performance (with a ball) observed with elite performers in these sports (Fujii *et al.*, 2010). In racquet sports and team sports such as hockey, acceleration and running mechanics will similarly be constrained by holding a racquet or a stick. Attention should therefore be given to the necessary technical modifications to running technique required when holding the ball or implement employed in the sport in order to develop the specific movement abilities involved. For example, it appears that skilled basketball players increase their shoulder rotation when running whilst dribbling the ball to maintain normal rotation of the hip girdle (Fujii *et al.*, 2010). It has been advocated previously that the ball or implement of the sport should be incorporated during acceleration and speed drills, particularly in the later phases of acceleration and speed development (Sheppard and Young, 2006).

It is also vital to observe the events that surround the expression of speed and acceleration movement in competition (Gamble, 2009d), for example identifying if acceleration movements are typically performed from a stationary position or if the athlete is in motion; if the athlete is in motion it is important to identify the direction and speed of the preceding movement. Once identified, these conditions can be integrated into acceleration and speed development sessions, so that acceleration movements are performed from a variety of starting positions and preceding movements at different velocities (Cronin and Hansen, 2006).

Finally, it is important to consider that acceleration and speed movements in competition environments are typically initiated in response to events occurring in the match situation. As a result, there will be an element of anticipation and decision-making even when executing straight-line speed movements. According to the definition proposed by Sheppard and Young (2006), these speed and acceleration movements in a competition context can therefore be classified as agility movements on the basis that their expression involves the elements of reaction and decision-making. Reactive starts should therefore be employed in athletes' training when developing straight-line acceleration and speed. Similarly, the strength and conditioning specialist should consider progressions that incorporate the preparatory preload and split step movements that athletes employ in many sports.

11
DEVELOPING CHANGE OF DIRECTION CAPABILITIES AND EXPRESSION OF SPORTS AGILITY

Introduction

Although there is some agreement regarding the key elements of sound sprinting technique (Thompson et al., 2009), consensus with respect to the critical aspects of change of direction movement technique remains elusive. The situation is further complicated by the observation that change of direction movement mechanics appear to differ according to the sport – for example, differences appear to exist in the kinetics of change of direction movements even between two team sports (soccer and basketball) with broadly similar movement demands (Cowley et al., 2006).

The importance of change of direction performance on successful competition in various intermittent sports is repeatedly seen in investigations of talent identification and talent development. Of all performance test measures, athletes' scores on change of direction measures are often the single best predictors of success and are the variables that most often successfully differentiate between elite and sub-elite competitors (Brughelli et al., 2008).

It is unclear from the literature exactly what constitutes the best approach to developing change of direction speed and agility for a given sport (Serpell et al., 2011). However, studies have demonstrated that there is a need for dedicated training to develop these abilities. It is evident that straight-line speed training alone will not provide adequate development of change of direction performance, particularly in the case of complex change of direction tasks involving many directional changes (Young et al., 2001). Of the training modes employed in studies investigating change of direction performance, training interventions that have featured bounding activities and/or movement skills training have typically reported the greatest success in eliciting significant improvements in change of direction test scores (Brughelli et al., 2008).

Finally, to ensure that change of direction movement skills acquired in training ultimately translate into sports agility, it is important that these abilities be developed as adaptive sports skills. This would appear to necessitate a similar approach to that seen in the domains of coaching and sports skill acquisition. To this end, a variety of approaches to motor learning have been advocated by different authors in the literature with regards to developing agility (Holmberg, 2009; Jeffreys, 2006).

Change of direction movement mechanics

Human running has been conceptualised in terms of a planar spring–mass model in which the kinetic chain of lower limb segments together act like a spring with the athlete's centre of mass on top, so that the running action is essentially a forwards bouncing motion (Brughelli and Cronin, 2008). The situation for non-linear running and change of direction movement is obviously more complex. Employing the spring–mass model, the athlete must manipulate the orientation of their torso and the position of their supporting foot with respect to their centre of mass at foot strike so that they are able to translate their forward momentum into motion in the desired direction. This is analogous to the effects of forward body lean on net ground reaction force and horizontal propulsion identified when performing straight-line acceleration (Kugler and Janshen, 2010).

Specifically, the orientation of the body and the degree of lean in the intended direction of movement will dictate the amount of propulsion that the athlete is able to generate during the acceleration movements involved in change of direction activities in much the same way as is observed with acceleration in a forward direction (Kugler and Janshen, 2010). In addition to manipulating the position and orientation of the supporting limb and torso prior to touchdown, changing the direction of movement when running also demands generation of medial-lateral ground reaction forces to propel the athlete in the new direction (McLean *et al.*, 2004). This involves quite different muscle recruitment and muscle action to that which occurs during propulsion in straight-line sprinting.

During the first part of the recovery action, once the foot has left the ground similar movement strategies as seen with straight-line running may be employed to minimise the moment of inertia of the lower limb (van Ingen Schenau *et al.*, 1994). Specifically, in much the same way as with forwards running, the athlete will flex the lower limb to reduce its moment of inertia during the initial recovery action. Retaining the unloaded lower limb in a position close to the line of the body and the axis of rotation when executing a turning movement, and delaying the forwards swing of the leg until the pivoting motion is complete, will also help to reduce the inertia of the lower limb.

Depending on the athlete's initial approach speed in a forwards direction when they initiate the change of direction, and the degree of change of direction required, executing change of direction movements may also involve braking forces in an anterior-posterior (i.e. negative or backwards) direction. With respect to kinematic aspects, how these deceleration or 'weight-acceptance' movements are executed will also impact considerably upon torques throughout the kinetic chain. Significant changes in lower limb joint kinetics and kinematics have been reported previously as a result of modifications in technique for the sidestep cutting movement (Dempsey *et al.*, 2009). The movement strategies employed can therefore influence the muscular demand and efficiency of the deceleration phase of change of direction movements. In turn, this may improve the athlete's ability to subsequently execute the transition to the concentric phases of the change of direction movement.

Types of sports agility

Reactive agility: interception movements

The timing of initiation of interception movements will be determined in different ways depending on the nature of the sport. For example, in racquet sports the initiation of the movement response is predictable and is based upon the arrival of the ball to the opponent and the subsequent initiation of the shot by the opponent (Gillet *et al.*, 2010). For interceptive movements the degree of certainty, in particular with regard to the timing of the initiation of the movement response, allows athletes to perform preparatory 'preload' movements that improve their ability to rapidly initiate the required movement.

One example of this is the 'split step' performed in tennis (and other racquet sports such as squash). This movement begins with an 'unweighting' movement (Kovacs, 2009) in which the player drops their centre of gravity and allows their feet to leave the floor; this serves to preload the leg extensor muscles upon touchdown (Gillet *et al.*, 2010). During the course of performing this 'dipping' motion the player will often alter the orientation of the lower limbs just prior to landing to touch down first with the foot farthest from the anticipated direction of motion and reposition the lower limbs to drive off in the new direction (Kovacs, 2009).

In other sports, such as team sports, the situation is slightly more complex. When intercepting the ball, similar timing constraints to those in raquet sports will often be involved, and thus it may be possible for the athlete to perform a preparatory preload movement. However, in the case that the athlete is moving to intercept an opponent the timing of the original movement response and subsequent adaptive movements is far less predictable and therefore it is unlikely that any preparatory movement will be possible.

There is often a degree of anticipation involved in the execution of interceptive movements. That said, the extent to which anticipation is employed to initiate movement responses is dependent upon the athlete's ability to attend to and interpret advance cues derived from the movement behaviour exhibited by their opponent (Holmberg, 2009). In the event that the athlete is able to 'read' the movement response of their opponent or motion of the ball they will be able to pre-plan their movement response and adjust their starting position and posture in advance. This 'predictive movement strategy' that has been observed with elite tennis players allows the player to initiate their movement response in advance, which ultimately enables them to intercept balls travelling at such a velocity that they would otherwise have insufficient reaction time to do so (Gillet *et al.*, 2010).

That said, skilled performers still adapt their anticipated movement strategy during the movement. For example, in racquet sports pre-planned movements initiated in advance of the opponent's anticipated shot selection are shown to be refined in a reactive manner based upon the actual trajectory or motion of the ball (Gillet *et al.*, 2010). Furthermore, expert players in these sports demonstrate superior ability to react to unexpected deviations late in the movement and initiate the required corrective action in motion (Le Runigo *et al.*, 2010).

Similarly, in cases in which movement responses are not anticipated or wrongly anticipated (i.e. the athlete guesses wrong or is eluded by their opponent), the athlete will be required to first recover and then initiate the correct movement response. This type of 'scrambling' reactive agility movement would appear to comprise specific abilities. It follows that the capacity to perform these scrambling reactive movements might be developed through appropriate training in the same way as any other aspect of agility movement.

Evasion agility movement

Evasion agility has been far less widely studied. The initiation of these movements is to a degree self-timed by the athlete – although the behaviour of the opposing players will also influence the timing with which evasive movements are initiated. To a degree, athletes may therefore employ pre-planned movement strategies when they perform evasive movements. Anecdotally, many players in intermittent sports develop favoured evasive 'moves' or movement strategies that they will employ in a given game situation in an attempt to 'wrong foot' their opponent(s). Specialised movement skills have been reported in sports that require evasive agility. One such example is the 'lateral false step', which is identified as being performed by players in team sports, notably basketball (Golden *et al.*, 2009).

However, in much the same way as described for interceptive movements, the athlete will also likely modify any planned movement strategy in response to the reaction and motion of the defending player(s). Thus, these movements appear to similarly comprise elements of both planning and anticipation; however, reaction remains an integral component of this form of agility. It follows that the process through which these abilities are developed should reflect the fact that evasion agility ultimately constitutes 'open' adaptive movement skills (Serpell *et al.*, 2011).

Identifying the specific movement skills for the sport

Agility movements are specific not only to the sport but also to the context and associated requirements of the particular game situation in the sport. Performance on different change of direction performance measures is often shown not to be strongly related, particularly when the change of direction activities differ significantly in terms of complexity (number of changes of direction, direction of movements involved, etc.) (Brughelli *et al.*, 2008). Accordingly, it has been stated that 'exercise selection based on *specific task dilemmas* is essential to skill acquisition' (Holmberg, 2009, p. 74, italics added for emphasis). In view of these observations, developing change of direction movement skills most effectively requires an intimate understanding of the nature of the particular agility movements that are characteristic of the sport.

Therefore, a crucial first step that must be undertaken when approaching change of direction and agility development is to identify the characteristic change of direction movements that are commonly employed in the particular sport. The component movement mechanics employed to execute a particular change of direction movement will tend to differ between sports as a result of the constraints placed upon athletes in those sports. For example, as discussed previously, those movements employed in an evasion sport and their associated motor control demands will likely be different from the interception movements that occur in racquet sports.

Categorising component movements

Numerous constraints are associated with the sport itself based upon the specific demands of operating in a particular competitive setting. These constraints can vary widely between sports, may vary further according to the playing positions within a sport, and for outdoor sports can even be altered by environmental conditions. Such constraints include the dimensions of the playing area and nature of the playing surface, the number of opponents, the rules of the sport, the nature of the ball for ball sports and, for striking sports, the type of implement involved.

To assist when identifying the pre-planned change of direction and reactive agility movements observed in the sport, these movements can be categorised on a variety of factors or task constraints. For example, defining factors include whether the particular movement is executed from a stationary position, whether there is a preparatory 'preload' or countermovement or, alternatively, whether the player is in motion when the movement is initiated. In the last case, the change of direction action will often feature a preceding movement before the acceleration movement in the new direction. What form this preceding movement takes will in turn depend in part upon the athlete's approach velocity and therefore the amount of inertia they are carrying into the change of direction action. Depending upon the athlete's momentum, and the degree of change of direction required, the athlete may need to first decelerate their momentum before accelerating into the new direction of movement. In this case the change of direction movement will feature a preceding deceleration or 'weight-acceptance' component. Alternatively, if their initial velocity is not too excessive and the cutting angle is fairly acute they may be able to translate their momentum directly into speed in the new direction of movement. This will involve a considerably different transition movement, akin to performing a preload split step-type movement whilst in motion.

With respect to the acceleration portion of the change of direction movement a key factor is whether the change of direction involves the athlete changing the direction they are facing. For example, with a shuffling movement the athlete remains facing in the same direction, whereas during a conventional cutting movement the athlete will pivot and turn to face the new direction of motion as they perform the movement. In the latter 'cutting' change of movement, a further critical factor is whether the athlete leads with the leg nearest to the intended direction of movement or whether they lead with the opposite leg (i.e. the leg farthest from the intended direction of motion). These acceleration movement techniques have been variously termed in the literature, depending to some extent on the convention in the particular sport. For example, in tennis the technique of initiating a lateral (90-degree) turn with the near lead leg is termed a 'jab step', whereas the movement bringing the far leg across the body to lead the movement is termed a 'pivot step' (Kovacs, 2009).

The cognitive and perceptual constraints involved in the specific agility tasks required in a given sport should also be identified and accounted for. Perception, anticipation and decision-making will all influence the nature and effectiveness of the movement response employed during agility tasks, in training as in competition. Categorising the specific component movements identified for the sport and athlete based upon these parameters can aid the strength and conditioning specialist in systematically addressing change of direction movement skill development (Table 11.1).

TABLE 11.1 Parameters to categorise change of direction movement

Parameters	Primary movement characteristics	Secondary movement characteristics
Timing of initiation	Self-determined	
	Reactive	
Nature of movement response	Pre-planned	
	Adaptive (but self-determined)	
	Reactive	
Initiation of change of direction movement	Stationary starting position	Static start
		Preparatory movement or preload action
	In motion	Define approach velocity
Type of movement	Side-shuffling/tracking motion facing opponent	
	Pivot and acceleration	Define degree of turn or 'cut'
		Identify lead leg (leg nearest to or farthest from new direction of motion)

Approaching change of direction movement skills development

It has been demonstrated that programmed training featuring solely closed-movement skill drills is effective in improving measures of change of direction performance, independently of concurrent development of physical capabilities (Bloomfield *et al.*, 2007). Interestingly, this study also demonstrated that specialised equipment (hurdles, ladders, etc.) was not required to successfully elicit these improvements. The decisive factors proved to be the instruction and deliberate practice of specific movement techniques, and these elements were not reliant on specialised equipment (Bloomfield *et al.*, 2007). The majority of movement drills that employ hurdles and other equipment can be adapted. For example, depending on the sports setting, the strength and conditioning specialist might employ court markings or lines on the pitch when undertaking footwork drills typically performed using agility ladder equipment (Gamble, 2009d).

Therefore, once the strength and conditioning specialist has identified and categorised the characteristic movement skills for the sport and athlete the next step is instruction and deliberate practice of the specific techniques. This might begin by concentrating on the component acceleration movement involved in the change of direction movements. To isolate this specific part of the movement it follows that this should be undertaken initially from a stationary position. For example, a racquet sport such as squash requires the ability to accelerate in multiple directions. The initial movements introduced might therefore feature 45-degree, 90-degree, 135-degree and 180-degree acceleration movements, and the athlete should develop the ability to execute these movements with either lead leg (i.e. the leg nearer to or farther from the intended direction of movement) (Figures 11.1 and 11.2). These acceleration movements are initiated in a variety of ways in sport: the athlete may be in a stationary position initially, they may precede the action with a preparatory

FIGURE 11.1 ¼, ½ and ¾ turns, near lead leg.

FIGURE 11.2 ¼, ½ and ¾ turns, far lead leg.

preload movement or they may be in motion. Whatever the scenario that precedes the movement, the ability to execute these acceleration movements with a high degree of technical proficiency is an essential prerequisite.

Once the range of acceleration movements that occur in the sport have been mastered from a stationary position, technical practice can be progressed by preceding the acceleration movement with the types of initiating movement that occur in the sport. Using the racquet sport example, this may be achieved initially by performing the movement from a stationary position but introducing a preparatory 'preload' movement such as a variation of the split step movement that is frequently employed in these sports (Gillet *et al.*, 2010; Kovacs, 2009). The logical next progression would be to initiate the range of acceleration movements developed whilst in motion. The initial movement might be in a variety of directions, depending on what is appropriate for the sport. In this scenario progression can be achieved by manipulating the initial approach velocity – that is, introducing different directions of movement and increasing speed. Depending upon the initial direction and speed of motion, executing the acceleration movement may involve a deceleration or weight-acceptance component.

In all of the examples of programmed deliberate practice described above, the athlete performs the movements in a self-paced fashion, that is, movements are pre-planned and the timing of execution of the movement is predetermined by the athlete. Although the effectiveness of this approach is proven for the acquisition of movement skills, and therefore would appear a necessary element of developing agility performance, there is equally a need for further progression in order to develop these component movement skills into the adaptive sports skills required for these abilities to be expressed under competition conditions.

Closed- versus open-skill practice for developing agility movement

Repetition of pre-planned movements under self-paced and predictable 'closed-skill' conditions is beneficial for acquiring the requisite component movement skills that comprise a particular sports agility task from the point of view of instructing, correcting and reinforcing correct movement patterns. However, there are clear limitations of this programmed closed-skill movement practice approach in terms of its transferability to the inherently unpredictable conditions that athletes encounter during competition. Agility in sport is essentially an open motor skill (Serpell *et al.*, 2011). Change of direction training featuring closed drills in isolation would not therefore be sufficient to provide the development of sensory, perceptual and decision-making aspects required for agility.

Ultimately the approach taken to developing agility should therefore aim to develop these capabilities as adaptive motor skills. Employing a more 'open-skill' setting would appear a more appropriate and effective means to provide concurrent development of perceptual and decision elements. Incorporating the coupling of perception and action would appear a key aspect of developing the adaptive (open) motor skills required for the athlete to be able to express their agility movement capabilities in a competition context.

Recent data from a study that employed video projections of a moving opponent and a number of different game-related scenarios during reactive agility training for elite-level team sports players lend support to this contention. The significant improvements in a reactive agility test following this short-term (3-week) training intervention were achieved by improved reaction times – the movement time component of players' scores was largely unchanged (Serpell *et al.*, 2011). It is therefore apparent that the visual stimulus used in this mode of training was successful in developing the perceptual and decision-making aspects involved in agility performance in the sport, and these changes were reflected in improved performance on a related reactive agility test measure.

However, an entirely open-skill practice setting in which the athlete is free to operate without intervention or immediate instruction would not seem amenable to developing and reinforcing correct movement techniques. In accordance with this, a study has shown that this type of open-skill environment is inferior to deliberate closed-skill practice in improving measures of change of direction performance (Bloomfield *et al.*, 2007). It should, however, be stated that the study by Bloomberg and colleagues featured subjects who could be considered novice performers. Open-skill conditions would appear to be more conducive to those experienced in change of direction movement.

Effectively there would seem to be a continuum between the two extremes of closed (pre-planned and self-paced) deliberate movement practice and the random open-skill conditions described. Agility movement skill development might begin with closed-skill practice at the outset and then as movement competencies develop the athlete can then be progressively exposed to conditions in which movements are less self-paced with respect to the speed of execution and less predictable in terms of when they are initiated, and which provide less opportunity to pre-plan movement responses.

Programming unpredictability: transfer training for agility development

Alongside the acquisition of component movement skills there is a need for the athlete to be progressively exposed to an unpredictable environment to allow them to develop the ability to execute these movement skills under reactive conditions. Ultimately, the total time to complete an agility movement task will depend on not only the time interval taken to complete the agility movement, but also the time elapsed whilst the athlete detects and processes task-relevant cues, and then decides and initiates the appropriate movement response. It follows that this perception and decision-making element of agility movement cannot be neglected if the athlete is to develop the ability to express their agility under competition conditions in the sport.

Some authors have described the requirements of agility tasks and the agility training environment employed in terms of 'degrees of freedom', that is, the number of perceptual and movement variables involved (Holmberg, 2009). For example, in reference to the continuum of movement skill tasks, the closed-skill drills at one extreme have effectively zero degrees of freedom – the movement is pre-planned and its initiation and speed of execution is determined by the athlete. At the opposite end of the continuum is the competition environment, which involves multiple degrees of freedom, with numerous movement and perceptual variables involved in any agility task required by the particular game situation.

Applying this concept allows the strength and conditioning specialist to categorise open-skill agility tasks of varying complexity. This in turn provides a framework that can be employed to manipulate perceptual and movement variables in a systematic fashion. This will also allow a coherent progression in the prescription of agility training modes.

Stimulus–response: reaction to external cues

Returning to the original definition of agility as 'change of velocity or direction in response to a stimulus' (Sheppard and Young, 2006, p. 922), an obvious means to progress self-paced closed-skill drills employed during programmed movement practice is to introduce the element of reaction. A range of external cues may be employed to trigger the initiation of the learned movement skill. It has been suggested by different authors that the strength and conditioning specialist should select the most task-relevant cue for the sport for it to be most relevant. There would seem to be a range of options with respect to what external cues may be employed. The most simple is a verbal 'Go' command delivered by the coach. Further coach-led cues include verbal or visual directional cues alongside a 'Go' command (Figure 11.3). Visual cues may be movement-based, for example the coach initiates the movement response by taking a step to indicate the direction that the athlete is required to move in.

The efficacy of this approach for developing perceptual and decision-making aspects is supported by a growing number of studies employing 'reactive agility' training interventions that incorporate video projections so that the players' movement responses are executed in reaction to the on-screen actions of an opponent in a variety of game scenarios (Serpell *et al.*, 2011). Partner drills work in a similar way and will also facilitate development of the athlete's ability to detect and process relevant cues derived from motion of the opposing players' body segments (Holmberg, 2009). This is identified as a key component of agility for interceptive movements and conversely also evasion movement agility (Serpell *et al.*, 2011). Partner drills will, however, tend to involve greater task complexity in that they will typically involve a greater number of movement variables, as discussed in the following section.

Stimulus–response: manipulating number and variety of movement responses

In addition to perceptual degrees of freedom, movement variables can be manipulated in order to vary and increase the challenge placed upon the athlete. This can be achieved by specifying what constitutes the correct movement response(s). Similarly, the strength and conditioning specialist can alter task demands by increasing the number of available movement responses or 'perception–action couplings' that the athlete has to select from. Reaction times when undertaking multiple response tasks are shown to vary in direct proportion to the number of possible responses (Le Runigo *et al.*, 2010). Hence, as the number of movement responses is increased, the perceptual demands associated with information–response coupling will also be concurrently increased. For example, simple reaction tasks (e.g. the same movement response, moving to either the right or left) can be progressed to more advanced perception–action challenges that might feature a number of movement responses (e.g. ¼ turn, ½ turn, ¾ turn) in a variety of directions.

As before, ultimately the progression will involve the introduction of partner drills, in which motion of another player dictates both the timing of initiation and also the selection of the movement response. Examples include 'shadow' or 'mirror' drills in which reactive movement responses are executed in response to movement of the 'lead' player (Holmberg, 2009). This offers the means to develop the specific abilities involved in

FIGURE 11.3 Horizontal jump into reactive 45-degree or 90-degree cut.

regulating and adapting movement responses in reaction to unanticipated deviations once the movement response is under way. Superior adaptive movement capacity is a characteristic of expert performers and comprises specific abilities requiring targeted development (Le Runigo et al., 2010). These drills can also be used concurrently as a tool for developing evasion movement capabilities for the athlete acting as the 'lead' player.

The strength and conditioning specialist can be creative in the design of these drills in order to simulate competition conditions. Different authors have highlighted the potential benefits of replicating the critical conditions and task constraints encountered during competition with respect to the perception and decision-making involved in the coupling of task stimuli and movement responses (Holmberg, 2009). From the point of view of developing these abilities there are clear advantages to be derived from replicating game scenarios so that the athlete is exposed to comparable 'perception–action coupling' conditions when initiating and regulating movement responses during the training task (Serpell et al., 2011).

PART IV
Designing the programme

12
PLANNING AND SCHEDULING
Periodisation of training

Introduction

Training variation is a critical aspect of effective training prescription (Fleck, 1999; Stone *et al*., 2000) to avoid diminished training responses and in more serious cases the detrimental effects on performance associated with training maladaptation (Maughan and Gleeson, 2004e). Periodisation offers a framework for manipulating training prescription to provide planned and systematic variation of training parameters (Brown and Greenwood, 2005; Plisk and Stone, 2003; Rhea *et al*., 2002). In addition to avoiding potential negative effects of training monotony, this approach also affords the coach the means to progressively direct training adaptations over successive training cycles to specific training outcomes. Finally, periodisation provides the facility to integrate multiple training components into the planning and scheduling of the training year.

Development of speed and agility performance is multidimensional, comprising numerous elements as discussed in the preceding chapters. To optimise speed and agility development each of these various discrete training components must be emphasised in a coherent and sequential manner. The manner in which these multiple training components are integrated into the athlete's training at different phases in the training year or macrocycle is vital to ensure that the athlete arrives into the key phases of the competition period in the best possible condition (Zatsiorsky and Kraemer, 2006). When designing the periodised training plan, consideration must also be given to the particular training adaptations induced by these multiple training components and how they interact (Reilly *et al*., 2009). For example, different forms of training when undertaken concurrently can interfere with each other because of the acute fitness and fatigue effects associated with the respective training modes.

As well as considering the interaction *between* different areas of training at a particular moment in time, the interaction over time of different training modes that exist *within* each area of physical preparation must also be considered carefully with respect to transference of training effects (Bondarchuk, 2007). This phenomenon has been described in terms of cumulative and residual training effects (Issurin, 2010) Specifically, the physical development undertaken in a particular aspect of performance during each training cycle can impact positively (and negatively) on the training adaptation that occurs in that area during successive training cycles (Bondarchuk, 2007). The residual training effects of preceding training phases may serve to potentiate the subsequent training block, and training effects are superimposed in a way that leads to enhanced performance (Zatsiorsky and Kraemer, 2006).

The challenge, therefore, is to plan and sequence training mesocycles so that training effects are cumulative and additive, as opposed to being conflicting and ultimately counterproductive (Reilly *et al.*, 2009). Effective planning and appropriate scheduling of training blocks early in the training year may serve to lay a foundation for subsequent training blocks in a way that ultimately allows for enhanced levels of performance at the culmination of the training year and competition season.

Planning and scheduling training cycles

Fundamentally, periodisation comprises the organisation and sequencing of training blocks. This requires coordinating the timing with which different training modes are introduced, which requires both long-term and medium-term planning. In addition, there is a further need for short-term planning when it comes to scheduling the training week. Different forms of training when undertaken concurrently can counteract each other, which may result in a blunted training response. Training for strength/power and endurance training, in particular, involve conflicting responses in terms of both the hormonal milieu and the intracellular processes that result. Minimising this negative interaction between opposing training stimuli requires careful scheduling (Reilly *et al.*, 2009).

The athlete's competition calendar will to some extent dictate the structure of the training year. However, the duration of each respective training block will also be determined by biological constraints, that is, the time frames necessary for the intended morphological, physiological or neural adaptation to take place (Bondarchuk, 2007). Reconciling these two conflicting scheduling constraints – that is, what is demanded by the competition calendar versus what is required to achieve the necessary training adaptation – will require consultation with the sports coach and athlete. One particular area on which it is necessary to reach an understanding is that the emphasis of the athlete's training during certain blocks in the year may be such that they will not always be in a condition to express their physical capabilities to the full extent when they compete during these periods.

The first consideration when planning an athlete's training is to establish their training history, both in general and also with regard to their previous experience with each aspect of training (strength and speed–strength training, plyometrics, different forms of metabolic conditioning, etc.). Relatively basic training prescription with only periodic variation is sufficient for younger athletes or athletes who do not have a long training history for a particular physical capacity (Kraemer and Fleck, 2005; Plisk and Stone, 2003). This is not the case for more advanced athletes, who often require marked variation in training parameters both within and between training cycles to optimise training responses (Gamble, 2006b). The periodisation scheme that is optimal for a given individual will therefore differ based upon the degree of training variation it provides.

Selecting periodisation schemes

Approaches to periodisation that are traditionally employed were developed for sports and athletic events that are relatively simple in terms of the variety of training involved (e.g. field sports events, endurance sports). Equally, these sports have a clearly delineated training and competition calendar, featuring a relatively short competition season. As described in the preceding chapters, development of sports speed and agility encompasses a much broader and more diverse range of training approaches. Furthermore, athletes for whom speed and agility are important commonly participate in sports (e.g. team sports, racquet sports) that involve numerous other challenges to planning and periodisation. Such constraints include the extended nature of the competition season, as well as the number and density of competitions involved (Gamble, 2006b).

With these considerations and constraints in mind, there a number of different options available to the strength and conditioning specialist with respect to the periodisation scheme employed in a given training cycle. A brief description of the most common approaches to periodisation is presented in the following sections.

Linear periodisation

Classically, linear periodisation schemes provide variation in training parameters between successive training cycles. The general trend over time is for intensity to be progressively increased with concomitant reductions in volume. Reverse periodisation schemes have been investigated that feature the opposite pattern (i.e. high intensity at the outset followed by progressive reductions in intensity prescribed); however, this approach has typically been proven to be inferior to other periodisation methods (Prestes *et al.*, 2009; Rhea *et al.*, 2003). Although training prescription with linear periodisation is varied between successive mesocycles there is minimal variation within each microcycle. There is some suggestion that this approach may not provide a sufficient level of variation for highly trained athletes.

In recent years innovations have seen modifications to the traditional linear periodisation approach, which provide more frequent alterations in training stimuli. One such example is a condensed version of the classical linear periodisation approach that features 2-week 'mesocycles' so that training prescription is markedly altered at 2-week intervals (Allerheiligan *et al.*, 2003). Favourable results have been reported with a similar but more progressive approach that featured increments in intensity occurring at weekly intervals (Prestes *et al.*, 2009).

The summated mesocycles approach described by Plisk and Stone (2003) represents a bridge between modified linear periodisation and the blocked periodisation method described in the following section. Essentially, there is a consistent linear increase in training load each week over a period of 2–4 weeks followed by an unloading week at markedly lower volume load. This pattern is repeated so that over time successive summated mesocycles form a wave-shaped progression, with higher or lower peaks in volume load with each successive cycle, depending on the objective of the particular phase of training within the training year (Plisk and Stone, 2003).

Blocked periodisation

Blocked periodisation involves dividing the training year into blocks of time ranging from 6 to 16 weeks; within each block the athlete performs a series of concentrated training mesocycles lasting from 2 to 4 weeks in a specified sequence (Issurin, 2010). The mesocycles within each training block concentrate on a limited number of training goals (i.e. two or three) to the exclusion of others. The individual mesocycles within each training block have been variously termed, but the general characteristics of each mesocycle are described below (Issurin, 2010):

- 'general' or 'accumulation' block: 2–6 weeks in duration, relatively higher volumes and lower intensities, focus on general preparation methods;
- 'specific', 'transmutation' or 'transformation' block: 2–4 weeks in duration, high-intensity training, focus on special conditioning modes and sport-specific training;
- 'realisation', 'restoration' or 'competition' block: 1–2 weeks in duration, training intensity remains high but training volume markedly reduced (i.e. taper), focus on highly specific 'transfer training' modes.

This approach is therefore broadly similar to the condensed modified linear periodisation schemes in the previous section, and this sequential pattern is designed to be repeated throughout multiple training blocks for an extended period.

Non-linear undulating periodisation

Non-linear undulating periodisation involves variable changes in volume load both within and between training cycles as a result of fluctuations in training intensity within each training microcycle. Non-linear undulating periodisation is suggested to be more appropriate for highly trained athletes because of the greater level of training variation afforded by this approach (Monteiro *et al.*, 2009). This approach is also advocated for team sports and other sports that have a prolonged competition season.

Both daily and weekly undulating periodisation schemes are employed (Buford *et al.*, 2007). Daily undulating periodisation involves variation on a daily basis so that the training stimulus provided by each session within the training week is markedly different (Apel *et al.*, 2011). Weekly undulating periodisation involves large fluctuations in training intensity prescribed between consecutive weeks; however, the programming of sessions within each week remains consistent. What differentiates this approach from the condensed modified linear periodisation models and the summated mesocycle approach described in the previous sections is that the weekly changes in intensity do not follow a linear progression.

Summary

The lack of studies of sufficient length means that there are not sufficient data to make recommendations about the best approach to periodisation for athletes' training for a given sport or athlete (Cissik *et al.*, 2008). A variety of periodisation methods (linear, weekly undulating, daily undulating) were reported to be equally effective for a short-term

(9-week) training intervention in recreationally trained subjects (Buford et al., 2007). Other studies that have compared periodisation methods have variously reported that linear periodisation produced superior results (Apel et al., 2011; Hoffman et al., 2003) or conversely that undulating periodisation was the more effective method (Rhea et al., 2002).

By definition, periodisation concerns variation of training; it would therefore appear contradictory that any single periodised training scheme could elicit optimum results when applied in isolation for an extended period (Gamble, 2006b). It is evident that certain strategies will be more suited to particular individuals based upon their level of training experience (Plisk and Stone, 2003). Equally, it is possible that the periodisation scheme that is most appropriate may differ according to the particular form of training – for example metabolic conditioning versus plyometric training.

In view of these observations, a blend of periodisation strategies may represent the best approach to optimise athletes' long-term training (Plisk and Stone, 2003). Periods in the off season and pre-season without competitive fixtures will undoubtedly allow different approaches to periodised training from those that will be conducive for adequate recovery when competitions are scheduled (Gamble, 2006b). Implementing a variety of periodisation schemes for different training mesocycles throughout the training year according to the needs of the respective phase of an athlete's preparation would therefore appear to be the best strategy.

Approaching periodisation at macrocycle, mesocycle and microcycle level

When applying a staged approach to the development of speed and agility capabilities each training block is designed to develop a particular aspect or attribute in a way that serves as the foundation for subsequent development in later training cycles. As well as the interaction between training for different physical and physiological attributes (strength training, speed–strength training, metabolic conditioning, etc.), there are also discrete properties within each respective training component, and an array of training modes to develop them. On a longitudinal basis the periodisation of training modes should incorporate progression of these individual training modes within each area of physical development. There are therefore different layers of planning and scheduling both between and within each area of physical development.

Periodisation of training comprises planned variation and scheduling at levels from macrocycle to mesocycle and microcycle. For example, planning at the level of the macrocycle is influenced by scheduling constraints such as the key dates in the competition season. Planning at microcycle level concerns not only structuring individual sessions to meet the goals of a particular phase of the training mesocycle but also scheduling the training week to account for the respective demands of competition, different training sessions and technical/tactical practices.

Planning the training macrocycle

Planning at the level of the macrocycle encompasses scheduling and structuring the training year, and also beyond, that is, long-term or multi-year planning (Issurin, 2010).

Essentially, the aim is that each year's training serves to build upon the development achieved over the previous year(s) rather than merely repeating the same yearly cycle. The strength and conditioning specialist should therefore consider the overall planning of training prescription not only within each training year, but also between successive annual cycles. The time frame involved might vary depending on the particular circumstances, but a quadrennial (i.e. 4-year) cycle is common for planning in many sports (Issurin, 2010).

As discussed in a previous section, the athlete's training history with different forms of training relevant to speed and agility development will influence not only the starting point but also the degree of variation and rate of progression for each aspect of training. It is possible that the athlete might be classed as 'experienced' for one aspect of training, for example strength training, but relatively untrained for another, such as plyometric training. This will necessitate a different approach to prescription, planned variation and progression for each of the respective components identified for developing speed and agility expression.

Periodisation models typically focus on manipulating training intensity (e.g. percentage of one-repetition maximum) and total training volume and frequency. However, periodisation concerns all aspects of training prescription and should be applied accordingly. In addition to alterations in training intensity and volume, periodic changes in the training modes employed offers another means to systematically vary the training stimulus to facilitate continued training adaptation (Zatsiorsky and Kraemer, 2006). In the classical periodised models there is a sequential shift from 'general' training modes during general preparation cycles to increasingly 'specific' training modes, particularly as the athlete approaches key phases in the competition period.

Indices of SSC and power performance appear more prone to detraining effects, for example in comparison with maximum strength measures (Sáez-Sáez de Villarreal et al., 2008). Another study likewise identified that measures of power are more sensitive to detraining than maximum strength (Izquierdo et al., 2007). This is an important consideration, particularly given that speed and agility performance are both heavily dependent upon these capabilities. In view of these findings, it would seem prudent to include some form of speed–strength training throughout, with the exception of the off season and early pre-season. Similarly, plyometric training should be introduced before the competition season and continued thereafter. Given the wide array of training modes that can be selected from (see Chapter 6), it should still be possible to programme the necessary training variation required to avoid stagnation effects.

Training mesocyles

Broadly, planning at mesocycle level should feature a progression so that the foundation development of physical and physiological capabilities undertaken early in the training year is translated over time into enhanced speed and agility expression meeting the specific demands of the sport (Zatsiorsky and Kraemer, 2006). This can be achieved through a coherent and sequential shift in training prescription between successive mesocycles from the general preparation modes early in the year through to the highly specific training approaches employed at the culmination of the competition season.

In this way, periodisation of training modes or training content prescribed for successive mesocycles throughout the training year for strength training and speed–strength training particularly will tend to correspond in broad terms to the classical linear periodisation model. The approach taken to periodising other training parameters (frequency, intensity volume) will, however, tend to vary for different phases in the training macrocycle (Tables 12.1–12.4). In addition, as noted previously, the approach to periodisation that is most appropriate may differ according to the type of training. For example, for metabolic conditioning the blocked periodisation model might be adopted so that a blend of conditioning methods are sequentially undertaken prior to a taper period, with this pattern repeated over successive phases of training. Similarly, during an extended season of competition, a summated mesocycles approach might be employed for the scheduling of volume load for strength and speed–strength training (Gamble, 2006b). Conversely, a weekly or daily undulating periodisation approach could be adopted when planning the intensity/volume of speed and change of direction training sessions during this period.

Scheduling at microcycle level

Scheduling each training microcycle requires consideration of the interaction between different forms of training. One example of negative interaction between conflicting forms of training is the interference effects observed between aerobic conditioning and strength/power training. A preceding bout of high-intensity endurance exercise has been reported to impair subjects' ability to perform strength training (Leveritt and Abernethy, 1999). These interference effects are associated with conflicting hormonal responses to strength versus endurance training (Kraemer et al., 1995). As a result, when strength training is performed on the same day following endurance training, the resulting training adaptation, with respect to power development in particular, is compromised.

Other considerations relating to the effects of neuromuscular fatigue include the time course of fatigue effects and the degree to which neural fatigue impairs the athlete's ability to perform a particular type of training. Some training modes are more prone to the detrimental effects of neural fatigue than others. One example of training that is highly susceptible to the effects of neural fatigue is fast SSC plyometric training. In general, the training week should be relatively front loaded, so that the more demanding exercises from a neuromuscular point of view are placed early in the week. Similarly, these forms of training should be scheduled first in the day. Other forms of training, for example metabolic conditioning, that are less sensitive to the influence of neural fatigue can follow these sessions later in the day, and can also be placed later in the training week.

It is equally important that there be flexibility in planning at the level of the microcycle. Specifically, the strength and conditioning specialist should be responsive to the state of the athlete on any given day. Ultimately, allowances must be made in the event of injury or illness, and equally for the acute effects of residual fatigue and other stressors. When necessary, modifications should be made to the plan for the training day and the particular session so that these factors can be accommodated.

TABLE 12.1 Representative off-season training mesocycle

	Training modes	Periodisation of intensity, volume, frequency
Strength training	'General strength development' training modes (see Chapter 5) Corrective exercises to address any issues identified during screening	Linear
Speed–strength training	N/A	N/A
Plyometric training	N/A	N/A
Metabolic conditioning	Aerobic interval training (see Chapter 7) Combination of cross-training modes and running conditioning	Linear
Speed training	N/A	N/A
Change of direction training and agility development	N/A	N/A

N/A, not applicable.

TABLE 12.2 Representative pre-season training mesocycle

	Training modes	Periodisation of intensity, volume, frequency
Strength training	Progression from 'general strength development' in early pre-season to 'special preparation phase strength development' training modes (see Chapter 5) Corrective exercises to address any issues identified during screening	Linear
Speed–strength training	Introduction of bilateral ballistic resistance training modes and basic Olympic-style lifts at the midpoint of pre-season (see Chapter 6)	Linear
Plyometric training	Introduction of bilateral slow SSC training modes mid-pre-season followed by progression to unilateral slow SSC training modes (see Chapter 6)	Linear
Metabolic conditioning	Progression from aerobic interval to anaerobic interval training modes to repeated sprint conditioning late pre-season (see Chapter 7) Combination of conditioning modes including skill-based games and conditioning drills at appropriate intensities	Linear

Speed training	Introduction of technique development drills and instruction/development of acceleration mechanics mid-pre-season, followed by progression to higher-speed sprint repetitions and acceleration drills (see Chapter 10)	Linear
Change of direction training and agility development	Introduction of movement skills training mid-pre-season, followed by progression to reactive agility drills (see Chapter 11)	Linear

TABLE 12.3 Representative competition or 'in-season' training mesocycle

	Training modes	*Periodisation of intensity, volume, frequency*
Strength training	Progression from 'special preparation phase strength development' to 'transfer training' modes (see Chapter 5)	Summated mesocycles
Speed–strength training	Progression to advanced Olympic-style lifts and unilateral ballistic resistance training modes and introduction of resisted sprint training modes (see Chapter 6)	Modified linear
Plyometric training	Progression from unilateral slow SSC training modes to fast SSC training modes (see Chapter 6)	Modified linear
Metabolic conditioning	Cycling of aerobic interval training, anaerobic interval training and repeated sprint conditioning (see Chapter 7) Combination of conditioning games, skill-based conditioning drills and movement-specific high-intensity conditioning drills, depending on respective block	Blocked periodisation
Speed training	Progression to game-related acceleration and speed work (see Chapter 10)	Weekly undulating periodisation
Change of direction training and agility development	Progression to more challenging and context-specific reactive agility drills and partner drills (see Chapter 11)	Daily undulating periodisation

TABLE 12.4 Representative 'peaking' training mesocycle

	Training modes	Periodisation of intensity, volume, frequency
Strength training	'Transfer training' modes (see Chapter 5)	Summated mesocycles
Speed–strength training	Unilateral ballistic resistance training modes and resisted sprint training modes (see Chapter 6)	Summated mesocycles
Plyometric training	Predominantly unilateral fast SSC training modes (see Chapter 6)	Summated mesocycles
Metabolic conditioning	Repeated sprint conditioning and speed-endurance training (see Chapter 7) Movement-specific high-intensity conditioning drills	Daily undulating periodisation
Speed training	High-intensity game-related acceleration and speed work (see Chapter 10)	Daily undulating periodisation
Change of direction training and agility development	High-intensity game-specific reactive agility and partner drills (see Chapter 11)	Daily undulating periodisation

REFERENCES

Aagaard, P., J.L. Andersen, P. Dyhre-Poulson, A.-M. Leffers, A. Wagner, S.P. Magnusson, J. Halkjaer-Kristensen and E.B. Simonsen. 2001. A Mechanism for Increased Contractile Strength of Human Pennate Muscle in Response to Strength Training: Changes in Muscle Architecture, *Journal of Physiology*, 534(2): 621–623.

Abernethy, P., G. Wilson and P. Logan.1995. Strength and Power Assessment: Issues, Controversies and Challenges, *Sports Medicine*, 19(6): 410–417.

Agel, J., E.A. Arendt and B. Bershadsky. 2005. Anterior Cruciate Ligament Injury in National Collegiate Athletic Association Basketball and Soccer: A 13-Year Review, *American Journal of Sports Medicine*, 33(4): 524–531.

Alcaraz, P.E., J.M. Palao and J.L.L. Elvira. 2009. Determining the Optimal Load for Resisted Sprint Training with Sled Towing, *Journal of Strength & Conditioning Research*, 23(2): 480–485.

Allerheiligan, B. 2003. In-Season Strength Training for Power Athletes, *Strength & Conditioning Journal*, 25(3): 23–28.

Anderson, K. and D.G. Behm. 2005. The Impact of Instability Resistance Training on Balance and Stability, *Sports Medicine*, 35(1): 43–53.

Apel, J.M., R.M. Lacey and R.T. Kell. 2011. A Comparison of Traditional and Weekly Undulating Periodized Strength Training Programs with Total Volume and Intensity Equated, *Journal of Strength & Conditioning Research*, 25(3): 694–703.

Arnason, A., S.B. Sigurdsson, A. Gudmundsson, I. Holme, L. Engebretsen and R. Bahr. 2004. Risk Factors for Injuries in Football, *American Journal of Sports Medicine*, 32(1 Suppl.): S5–S16.

Axler, C.T. and S.M. McGill. 1997. Low Back Loads over a Variety of Abdominal Exercises: Searching for the Safest Abdominal Challenge, *Medicine & Science in Sports & Exercise*, 29(6): 804–811.

Baker, D. 1996. Improving Vertical Jump Performance through General, Special, and Specific Strength Training: A Brief Review, *Journal of Strength & Conditioning Research*, 10(2): 131–136.

Baker, D. 2001. A Series of Studies on the Training of High-Intensity Muscle Power in Rugby League Football Players, *Journal of Strength & Conditioning Research*, 15(2): 198–209.

Baker, D. 2003. Acute Negative Effect of Hypertrophy-Oriented Training Bout on Subsequent Upper-Body Power Output, *Journal of Strength & Conditioning Research*, 17(3): 527–530.

Balsom, P.D., J.Y. Seger, B. Sjodin and B. Ekblom. 1992. Maximal-Intensity Intermittent Exercise: Effect of Recovery Duration, *International Journal of Sports Medicine*, 13(7): 528–533.

Bangsbo, J., F.M. Iaia and P. Krustrup. 2008. The Yo-Yo Intermittent Recovery Test: A Useful Tool for Evaluation of Physical Performance in Intermittent Sports, *Sports Medicine*, 38(1): 37–51.

Barber-Westin, S.D., M. Galloway, F.R. Noyes, G. Corbett and C. Walsh. 2005. Assessment of Lower Limb Neuromuscular Control in Prepubescent Athletes, *American Journal of Sports Medicine*, 33(12): 1853–1860.

Barber-Westin, S.D., F.R. Noyes and M. Galloway. 2006. Jump-Land Characteristics and Muscle Strength Development in Young Athletes, *American Journal of Sports Medicine*, 34(3): 375–384.

Barr, K.P., M. Griggs and T. Cadby. 2005. Lumbar Stabilization: Core Concepts and Current Literature, Part 1, *American Journal of Physical Medicine and Rehabilitation*, 84: 473–480.

Behm, D.G. 1995. Neuromuscular Implications and Applications of Resistance Training, *Journal of Strength & Conditioning Research*, 9(4): 264–274.

Behm, D.G., A.M. Leonard, W.B. Young, W.A.C. Bonsey and S.N. Mackinnon. 2005. Trunk Muscle Electromyographic Activity with Unstable and Unilateral Exercises, *Journal of Strength & Conditioning Research*, 19(1): 193–201.

Belli, A., H. Kyrolainen and P.V. Komi. 2002. Movement and Power of Lower Limb Joints in Running, *International Journal of Sports Medicine*, 23: 136–141.

Bennett, J.P., M.G.L. Sayers and B.J. Burkett. 2009. The Impact of Lower Extremity Mass and Inertia Manipulation on Sprint Kinematics, *Journal of Strength & Conditioning Research*, 23(9): 2542–2547.

Berryman, N., D. Maurel and L. Bosquet. 2010. Effect of Plyometric vs. Dynamic Weight Training on the Energy Cost of Running, *Journal of Strength & Conditioning Research*, 24(7): 1818–1825.

Besier, T.F., D.G. Lloyd, T.R. Ackland and J.L. Cochrane. 2001. Anticipatory Effects on Knee Joint Loading during Running and Cutting Maneuvres, *Medicine & Science in Sports & Exercise*, 33(7): 1176–1181.

Billat, V.L. 2001a. Interval Training for Performance: A Scientific and Empirical Practice. Special Recommendations for Middle- and Long-Distance Running, Part I: Aerobic Interval Training, *Sports Medicine*, 31(1): 13–31.

Billat, V.L. 2001b. Interval Training for Performance: A Scientific and Empirical Practice. Special Recommendations for Middle- and Long-Distance Running, Part II: Anaerobic Interval Training, *Sports Medicine*, 31(2): 75–90.

Billaut, F. and F.A. Basset. 2007. Effect of Different Recovery Patterns on Repeated-Sprint Ability and Neuromuscular Responses, *Journal of Sports Sciences*, 25(8): 905–913.

Bishop, D. 2003a. Warm Up I: Potential Mechanisms and the Effects of Passive Warm Up on Exercise Performance, *Sports Medicine*, 33(6): 439–454.

Bishop, D. 2003b. Warm Up II: Performance Changes Following Active Warm Up and How to Structure the Warm Up, *Sports Medicine*, 33(7): 483–498.

Bishop, D., M. Spencer, R. Duffield and S. Lawrence. 2001. The Validity of a Repeated Sprint Ability Test, *Journal of Science & Medicine in Sport*, 4(1): 19–29.

Bishop, D., J. Edge and C. Goodman. 2004. Muscle Buffer Capacity and Aerobic Fitness Are Associated with Repeated Sprint Ability in Women, *European Journal of Applied Physiology*, 92: 540–547.

Bloomfield, J., R. Polman, P. O'Donoghue and L. McNaughton. 2007. Effective Speed and Agility Conditioning Methodology for Random Intermittent Dynamic Type Sports, *Journal of Strength & Conditioning Research*, 21(4): 1093–1100.

Boddington, M.K., M.I. Lambert, A. St Clair Gibson and T.D. Noakes. 2001. Reliability of a 5-m Multiple Shuttle Test, *Journal of Sports Sciences*, 19: 223–228.

Bogdanis, G.C., M.E. Nevill, L.H. Boobis and H.K.A. Lakomy. 1996. Contribution of Phosphocreatine and Aerobic Metabolism to Energy Supply during Repeated Sprint Exercise, *Journal of Applied Physiology*, 80(3): 876–884.

Bondarchuk, A. 2007. *Transfer of Training in Sports*, Muskegon, MI: Ultimate Athlete Concepts.

Bradley, P.S., P.D. Olsen and M.D. Portas. 2007. The Effect of Static, Ballistic, and Proprioceptive Neuromuscular Facilitation Stretching on Vertical Jump Performance, *Journal of Strength & Conditioning Research*, 21(1): 223–226.

Brechue, W.F., J.L. Mayhew and F.C. Piper. 2010. Characteristics of Sprint Performance in College Football Players, *Journal of Strength & Conditioning Research*, 24(5): 1169–1178.

Bressel, E., J.C. Yonker, J. Kras and E.M. Heath. 2007. Comparison of Static and Dynamic Balance in Female Collegiate Soccer, Basketball, and Gymnastics Athletes, *Journal of Athletic Training*, 42(1): 42–46.

Brown, C.N. and R. Mynark. 2007. Balance Deficits in Recreational Athletes with Chronic Ankle Instability, *Journal of Athletic Training*, 42(3): 367–373.

Brown, L.E. and M. Greenwood. 2005. Periodization Essentials and Innovations in Resistance Training Protocols, *Strength & Conditioning Journal*, 27(4): 80–85.

Brown, T.D., J.D. Vescovi and J.L. Vanheest. 2004. Assessment of Linear Sprinting Performance: A Theoretical Paradigm, *Journal of Sports Science and Medicine*, 3: 203–210.

Brughelli, M. and J. Cronin. 2008. Influence of Running Velocity on Vertical, Leg and Joint Stiffness: Modelling and Recommendations for Future Research, *Sports Medicine*, 38(8): 647–657.

Brughelli, M., J. Cronin, G. Levin and A. Chaouachi. 2008. Understanding Change of Direction Ability in Sport: A Review of Resistance Training Studies, *Sports Medicine*, 38(12): 1045–1063.

Buchheit, M. 2008. The 30–15 Intermittent Fitness Test: Accuracy for Individualising Interval Training of Young Intermittent Sport Players, *Journal of Strength & Conditioning Research*, 22(2): 365–374.

Buford, T.W., S.J. Rossi, D.B., Smith and A.J. Warren. 2007. A Comparison of Periodization Models during Nine Weeks with Equated Volume and Intensity for Strength, *Journal of Strength & Conditioning Research*, 21(4): 1245–1250.

Bundle, M.W., R.W. Hoyt and P.G. Weyand. 2003. High-Speed Running Performance: A New Approach to Assessment and Prediction, *Journal of Applied Physiology*, 95: 1955–1962.

Burgomaster, K.A., K.R. Howarth, S.M. Phillips, M. Rakobowchuk, M.J. MacDonald, S.L. McGee and M.J. Gibala. 2008. Similar Metabolic Adaptations during Exercise after Low Volume Sprint Interval and Traditional Endurance Training in Humans, *Journal of Physiology*, 586(1): 151–160.

Carey, D.G., M.M. Drake, G.J. Pliego and R.L. Raymond. 2007. Do Hockey Players Need Aerobic Fitness? Relation between VO_2max and Fatigue during High-Intensity Intermittent Ice Skating, *Journal of Strength & Conditioning Research*, 21(3): 963–966.

Carter, J.M., W.C. Beam, S.G. McMahan, M.L. Barr and L.E. Brown. 2006. The Effects of Stability Ball Training on Spinal Stability in Sedentary Individuals, *Journal of Strength & Conditioning Research*, 20(2): 429–435.

Castagna, C., F.M. Impellizeri, K. Chamari, D. Carlomagno and E. Rampinini. 2006. Aerobic Fitness and Yo-Yo Continuous and Intermittent Test Performances in Soccer Players: A Correlation Study, *Journal of Strength & Conditioning Research*, 20(2): 320–325.

Castagna, C., V. Manzi, S. D'Ottavio, G. Annino, E. Padua and D. Bishop. 2007. Relation between Maximal Aerobic Power and the Ability to Repeat Sprints in Young Basketball Players, *Journal of Strength & Conditioning Research*, 21(4): 1172–1176.

Chaouachi, A., C. Castagna, M. Chtara, M. Brughelli, O. Turki, O. Galy, K. Chamari and D.G. Behm. 2010. Effect of Warm-Ups Involving Static or Dynamic Stretching on Agility, Sprinting and Jumping Performance in Trained Individuals, *Journal of Strength & Conditioning Research*, 24(8): 2001–2011.

Chappell, J.D., B. Yu, D.T. Kirkendall and W.E. Garrett. 2002. A Comparison of Knee Kinetics between Male and Female Recreational Athletes in Stop-Jump Tasks, *American Journal of Sports Medicine*, 30(2): 261–267.

Chiu, L.Z.E., A.C. Fry, L.W. Weiss, B.K. Schilling, L.E. Brown and S.L. Smith. 2003. Postactivation Potentiation Response in Athletes and Recreationally Trained Individuals, *Journal of Strength & Conditioning Research*, 17(4): 671–677.

Cholewicki, J. and S.M. McGill. 1996. Mechanical Stability of the In Vivo Lumbar Spine: Implications for Injury and Chronic Low Back Pain, *Clinical Biomechanics*, 11(1): 1–15.

Cholewicki, J. and J.J. Vanvliet. 2002. Relative Contribution of Trunk Muscles to the Stability of the Lumbar Spine during Isometric Exertions, *Clinical Biomechanics*, 17(2): 99–105.

Cissik, J.M. 2005. Means and Methods of Speed Training: Part II, *Strength & Conditioning Journal*, 27(1): 18–25.

Cissik, J., A. Hedrick and M. Barnes. 2008. Challenges Applying the Research on Periodization, *Strength & Conditioning Journal*, 30(1): 45–51.

Cook, G. 2003. Mobility and Stability Testing. In: *Athletic Body in Balance*, Champaign, IL: Human Kinetics, pp. 26–38.

Cormie, P., R. Deane and J.M. McBride. 2007a. Methodological Concerns for Determining Power Output in the Jump Squat, *Journal of Strength & Conditioning Research*, 21(2): 424–430.

Cormie, P., J.M. McBride and G.O. McCaulley. 2007b. Validation of Power Measurement Techniques in Dynamic Lower Body Resistance Exercises, *Journal of Applied Biomechanics*, 23: 103–118.

Cormie, P., J.M. McBride and G.O. McCaulley. 2007c. The Influence of Body Mass on Calculation of Power during Lower-Body Resistance Exercises, *Journal of Strength & Conditioning Research*, 21(4): 1042–1049.

Cormie, P., M.R. McGuigan and R.U. Newton. 2008. The Influence of Initial Strength Level on the Ability to Adapt to Power Training, *Proceedings of the 6th International Conference on Strength Training*, Colorado Springs, pp. 59–60.

Cormie, P., M.R. McGuigan and R.U. Newton. 2010a. Changes in the Eccentric Phase Contribution to Improved SSC Performance after Training, *Medicine & Science in Sports & Exercise*, 42(9): 1731–1744.

Cormie, P., M.R. McGuigan and R.U. Newton. 2010b. Influence of Strength on the Magnitude and Mechanisms of Adaptation to Power Training, *Medicine & Science in Sports & Exercise*, 42(8): 1566–1581.

Cowley, H.R., K.R. Ford, G.D. Myer, T.W. Kernozek and T.E. Hewett. 2006. Differences in Neuromuscular Strategies between Landing and Cutting Tasks in Female Basketball and Soccer Athletes, *Journal of Athletic Training*, 41(1): 67–73.

Cowley, P.M. and T.C. Swensen. 2008. Development and Reliability of Two Core Stability Field Tests, *Journal of Strength & Conditioning Research*, 22(2): 619–624.

Cronin, J.B. and K.T. Hansen. 2005. Strength and Power Predictors of Sports Speed, *Journal of Strength & Conditioning Research*, 19(2): 349–357.

Cronin, J.B. and G. Sleivert. 2005. Challenges in Understanding the Influence of Maximal Power Training on Improving Athletic Performance, *Sports Medicine*, 35(3): 215–234.

Cronin, J.B. and K.T. Hansen. 2006. Resisted Sprint Training for the Acceleration Phase of Sprinting, *Strength & Conditioning Journal*, 28(4): 42–51.

Cronin, J., P.J. McNair and R.N. Marshall. 2001. Developing Explosive Power: A Comparison of Technique and Training, *Journal of Science & Medicine in Sport*, 4(1): 59–70.

Cronin, J.B., P.J. McNair and R.N. Marshall. 2003. Force–Velocity Analysis of Strength-Training Techniques and Load: Implications for Training Strategy and Research, *Journal of Strength & Conditioning Research*, 17(1): 148–155.

Cronin, J., T. Ogden, T. Lawton and M. Brughelli. 2007. Does Increasing Maximal Strength Improve Sprint Running Performance, *Strength & Conditioning Journal*, 29(3): 86–95.

Cusi, M.F., C.J. Juska-Butel, D. Garlick and G. Argyrous. 2001. Lumbopelvic Stability and Injury Profile in Rugby Union Players, *New Zealand Journal of Sports Medicine*, 29(1): 14–18.

Danneels, L.A., G.G. Vanderstraeten, D.C. Cambier, E.E. Witrvrouw, J. Bourgois, W. Dankaerts and H.J. de Cuyper. 2001. Effects of Three Different Training Modalities on the Cross Sectional Area of the Lumbar Multifidus Muscle in Patients with Chronic Low Back Pain, *British Journal of Sports Medicine*, 35: 186–191.

Dayne, A.M., J.M. McBride, J.L. Nuzzo, N.T. Triplett, J. Skinner and A. Burr. 2011. Power Output in the Jump Squat in Adolescent Male Athletes, *Journal of Strength & Conditioning Research*, 25(3): 585–589.

Deane, R.S., J.W. Chow, M.D. Tillman and K.A. Fournier. 2005. Effects of Hip Flexor Training on Sprint, Shuttle Run, and Vertical Jump Performance, *Journal of Strength & Conditioning Research*, 19(3): 615–621.

Delecluse, C., H. van Coppenolle, E. Willems, M. van Leemputte, R. Diels and M. Goris. 1995. Influence of High-Resistance and High-Velocity Training on Sprint Performance, *Medicine & Science in Sports & Exercise*, 27(8): 1203–1209.

Dempsey, A.R., D.G. Lloyd, B.C. Elliott, J.R. Steele and B.J. Munro. 2009. Changing Sidestep Cutting Technique Reduces Knee Valgus Loading, *American Journal of Sports Medicine*, 37(11): 2192–2200.

DiStefano, L.J., M.A. Clark and D.A. Padua. 2009. Evidence Supporting Balance Training in Healthy Individuals: A Systematic Review, *Journal of Strength & Conditioning Research*, 23(9): 2718–2731.

Divert, C., G. Mornieux, H. Baur, F. Mayer and A. Belli. 2005. Mechanical Comparisons of Barefoot and Shod Running, *International Journal of Sports Medicine*, 26: 593–598.

Drinkwater, E.J., T. Lane and J. Cannon. 2009. Effect of an Acute Bout of Plyometric Exercise on Neuromuscular Fatigue and Recovery in Recreational Athletes, *Journal of Strength & Conditioning Research*, 23(4): 1181–1186.

Dupont, G., A. McCall, F. Prieur, G.P. Millet and S. Berthoin. 2010. Faster Oxygen Uptake Kinetics during Recovery Is Related to Better Repeated Sprinting Ability, *European Journal of Applied Physiology*, 110(3): 627–634.

Ebben, W.P., C. Simenz and R.L. Jensen. 2008. Evaluation of Plyometric Intensity Using Electromyography, *Journal of Strength & Conditioning Research*, 22(3): 861–868.

Edge, J., D. Bishop, S. Hill-Haas, B. Dawson and C. Goodman. 2006a. Comparison of Muscle Buffer Capacity and Repeated-Sprint Ability of Untrained, Endurance-Trained and Team-Sport Athletes, *European Journal of Applied Physiology*, 96: 225–234.

Edge, J., D. Bishop and C. Goodman. 2006b. The Effects of Training Intensity on Muscle Buffer Capacity in Females, *European Journal of Applied Physiology*, 96: 97–105.

Emery, C.A. 2003. Is There a Clinical Standing Balance Measurement Appropriate for Use in Sports Medicine? A Review of the Literature, *Journal of Science & Medicine in Sport*, 6(4): 492–504.

Evans, K., K.M. Refshauge and R. Adams. 2007. Trunk Muscle Endurance Tests: Reliability and Gender Differences in Athletes, *Journal of Science & Medicine in Sport*, 10: 447–455.

Farrow, D., W. Young and L. Bruce. 2005. The Development of a Test of Reactive Agility for Netball: A New Methodology, *Journal of Science & Medicine in Sport*, 8(1): 52–60.

Fenwick, C.M.J., S.H.M. Brown and S.M. McGill. 2009. Comparison of Different Rowing Exercises: Trunk Muscle and Activation and Lumbar Spine Motion, Load and Stiffness, *Journal of Strength & Conditioning Research*, 23(5): 1408–1417.

Fleck, S.J. 1999. Periodized Strength Training: A Critical Review, *Journal of Strength & Conditioning Research*, 13(1): 82–89.

Fletcher, I.M. and B. Jones. 2004. The Effect of Different Warm-Up Stretch Protocols on 20 Meter Sprint Performance in Trained Rugby Union Players, *Journal of Strength & Conditioning Research*, 18(4): 885–888.

Fletcher, I.M. and R. Anness. 2007. The Acute Effects of Combined Static and Dynamic Stretch Protocols on Fifty-Meter Sprint Performance in Track-and-Field Athletes, *Journal of Strength & Conditioning Research*, 21(3): 784–787.

Ford, K.R., G.D. Myer and T.E. Hewett. 2003. Valgus Knee Motion during Landing in High School Female and Male Basketball Players, *Medicine & Science in Sports & Exercise*, 35(10): 1745–1750.

Ford, K.R., G.D. Myer and T.E. Hewett. 2010. Longitudinal Effects of Maturation on Lower Extremity Joint Stiffness in Adolescent Athletes, *American Journal of Sports Medicine*, 38(9): 1829–1837.

Foster, C., L.L. Hector, R. Welsh, M. Schrager, M.A. Green and A.C. Snyder. 1997. Effects of Specific versus Cross-Training on Running Performance, *European Journal of Applied Physiology*, 70: 367–372.

Fouré, A., A. Nordez and C. Cornu. 2010. Plyometric Training Effects on Achilles Tendon Stiffness and Dissipative Properties, *Journal of Applied Physiology*, 109: 849–854.

Frost, D.M., J.B. Cronin and G. Levin. 2008. Stepping Backward Can Improve Sprint Performance over Short Distances, *Journal of Strength & Conditioning Research*, 22(3): 918–922.

Fujii, K., Y. Yamada and S. Oda. 2010. Skilled Basketball Players Rotate Their Shoulders More during Running while Dribbling, *Perceptual and Motor Skills*, 110(3): 983–984.

Gabbett, T. and D. Benton. 2009. Reactive Agility of Rugby League Players, *Journal of Science & Medicine in Sport*, 12: 212–214.

Gabbett, T.J., J.M. Sheppard, K.R. Pritchard-Peschek, M.D. Leveritt and M.J. Aldred. 2008. Influence of Closed Skill and Open Skill Warm-Ups on the Performance of Speed, Change of Direction, Vertical Jump, and Reactive Agility in Team Sports Athletes, *Journal of Strength & Conditioning Research*, 22(5): 1413–1415.

Gamble, P. 2004. A Skill-Based Conditioning Games Approach to Metabolic Conditioning for Elite Rugby Football Players, *Journal of Strength & Conditioning Research*, 18(3): 491–497.

Gamble, P. 2006a. Implications and Applications of Training Specificity for Coaches and Athletes, *Strength & Conditioning Journal*, 28(3): 54–58.

Gamble, P. 2006b. Periodization of Training for Team Sports Athletes, *Strength & Conditioning Journal*, 28(5): 56–66.

Gamble, P. 2007. An Integrated Approach to Training Core Stability, *Strength and Conditioning Journal*, 29(1): 58–68.

Gamble, P. 2009a. Physiological and Performance Testing, In: *Strength and Conditioning for Team Sports: Sport-Specific Physical Preparation for High Performance*, Oxford: Routledge, pp. 10–37.

Gamble, P. 2009b. Physical Preparation for Youth Sports, In: *Strength and Conditioning for Team Sports: Sport-Specific Physical Preparation for High Performance*, Oxford: Routledge, pp. 197–221.

Gamble, P. 2009c. Training for Power, In: *Strength and Conditioning for Team Sports, Sport-Specific Physical Preparation for High Performance*, Oxford: Routledge, pp. 78–99.

Gamble, P. 2009d. Agility and Speed Training, In: *Strength and Conditioning for Team Sports: Sport-Specific Physical Preparation for High Performance*, Oxford: Routledge, pp. 100–118.

Gamble, P. 2009e. Metabolic Conditioning for Team Sports, In: *Strength and Conditioning for Team Sports: Sport-Specific Physical Preparation for High Performance*, Oxford: Routledge, pp. 60–77.

Gamble, P. 2009f. Lumbopelvic 'Core' Stability, In: *Strength and Conditioning for Team Sports: Sport-Specific Physical Preparation for High Performance*, Oxford: Routledge, pp. 119–138.

Gamble, P. 2009g. Training for Injury Prevention. In: *Strength and Conditioning for Team Sports: Sport-Specific Physical Preparation for High Performance*, Oxford: Routledge, pp. 158–196.

Garhammer, J. 1993. A Review of Power Output Studies of Olympic and Powerlifting: Methodology, Performance Prediction, and Evaluation Tests, *Journal of Strength & Conditioning Research*, 7(2): 76–89.

Gibala, M.J., J.P. Little, M. van Essen, G.P. Wilkin, K.A. Burgomaster, A. Safdar, S. Raha and M.A. Tarnopolsky. 2006. Short-Term Sprint Interval versus Traditional Endurance Training: Similar Initial Adaptations in Human Skeletal Muscle and Exercise Performance, *Journal of Physiology*, 575(3): 901–911.

Gillet, E., D. Leroy, R. Thouvarecq, F. Megrot and J.-F. Stein. 2010. Movement-Production Strategy in Tennis: A Case Study, *Journal of Strength & Conditioning Research*, 24(7): 1942–1947.

Girard, O., J.-P. Micallef and G.P. Millet. 2011. Changes in Spring-Mass Model Characteristics during Repeated Running Sprints, *European Journal of Applied Physiology*, 111(1): 125–134.

Glaister, M. 2005. Multiple Sprint Work: Physiological Responses, Mechanisms for Fatigue and the Influence of Aerobic Fitness, *Sports Medicine*, 35(9): 757–777.

Golden, G.M., M.J. Pavol and M.A. Hoffman. 2009. Knee Joint Kinematics and Kinetics during a Lateral False-Step Maneuvre, *Journal of Athletic Training*, 44(5): 503–510.

Gray, S. and M. Nimmo. 2001. Effects of Active, Passive, or No Warm-Up on Metabolism and Performance during High-Intensity Exercise, *Journal of Sports Sciences*, 19: 693–700.

Hakkinen, K., P.V. Komi, M. Alen and H. Kauhanen. 1987. EMG, Muscle Fibre and Force Production Characteristics during a One Year Training Period in Elite Weight-Lifters, *European Journal of Applied Physiology*, 56: 419–427.

Hamada, T., D.G. Sale, J.D. MacDougall and M.A. Tarnopolsky. 2000. Postactivation Potentiation, Fiber Type, and Twitch Contraction Time in Human Knee Extensor Muscles, *Journal of Applied Physiology*, 88: 2131–2137.

Hamilton, R.T., S.J. Shultz, R.J. Schmitz and D.H. Perrin. 2008. Triple-Hop Distance as a Valid Predictor of Strength and Power, *Journal of Athletic Training*, 43(2): 144–151.

Hanna, C.M., M.L. Fulcher, C. Raina Elley and S.A. Moyes. 2010. Normative Values of Hip Strength in Adult Male Association Football Players Assessed by Handheld Dynamometry, *Journal of Science & Medicine in Sport*, 13: 299–303.

Hanson, A.M., D.A. Padua, J.T. Blackburn, W.E. Prentice and C.J. Hirth. 2008. Muscle Activation during Side-Step Cutting Maneuvers in Male and Female Soccer Athletes, *Journal of Athletic Training*, 43(2): 133–143.

Hardy, L.L., L. King, L. Farrell, R. MacNiven and S. Howlett. 2010. Fundamental Movement Skills among Australian Preschool Children, *Journal of Science & Medicine in Sport*, 13(5): 503–508.

Harris, G.R., M.H. Stone, H.S. O'Bryant, C.M. Proulx and R.L. Johnson. 2000. Short-Term Performance Effects of High Power, High Force, or Combined Weight Training Methods, *Journal of Strength & Conditioning Research*, 14(1): 14–20.

Harris, N.K., J.B. Cronin and W.G. Hopkins. 2007a. Power Outputs of a Machine Squat-Jump across a Spectrum of Loads, *Journal of Strength & Conditioning Research*, 21(4): 1260–1264.

Harris, N., J. Cronin and J. Keogh. 2007b. Contractile Force Specificity and Its Relationship to Functional Performance, *Journal of Sports Sciences*, 25(2): 201–212.

Hazell, T.J., R.E.K. MacPherson, B.M.R. Gravelle and P.W.R. Lemon. 2010. 10 or 30-s Sprint Interval Training Bouts Enhance both Aerobic and Anaerobic Performance, *European Journal of Applied Physiology*, 110(1): 153–160.

Hedrick, A. 1993. Literature Review: High Speed Resistance Training, *NSCA Journal*, 15(6): 22–30.

Hedrick, A. 1999. Using Free Weights to Improve Lateral Movement Performance, *Strength & Conditioning Journal*, 21(5): 21–25.

Helgerud, J., L.C. Engen, U. Wisloff and J. Hoff. 2001. Aerobic Endurance Training Improves Soccer Performance, *Medicine & Science in Sports & Exercise*, 33(11): 1925–1931.

Hennessy, L. and J. Kilty. 2001. Relationship of the Stretch-Shortening Cycle to Sprint Performance in Trained Female Athletes, *Journal of Strength & Conditioning Research*, 15(3): 326–331.

Hetzler, R.K., C.D. Stickley, K.M. Lundquist and I.F. Kimura. 2008. Reliability and Accuracy of Handheld Stopwatches Compared with Electronic Timing in Measuring Sprint Performance, *Journal of Strength & Conditioning Research*, 22(6): 1969–1976.

Hewett, T.E., T.N. Lindenfield, J.V. Riccobene and F.R. Noyes. 1999. The Effect of Neuromuscular Training on the Incidence of Knee Injury in Female Athletes: A Prospective Study, *American Journal of Sports Medicine*, 27(6): 699–706.

Hewett, T.E., G.D. Myer and K.R. Ford. 2005. Reducing Knee and Anterior Cruciate Ligament Injuries among Female Athletes, *Journal of Knee Surgery*, 18(1): 82–88.

Hewett, T.E., K.R. Ford and G.D. Myer. 2006a. Anterior Cruciate Injuries in Female Athletes, Part 2: A Meta-Analysis of Neuromuscular Interventions Aimed at Injury Prevention, *American Journal of Sports Medicine*, 34(3): 490–498.

Hewett, T.E., G.D. Myer and K.R. Ford. 2006b. Anterior Cruciate Injuries in Female Athletes, Part 1: Mechanisms and Risk Factors, *American Journal of Sports Medicine*, 34(2): 299–311.

Hewett, T.E., J.S. Tong and B.P. Boden. 2009. Video Analysis of Trunk and Knee Motion during Non-Contact Anterior Cruciate Ligament Injury in Female Athletes: Lateral Trunk and Knee Abduction Motion Are Combined Components of the Injury Mechanism, *British Journal of Sports Medicine*, 43: 417–422.

Hibbs, A.E., K.G. Thompson, D. French, A. Wrigley and I. Spears. 2008. Optimising Performance by Improving Core Stability and Core Strength, *Sports Medicine*, 38(12): 995–1008.

Higashihara, A., T. Ono, J. Kubota, T. Okuwaki and T. Fukubayashi. 2010. Functional Differences in the Activity of the Hamstring Muscles with Increasing Running Speed, *Journal of Sports Sciences*, 28(10): 1085–1092.

Hill-Haas, S.V., A.J. Coutts, B.T. Dawson and G.J. Rowsell. 2010. Time-Motion Characteristics and Physiological Responses of Small-Sided Games in Elite Youth Players: The Influence of Player Number and Rule Changes, *Journal of Strength & Conditioning Research*, 24(8): 2149–2156.

Hoff, J., U. Wisloff, L.C. Engen, O.J. Kemi and J. Helgerud. 2002. Soccer Specific Aerobic Endurance Training, *British Journal of Sports Medicine*, 36(3), 218–221.

Hoffman, J.R., S. Epstein, M. Einbinder and Y. Weinstein. 1999. The Influence of Aerobic Capacity on Anaerobic Performance and Recovery Indices in Basketball Players, *Journal of Strength & Conditioning Research*, 13(4), 407–411.

Hoffman, J.R., M. Wendell, J. Cooper and J. Kang. 2003. Comparison between Linear and Nonlinear In-Season Training Programs in Freshman Football Players, *Journal of Strength & Conditioning Research*, 17(3): 561–565.

Hoffman, J.R., J. Cooper, M. Wendell and J. Kang. 2004. Comparison of Olympic vs Traditional Power Lifting Training Programs in Football Players, *Journal of Strength & Conditioning Research*, 18(1): 129–135.

Holm, D.J., M. Stalbom, J.W.L. Keogh and J. Cronin. 2008. Relationship between the Kinetics and Kinematics of a Unilateral Horizontal Drop Jump to Sprint Performance, *Journal of Strength & Conditioning Research*, 22(5): 1589–1596.

Holmberg, P.M. 2009. Agility Training for Experienced Athletes: A Dynamical Systems Approach, *Strength & Conditioning Journal*, 31(5): 73–78.

Holmes, A. and E. Delahunt. 2009. Treatment of Common Deficits Associated with Chronic Ankle Instability, *Sports Medicine*, 39(3): 207–224.

Hori, N., R.U. Newton, W.A. Andrews, N. Kawamori, M.R. McGuigan and K. Nosaka. 2008. Does Performance of Hang Power Clean Differentiate Performance of Jumping, Sprinting and Changing of Direction?, *Journal of Strength & Conditioning Research*, 22(2): 412–418.

Hrysomallis, C. 2007. Relationship between Balance Ability, Training and Sports Injury Risk, *Sports Medicine*, 37(6): 547–556.

Hunter, J.P., R.N. Marshall and P.J. McNair. 2005. Relationships between Ground Reaction Force Impulse and Kinematics of Sprint Running Acceleration, *Journal of Applied Biomechanics*, 21: 31–43.

Iaia, F.M. and J. Bangsbo. 2010. Speed-Endurance Training Is a Powerful Stimulus for Physiological Adaptations and Performance Improvements in Athletes, *Scandinavian Journal of Medicine and Science in Sports*, 20(Suppl. 2): 11–23.

Imwalle, L.E., G.D. Myer, K.R. Ford and T.E. Hewett. 2009. Relationship between Hip and Knee Kinematics in Athletic Women during Cutting Maneuvres: A Possible Link to Noncontact Anterior Cruciate Ligament Injury and Prevention, *Journal of Strength & Conditioning Research*, 23(8): 2223–2230.

Issurin, V.B. 2010. New Horizons for the Methodology and Physiology of Training Periodization, *Sports Medicine*, 40(3): 189–206.

Ives, J.C. and G.A. Shelley. 2003. Psychophysics in Functional Strength and Power Training: Review and Implementation Framework, *Journal of Strength & Conditioning Research*, 17(1): 177–186.

Izquierdo, M., J. Ibanez, J.J. Gonzalez-Badillo, N.A. Ratamess, W.J. Kraemer, K. Hakkinen, H. Bonnabau, C. Granados, D.N. French and E.M. Gorostiaga. 2007. Detraining and Tapering Effects on Hormonal Responses and Strength Performance, *Journal of Strength and Conditioning Research*, 21(3): 768–775.

Jeffreys, I. 2006. Motor Learning: Applications for Agility, Part 2, *Strength & Conditioning Journal*, 28(6): 10–14.

Jeffreys, I. 2010. Should Post-Activation Potentiation Methods Be Used in Warm Up Practices for Collegiate Aged Team Sports Athletes. Unpublished doctoral thesis, University of Glamorgan, Wales.

Jensen, R.L. and W.P. Ebben. 2003. Kinetic Analysis of Complex Training Rest Interval Effect on Vertical Jump Performance, *Journal of Strength & Conditioning Research*, 17(2): 345–349.

Jones, A.M. and H. Carter. 2000. The Effect of Endurance Training on Parameters of Aerobic Fitness, *Sports Medicine*, 29(6): 373–386.

Jones, K., G. Hunter, G. Fleisig, R. Escamilla and L. Lemak. 1999. The Effects of Compensatory Acceleration on Upper-Body Strength and Power in Collegiate Football Players, *Journal of Strength & Conditioning Research*, 13(2): 99–105.

Jones, P., T.M. Bampouras and K. Marrin. 2009. An Investigation into the Physical Determinants of Change of Direction Speed, *Journal of Sports Medicine & Physical Fitness*, 49: 97–104.

Juker, D., S.M. McGill, P. Kropf and S. Thomas. 1998. Quantitative Intramuscular Myoelectric Activity of Lumbar Portions of Psoas and the Abdominal Wall during a Wide Variety of Tasks, *Medicine & Science in Sports & Exercise*, 30(2): 301–310.

Jungers, W.L. 2010. Barefoot Running Strikes Back, *Nature*, 463: 433–434.

Kawakami, Y., T. Muraoka, S. Ito, H. Kanehisa and T. Fukunaga. 2002. *In Vivo* Muscle Fibre Behaviour during Counter-Movement Exercise in Humans Reveals a Significant Role for Tendon Elasticity, *Journal of Physiology*, 540(2): 635–646.

Kawamori, N., A.J. Crum, P.A. Blumert, J.R. Kulik, J.T. Childers, J.A. Wood, M.H. Stone and G.G. Haff. 2005. Influence of Different Relative Intensities on Power Output during the Hang Power Clean: Identification of the Optimal Load, *Journal of Strength & Conditioning Research*, 19(3): 698–708.

Kibler, W.B., J. Press and A. Sciascia. 2006. The Role of Core Stability in Athletic Function, *Sports Medicine*, 36(3): 189–198.

Kilduff, L.P., H.R. Bevan, M.I.C. Kingsley, N.J. Owen, M.A. Bennett, P.J. Bunce, A.M. Hore, J.R. Maw and D.J. Cunningham. 2007. Postactivation Potentiation in Professional Rugby Players: Optimal Recovery, *Journal of Strength & Conditioning Research*, 21(4): 1134–1138.

Kistler, B.M., M.S. Walsh, T.S. Horn and R.H. Cox. 2010. The Acute Effect of Static Stretching on the Sprint Performance of Collegiate Men in the 60- and 100-m Dash after a Dynamic Warm-Up, *Journal of Strength & Conditioning Research*, 24(9): 2280–2284.

Kovacs, M.S. 2009. Movement for Tennis: The Importance of Lateral Training, *Strength & Conditioning Journal*, 31(4): 77–85.

Kraemer, W.J. 1997. A Series of Studies – the Physiological Basis for Strength Training in American Football: Fact over Philosophy, *Journal of Strength & Conditioning Research*, 11(3): 131–142.

Kraemer, W.J. and S.J. Fleck. 2005. *Strength Training for Young Athletes*, 2nd edn, Champaign, IL: Human Kinetics.

Kraemer, W.J., J.F. Patton, S.E. Gordon, E.A. Harman, M.R. Deschenes, K. Reynolds, R.U. Newton, N.T. Triplett and J.E. Dziados. 1995. Compatibility of High-Intensity Strength and Endurance Training on Hormonal and Skeletal Muscle Adaptations, *Journal of Applied Physiology*, 78(3): 976–989.

Kristensen, G.O., R. van den Tillar and G.J.C. Ettema. 2006. Velocity Specificity in Early-Phase Sprint Training, *Journal of Strength & Conditioning Research*, 20(4): 833–837.

Krustrup, P., M. Mohr, T. Amstrup, T. Rysgaard, J. Johansen, A. Steensberg, P.K. Pedersen and J. Bangsbo. 2003. The Yo-Yo Intermittent Recovery Test: Physiological Response, Reliability and Validity, *Medicine & Science in Sports & Exercise*, 35(4): 697–705.

Kubo, K., H. Kaneisha and T. Fukunaga. 2002. Effect of Stretching Training on the Viscoelastic Properties of Human Tendon Structure In Vivo, *Journal of Applied Physiology*, 92: 595–601.

Kubukeli, Z.N., T.D. Noakes and S.C. Dennis. 2002. Training Techniques to Improve Endurance Exercise Performances, *Sports Medicine*, 32(8): 489–509.

Kugler, F. and L. Janshen. 2010. Body Position Determines Propulsive Forces in Accelerated Running, *Journal of Biomechanics*, 43: 343–348.

Landry, S.C., K.A. McKean, C.L. Hubley-Kozey, W.D. Stanish and K.J. Deluzio. 2007. Neuromuscular and Lower Limb Biomechanical Differences Exist between Male and Female Adolescent Soccer Players during an Unanticipated Side-Cut Maneuvre, *American Journal of Sports Medicine*, 35(11): 1888–1900.

Laursen, P.B. 2010. Training for Intense Exercise Performance: High-Intensity or High-Volume Training?, *Scandinavian Journal of Medicine & Science in Sports*, 20(2): 1–10.

Lawson, B.R., T.M. Stephens II, D.E. Devoe and R.F. Reiser II. 2006. Lower-Extremity Bilateral Differences during Step-Close and No-Step Countermovement Jumps with Concern for Gender, *Journal of Strength & Conditioning Research*, 20(3): 608–619.

Lee, S.S.M. and S.J. Piazza. 2009. Built for Speed: Musculoskeletal Structure and Sprinting Ability, *Journal of Experimental Biology*, 212: 3700–3707.

Leetun, D.T., M.L. Ireland, J.D. Willson, B.T. Ballantyne and I.M. Davis. 2004. Core Stability Measures as Risk Factors for Lower Extremity Injury in Athletes, *Medicine & Science in Sports & Exercise*, 36(6): 926–934.

Legaz-Arrese, A., D. Munguia-Izquierdo, L.E. Carranza-Garcia and C.G. Torres-Davila. 2011. Validity of the Wingate Anaerobic Test for the Evaluation of Elite Runners, *Journal of Strength & Conditioning Research*, 25(3): 819–824.

Le Runigo, C., N. Benguigui and B.G. Bardy. 2010. Visuo-Motor Delay, Information–Movement Coupling, and Expertise in Ball Sports, *Journal of Sports Sciences*, 28(3): 327–337.

Leveritt, M. and P.J. Abernethy. 1999. Acute Effects of High-Intensity Endurance Exercise on Subsequent Resistance Activity, *Journal of Strength & Conditioning Research*, 13(1): 47–51.

Lieberman, D.E., M. Venkadesan, W.A. Werbel, A.I. Daoud, S. D'Andrea, I.S. Davis, R. Ojiambo Mang'eni and Y. Pitsiladis. 2010. Foot Strike Patterns and Collision Forces in Habitually Barefoot versus Shod Runners, *Nature*, 463: 531–535.

Lim, B.O., Y.S. Lee, J.G. Kim, K.O. An, J. Yoo and Y.H. Kwon. 2009. Effects of Sports Injury Prevention Training on the Biomechanical Risk Factors of Anterior Cruciate Ligament Injury in High School Female Basketball Players, *American Journal of Sports Medicine*, 37(9): 1728–1734.

Little, T. and A.G. Williams. 2005. Specificity of Acceleration, Maximum Speed and Agility in Professional Soccer Players, *Journal of Strength & Conditioning Research*, 19(1): 76–78.

Little, T. and A.G. Williams. 2006. Effects of Differential Stretching Protocols during Warm-Ups on High-Speed Motor Capacities in Professional Soccer Players, *Journal of Strength & Conditioning Research*, 20(1): 203–207.

Little, T. and A.G. Williams. 2007. Effects of Sprint Duration and Exercise:Rest Ratio on Repeated Sprint Performance and Physiological Responses in Professional Soccer Players, *Journal of Strength & Conditioning Research*, 21(2): 646–648.

Lockie, R.G., A.J. Murphy and C.D. Spinks. 2003. Effects of Resisted Sled Towing on Sprint Kinematics in Field-Sport Athletes, *Journal of Strength & Conditioning Research*, 17(4): 760–767.

McBride, J.M., T. Triplett-McBride, A. Davie and R.U. Newton. 2002. The Effect of Heavy- Versus Light-Load Jump Squats on the Development of Strength, Power and Speed, *Journal of Strength & Conditioning Research*, 16: 75–82.

McBride, J.M., G.O. McCaulley and P. Cormie. 2008. Influence of Preactivity and Eccentric Muscle Activity on Concentric Performance during Vertical Jumping, *Journal of Strength & Conditioning Research*, 22(3): 750–757.

McBride, J.M., D. Blow, T.J. Kirby, T.L. Haines, A.M. Dayne and N.T. Triplett. 2009. Relationship between Maximal Squat Strength and Five, Ten and Forty Yard Sprint Times, *Journal of Strength & Conditioning Research*, 23(6): 1633–1636.

McCann, M.R. and S.P. Flanagan. 2010. The Effects of Exercise Selection and Rest Interval on Postactivation Potentiation of Vertical Jump Performance, *Journal of Strength & Conditioning Research*, 24(5): 1285–1291.

McConnell, A. 2011. Getting Started. In: *Breathe Strong, Perform Better*, Human Kinetics, Champaign, IL.

McGill, S.M. 2006a. Fundamental Principles of Movement and Causes of Movement Error. In: *Ultimate Back Fitness and Performance*, 3rd edn, Waterloo, ON: Wabuno, pp. 127–149.

McGill, S.M. 2006b. Stage 4: Developing Ultimate Strength. In: *Ultimate Back Fitness and Performance*, 3rd edn, Waterloo, ON: Wabuno, pp. 239–273.

McGill, S.M. 2006c. Enhancing Lumbar Spine Stability. In: *Ultimate Back Fitness and Performance*, 3rd edn, Waterloo, ON: Wabuno, pp. 113–123.

McGill, S.M. 2006d. Stage 1: Groove Motion/Motor Patterns and Corrective Exercise. In: *Ultimate Back Fitness and Performance*, 3rd edn, Waterloo, ON: Wabuno, pp. 175–212.

McGill, S.M. 2006e. Evaluating and Qualifying the Athlete/Client. In: *Ultimate Back Fitness and Performance*, 3rd edn, Waterloo, ON: Wabuno, pp. 151–165.

McGill, S.M. 2006f. Helpful Facts: Anatomy, Injury Mechanisms and Effective Training. In: *Ultimate Back Fitness and Performance*, 3rd edn, Waterloo, ON: Wabuno, pp. 61–86.

McGill, S.M. 2007a. Evaluating the Patient. In: *Low Back Disorders: Evidence-Based Prevention and Rehabilitation* 2nd edn, Champaign, IL: Human Kinetics, pp. 189–212.

McGill, S.M. 2007b. Functional Anatomy of the Lumbar Spine. In: *Low Back Disorders: Evidence-Based Prevention and Rehabilitation* 2nd edn, Champaign, IL: Human Kinetics, pp. 35–71.

McGill, S.M. 2007c. Normal and Injury Mechanics of the Lumbar Spine. In: *Low Back Disorders: Evidence-Based Prevention and Rehabilitation* 2nd edn, Champaign, IL: Human Kinetics, pp. 72–111.

McGill, S.M. 2010. Core Training: Evidence Translating to Better Performance and Injury Prevention, *Strength & Conditioning Journal*, 32(3): 33–46.

McGill, S.M., A. Karpowicz, C.M.J. Fenwick and S.H.M. Brown. 2009. Exercises for the Torso Performed in a Standing Posture: Spine and Hip Motion and Motor Patterns and Spine Load, *Journal of Strength & Conditioning Research*, 23(2): 455–464.

McHugh, M.P. and C.H. Cosgrave. 2010. To Stretch or Not to Stretch: The Role of Stretching in Injury Prevention and Performance, *Scandinavian Journal of Medicine & Science in Sports*, 20: 169–181.

McLean, S.G., S.W. Lipfert and A.J. van den Bogert. 2004. Effect of Gender and Defensive Opponent on the Biomechanics of Sidestep Cutting, *Medicine & Science in Sports & Exercise*, 36(6): 1008–1016.

McMillan, K., J. Helgerud, R. MacDonald and J. Hoff. 2005. Physiological Adaptations to Soccer Specific Endurance Training in Professional Youth Soccer Players, *British Journal of Sports Medicine*, 39: 273–277.

Macpherson, R.E.K., T.J. Hazell, T.D. Olver, D.H. Paterson and P.W.R. Lemon. 2011. Run Sprint Interval Training Improves Aerobic Performance but Not Maximal Cardiac Output, *Medicine & Science in Sports & Exercise*, 43(1): 115–122.

Malisoux, L., M. Francaux, H. Nielens and D. Theisen. 2006. Stretch-Shortening Cycle Exercises: An Effective Training Paradigm to Enhance Power Output of Human Single Muscle Fibers, *Journal of Applied Physiology*, 100: 771–779.

Markovic, G., I. Jukic, D. Milanovic and D. Metikos. 2007. Effects of Sprint and Plyometric Training on Muscle Function and Athletic Performance, *Journal of Strength & Conditioning Research*, 21(2): 543–549.

Maughan, R. and M. Gleeson. 2004a. Middle Distance Events. In: *The Biochemical Basis of Sports Performance*, Oxford: Oxford University Press, pp. 91–114.

Maughan, R. and M. Gleeson. 2004b. The Endurance Athlete. In: *The Biochemical Basis of Sports Performance*, Oxford: Oxford University Press, pp. 115–147.

Maughan, R. and M. Gleeson. 2004c. The Games Player. In: *The Biochemical Basis of Sports Performance*, Oxford: Oxford University Press, pp. 150–170.

Maughan, R. and M. Gleeson. 2004d. Sporting Talent: The Genetic Basis of Athletic Capability. In: *The Biochemical Basis of Sports Performance*, Oxford: Oxford University Press, pp. 171–189.

Maughan, R. and M. Gleeson. 2004e. Adaptations to Training. In: *The Biochemical Basis of Sports Performance*, Oxford: Oxford University Press, pp. 191–221.

Mero, A. and P.V. Komi. 1994. EMG, Force, and Power Analysis of Sprint-Specific Strength Exercises, *Journal of Applied Biomechanics*, 10: 1–13.

Meylan, C., T. McMaster, J. Cronin, N.I. Mohammad, C. Rogers and M. Deklerk. 2009. Single-Leg Lateral, Horizontal, and Vertical Jump Assessment: Reliability, Interrelationships, and Ability to Predict Sprint and Change-of-Direction Performance, *Journal of Strength & Conditioning Research*, 23(4): 1140–1147.

Miller, M.G., J.L. Herniman, M.D. Ricard, C.C. Cheatham and T.J. Michael. 2006. The Effects of a 6-Week Plyometric Training Program on Agility, *Journal of Sports Science & Medicine*, 5: 459–465.

Millet, G.P., R.B. Candau, B. Barbier, T. Busso, J.D. Rouillon and J.C. Chatard. 2002. Modelling the Transfers of Training Effects on Performance in Elite Triathletes, *International Journal of Sports Medicine*, 23: 55–63.

Mirkov, D., A. Nedeljkovic, M. Kukolj, D. Ugarkovic and S. Jaric. 2008. Evaluation of the Reliability of Soccer-Specific Field Tests, *Journal of Strength & Conditioning Research*, 22(4): 1046–1050.

Monteiro, A.G., M.S. Aoki, A.L. Evangelista, D.A. Alveno, G.A. Monteiro, I.D.C. Picarro and C. Ugrinowitsch. 2009. Nonlinear Periodization Maximises Strength Gains in Split Resistance Training Routines, *Journal of Strength & Conditioning Research*, 23(4): 1321–1326.

Moore, A. and A. Murphy. 2003. Development of an Anaerobic Capacity Test for Field Sports Athletes, *Journal of Science & Medicine in Sport*, 6(3): 275–284.

Moran, K.A., M. Clarke, F. Reilly, E.S. Wallace, D. Brabazon and B. Marshall. 2009. Does Endurance Fatigue Increase the Risk of Injury When Performing Drop Jumps?, *Journal of Strength & Conditioning Research*, 23(5): 1448–1455.

Murphy, A.J. and G.J. Wilson. 1997. The Ability of Tests of Muscular Function to Reflect Training-Induced Changes in Performance, *Journal of Sports Sciences*, 15: 191–200.

Murphy, D.F., D.A.J. Connolly and B.D. Beynnon. 2003. Risk Factors for Lower Extremity Injury: A Review of the Literature, *British Journal of Sports Medicine*, 37: 13–29.

Myer, G.D., K.R. Ford, J.P. Palumbo and T.E. Hewett. 2005. Neuromuscular Training Improves Performance and Lower-Extremity Biomechanics in Female Athletes, *Journal of Strength & Conditioning Research*, 19(1): 51–60.

Myer, G.D., K.R. Ford, J.L. Brent and T.E. Hewett. 2006a. The Effect of Plyometric vs Dynamic Stabilisation and Balance Training on Power, Balance and Landing Force in Female Athletes, *Journal of Strength & Conditioning Research*, 20(2): 345–358.

Myer, G.D., K.R. Ford, S.G. McLean and T.E. Hewett. 2006b. The Effects of Plyometric versus Dynamic Stabilisation Training on Lower Extremity Biomechanics, *American Journal of Sports Medicine*, 34(3): 445–455.

Myers, C.A. and D. Hawkins. 2010. Alterations to Movement Mechanics Can Greatly Reduce Anterior Cruciate Ligament Loading without Reducing Performance, *Journal of Biomechanics*, 43: 2657–2664.

Nadler, S.F., G.A. Malanga, M. Deprince, T.P. Stitik and J.H. Feinberg. 2000. The Relationship between Lower Extremity Injury, Low Back Pain, and Hip Muscle Strength in Male and Female Collegiate Athletes, *Clinical Journal of Sports Medicine*, 10: 89–97.

Naughton, G., N.J. Farpour-Lambert, J. Carlson, M. Bradley and E. Van Praagh. 2000. Physiological Issues Surrounding the Performance of Adolescent Athletes, *Sports Medicine*, 30(5): 309–325.

Nelson, R.T. and W.D. Bandy. 2005. An Update on Flexibility, *Strength & Conditioning Journal*, 27(1): 10–16.

Nesser, T.W., K.C. Huxel, J.L. Tincher and T. Okada. 2008. The Relationship between Core Stability and Performance in Division I Football Players, *Journal of Strength & Conditioning Research*, 22(6): 1750–1754.

Newton, R.U. and W.J. Kraemer. 1994. Developing Explosive Muscular Power: Implications for a Mixed Methods Training Strategy, *Strength & Conditioning*, 16: 20–31.

Newton, R.U. and E. Dugan. 2002. Application of Strength Diagnosis, *Strength & Conditioning Journal*, 24(5): 50–59.

Newton, R.U., W.J. Kraemer, K. Hakkinen, B.J. Humphries and A.J. Murphy. 1996. Kinematics, Kinetics and Muscle Activation during Explosive Upper Body Movements, *Journal of Applied Biomechanics*, 12: 31–43.

Newton, R.U., W.J. Kraemer and K. Hakkinen. 1999. Effects of Ballistic Training on Preseason Preparation of Elite Volleyball Players, *Medicine & Science in Sports & Exercise*, 31(2): 323–330.

Newton, R.U., A. Gerber, S. Nimphius, J.K. Shim, B.K. Doan, M. Robertson, D.R. Pearson, B.W. Craig, K. Hakkinen and W.J. Kraemer. 2006. Determination of Functional Strength Imbalance of the Lower Extremities, *Journal of Strength & Conditioning Research*, 20(4): 971–977.

Nimphius, S., M.R. McGuigan and R.U. Newton. 2010. Relationship between Strength, Power, Speed, and Change of Direction Performance of Female Softball Players, *Journal of Strength & Conditioning Research*, 24(4): 885–895.

Noyes, F.R., S.D. Barber-Westin, C. Fleckenstein, C. Walsh and J. West. 2005. The Drop Jump Screening Test: Difference in Lower Limb Control by Gender and Effect of Neuromuscular Training in Female Athletes, *American Journal of Sports Medicine*, 33(2): 197–207.

Nummela, A., T. Keranen and L.O. Mikkelsson. 2007. Factors Related to Top Running Speed and Economy, *International Journal of Sports Medicine*, 28: 655–661.

Nuzzo, J.L., G.O. McCaulley, P. Cormie, M.J. Cavill and J.M. McBride. 2008. Trunk Muscle Activity during Stability Ball and Free Weight Exercises, *Journal of Strength & Conditioning Research*, 22(1): 95–102.

Okada, T., K.C. Huxel and T.W. Nesser. 2011. Relationship between Core Stability, Functional Movement, and Performance, *Journal of Strength & Conditioning Research*, 25(1): 252–261.

Oliver, J.L. 2009. Is a Fatigue Index a Worthwhile Measure of Repeated Sprint Ability?, *Journal of Science & Medicine in Sport*, 12: 20–23.

Oliver, J.L., N. Armstrong and C.A. Williams. 2009. Relationships between Brief and Prolonged Repeated Sprint Ability, *Journal of Science & Medicine in Sport*, 12: 238–243.

Otago, L. 2004. Kinetic Analysis of Landings in Netball: Is a Footwork Rule Change Required to Decrease ACL Injuries, *Journal of Science & Medicine in Sport*, 7(1): 85–95.

Paasuke, M., L. Saapar, J. Ereline, H. Gapeyeva, B. Requena and V. Oopik. 2007. Postactivation Potentiation of Knee Extensor Muscles in Power- and Endurance-Trained, and Untrained Women, *European Journal of Applied Physiology*, 101: 577–585.

Paavolainen, L., K. Hakkinen, I. Hamalainen, A. Nummela and H. Rusko. 1999. Explosive-Strength Training Improves 5-km Running Time by Improving Running Economy and Muscle Power, *Journal of Applied Physiology*, 86(5): 1527–1533.

Papaiakovou, G., A. Giannakos, C. Michailidis, D. Patikas, E. Bassa, V. Kalopisis, N. Anthrakidis and C. Kotzamanidis. 2009. The Effect of Chronological Age and Gender on the Development of Sprint Performance during Childhood and Puberty, *Journal of Strength & Conditioning Research*, 23(9): 2568–2573.

Peterson, M.D., M.R. Rhea and B.A. Alvar. 2004. Maximising Strength Development in Athletes: A Meta-Analysis to Determine the Dose–Response Relationship, *Journal of Strength & Conditioning Research*, 18(2): 377–382.

Peterson, M.D., B.A. Alvar and M.R. Rhea. 2006. The Contribution of Maximal Force Production to Explosive Movement among Young Collegiate Athletes, *Journal of Strength & Conditioning Research*, 20(4): 867–873.

Philippaerts, R.M., R. Vaeyans, M. Janssens, B. van Renterghem, D. Matthys, R. Craen, J. Bourgois, J. Vrijens, G. Beunen and R.M. Malina. 2006. The Relationship between Peak Height Velocity and Physical Performance in Youth Soccer Players, *Journal of Sports Sciences*, 24(3): 221–230.

Plisk, S.S. and M.H. Stone. 2003. Periodization Strategies, *Strength & Conditioning Journal*, 25(6): 19–37.

Pool-Goudzwaard, A.L., A. Vleeming, R. Stoeckart, C.J. Snijders and J.M.A. Mens. 1998. Insufficient Lumpopelvic Stability: A Clinical, Anatomical and Biomechanical Approach to a Specific Low Back Pain, *Manual Therapy*, 3(1): 12–20.

Popadic Gacesa, J.Z., O.F. Barak and N.G. Grujic. 2009. Maximal Anaerobic Power Test in Athletes of Different Sport Disciplines, *Journal of Strength & Conditioning Research*, 23(3): 751–755.

Prestes, J., C. De Lima, A.B. Frollini, F.P. Donatto and M. Conte. 2009. Comparison of Linear and Reverse Linear Periodization Effects on Maximal Strength and Body Composition, *Journal of Strength & Conditioning Research*, 23(1): 266–274.

Pyne, D.B., P.U. Saunders, P.G. Montgomery, A.J. Hewitt and K. Sheehan. 2008. Relationships between Repeated Sprint Testing, Speed, and Endurance, *Journal of Strength & Conditioning Research*, 22(5): 1633–1637.

Quarrie, K.L., P. Handcock, A.E. Waller, D.J. Chalmers, M.J. Toomey and B.D. Wilson. 1995. The New Zealand Rugby Injury and Performance Project. III. Anthropometric and Physical Performance Characteristics of Players, *British Journal of Sports Medicine*, 29(4): 263–270.

Quatman, C.E., K.R. Ford, G.D. Myer and T.E. Hewett. 2006. Maturation Leads to Gender Differences in Landing Force and Vertical Jump Performance, *American Journal of Sports Medicine*, 34(5): 806–813.

Rabita, G., A. Couturier and D. Lambertz. 2008. Influence of Training Background on the Relationship between Plantarflexor Intrinsic Stiffness and Overall Musculoskeletal Stiffness during Hopping, *European Journal of Applied Physiology*, 103: 163–171.

Rampinini, F., F.M. Impillizzeri, C. Castagna, G. Abt, K. Chamari, A. Sassi and S.M. Marcora. 2007. Factors Influencing Physiological Responses to Small-Sided Soccer Games, *Journal of Sports Sciences*, 25(6): 659–666.

Randell, A.D., J.B. Cronin, J.W.L. Keogh and N.D. Gill. 2010. Transference of Strength and Power Adaptation to Sports Performance: Horizontal and Vertical Force Production, *Strength & Conditioning Journal*, 42(4): 100–106.

Reilly, T., T. Morris and G. Whyte. 2009. The Specificity of Training Prescription and Physiological Assessment: A Review, *Journal of Sports Sciences*, 27(6): 575–589.

Rhea, M.R., S.D. Ball, W.T. Phillips and L.N. Burkett. 2002. A Comparison of Linear and Daily Undulating Periodized Programs with Equated Volume and Intensity for Strength, *Journal of Strength & Conditioning Research*, 16(2): 250–255.

Rhea, M., B. Alvar, L. Burkett and S. Ball. 2003. A Meta-Analysis to Determine the Dose–Response Relationship for Strength, *Medicine & Science in Sports & Exercise*, 35: 456–464.

Rimmer, E. and G. Sleivert. 2000. Effects of a Plyometrics Training Intervention Program on Sprint Performance, *Journal of Strength & Conditioning Research*, 14(3): 295–301.

Ross, A. and M. Leveritt. 2001. Long-Term Metabolic and Skeletal Muscle Adaptations to Short-Sprint Training: Implications for Sprint Training and Tapering, *Sports Medicine*, 31(15): 1063–1082.

Ross, A., M. Leveritt and S. Riek. 2001. Neural Influences on Sprint Running: Training Adaptations and Acute Responses, *Sports Medicine*, 31(6): 409–425.

Rubini, E.C., A.L.L. Costa and P.S.C. Gomes. 2007. The Effects of Stretching on Strength Performance, *Sports Medicine*, 37(3): 213–224.

Saeterbakken, A.H., R. van den Tillar and S. Seiler. 2011. Effect of Core Stability Training on Throwing Velocity in Female Handball Players, *Journal of Strength & Conditioning Research*, 25(3): 712–718.

Sáez-Sáez de Villarreal, E., J.J. Gonzalez-Badillo and M. Izquierdo. 2008. Low and Moderate Plyometric Training Frequency Produces Greater Jumping and Sprinting Gains Compared with High Frequency, *Journal of Strength & Conditioning Research*, 22(3): 715–725.

Sáez-Sáez de Villarreal, E., B. Requena and R.U. Newton. 2010. Does Plyometric Training Improve Strength Performance? A Meta-Analysis, *Journal of Science & Medicine in Sport*, 13(5): 513–522.

Santana, J.C., F.J. Vera-Garcia and S.M. McGill. 2007. A Kinetic and Electromyographic Comparison of the Standing Cable Press and Bench Press, *Journal of Strength & Conditioning Research*, 21(4): 1271–1279.

Santello, M., M.J.N. McDonagh and J.H. Challis. 2001. Visual and Non-Visual Control of Landing Movements in Humans, *Journal of Physiology*, 537(1): 313–327.

Schale, A.G., P.D. Blanch, D.A. Rath, T.V. Wrigley, R. Starr and K.L. Bennell. 2001. A Comparison of Overground and Treadmill Running for Measuring the Three-Dimensional Kinematics of the Lumbo–Pelvic–Hip Complex, *Clinical Biomechanics*, 16: 667–680.

Schmidtbleicher, D. 2008. Practical Aspects of Using Plyometric Training, *Proceedings of the 6th International Conference on Strength Training*, Colorado Springs, pp. 337–338.

Schmitz, R.J., S.J. Shultz and A.-D. Nguyen. 2009. Dynamic Valgus Alignment and Functional Strength in Males and Females during Maturation, *Journal of Athletic Training*, 44(1): 26–32.

Serpell, B.G., W.B. Young and M. Ford. 2011. Are the Perceptual and Decision-Making Aspects of Agility Trainable? A Preliminary Investigation, *Journal of Strength & Conditioning Research*, 25(5): 1240–1248.

Sheppard, J.M. and W.B. Young. 2006. Agility Literature Review: Classifications, Training and Testing, *Journal of Sports Sciences*, 24(9): 919–932.

Sheppard, J.M., W.B. Young, T.L.A. Doyle, T.A. Sheppard and R.U. Newton. 2006. An Evaluation of a New Test of Reactive Agility and Its Relationship to Sprint Speed and Change of Direction Speed, *Journal of Science & Medicine in Sport*, 9: 342–349.

Sierer, S.P., C.L. Battaglini, J.P. Mihalik, E.W. Shields and N.T. Tomasini. 2008. The National Football League Combine: Performance Differences between Drafted and Nondrafted Players Entering the 2004 and 2005 Drafts, *Journal of Strength & Conditioning Research*, 22(1): 6–12.

Silvers, H.C. and B.R. Mandelbaum. 2007. Prevention of Anterior Cruciate Ligament Injuries in the Female Athlete, *British Journal of Sports Medicine*, 41(Suppl. 1): i52–i59.

Simao, R., J. Spineti, B.F. De Salles, L.F. Oliveira, T. Matta, F. Miranda, H. Miranda and P.B. Costa. 2010. Influence of Exercise Order on Maximum Strength and Muscle Thickness in Untrained Men, *Journal of Sports Science and Medicine*, 9: 1–7.

Škof, B. and V. Strojnik. 2007. The Effect of Two Warm-Up Protocols on Some Biomechanical Parameters of the Neuromuscular System in Middle Distance Runners, *Journal of Strength & Conditioning Research*, 21(2): 394–399.

Sleivert, G. and M. Taingahue. 2004. The Relationship between Maximal Jump-Squat Power and Sprint Acceleration in Athletes, *European Journal of Applied Physiology*, 91: 46–52.

Spencer, M., D. Bishop and S. Lawrence. 2004. Longitudinal Assessment of the Effects of Field Hockey Training on Repeated Sprint Ability, *Journal of Science & Medicine in Sport*, 7(3): 323–334.

Spencer, M., D. Bishop, B. Dawson and C. Goodman. 2005. Physiological and Metabolic Responses of Repeated Sprint Activities: Specific to Field-Based Team Sports, *Sports Medicine*, 35(12): 1025–1044.

Spencer, M., M. Fitzsimons, B. Dawson, D. Bishop and C. Goodman. 2006. Reliability of a Repeated-Sprint Ability Test for Field-Hockey, *Journal of Science & Medicine in Sport*, 9: 181–184.

Sporis, G., I. Jukic, L. Milanovic and V. Vucetic. 2010. Reliability and Factorial Validity of Agility Tests for Soccer Players, *Journal of Strength and Conditioning Research*, 24(3): 679–686.

Spreuwenberg, L.P.B., W.J. Kraemer, B.A. Spierling, J.S. Volek, D.L. Hatfield, R. Silvestre, J.L. Vingren, M.S. Fragala, K. Hakkinen, R.U. Newton, C.M. Maresh and S.J. Fleck. 2006. Influence of Exercise Order in a Resistance-Training Exercise Session, *Journal of Strength & Conditioning Research*, 20(1): 141–144.

Stafidis, S. and A. Arampatzis. 2007. Muscle–Tendon Unit Mechanical and Morphological Properties and Sprint Performance, *Journal of Sports Sciences*, 25(9): 1035–1046.

Stanton, R., P.R. Reaburn and B. Humphries. 2004. The Effect of Short-Term Swiss Ball Training on Core Stability and Running Economy, *Journal of Strength & Conditioning Research*, 18(3): 522–528.

Stewart, D., A. Macaluso and G. De Vito. 2003. The Effect of an Active Warm-Up on Surface EMG and Muscle Performance in Healthy Humans, *European Journal of Applied Physiology*, 89: 509–513.

Stone, M.H. 1993. Literature Review: Explosive Exercises and Training, *NSCA Journal*, 15(3): 7–15.

Stone, N.M. and A.E. Kilding. 2009. Aerobic Conditioning for Team Sport Athletes, *Sports Medicine*, 39(8): 615–642.

Stone, M.H., J.A. Potteiger, K.C. Pierce, C.M. Proulx, H.S. O'Bryant, R.L. Johnson and M.E. Stone. 2000. Comparison of the Effects of Three Different Weight-Training Programs on the One Repetition Maximum Squat, *Journal of Strength & Conditioning Research*, 14(3): 332–337.

Stone, M.H., H.S. O'Bryant, L. McBoy, R. Coglianese, M. Lehmkuhl and B. Schilling. 2003. Power and Maximum Strength Relationships during Performance of Dynamic and Static Weighted Jumps, *Journal of Strength & Conditioning Research*, 17(1): 140–147.

Supej, M. 2010. Carving versus Side-Skidding Turn in Men's World Cup Giant Slalom, *Proceedings of the European Congress of Sports Sciences*, Antalya, p.68.

Tabata, I., K. Nishimura, M. Kouzaki, Y. Hirai, F. Ogita, M. Miyachi and K. Yamamoto. 1996. Effects of Moderate-Intensity Endurance Training and High-Intensity Intermittent Training on Anaerobic Capacity and VO$_2$max, *Medicine & Science in Sports & Exercise*, 28(10): 1327–1330.

Tabata, I., K. Irisawa, M. Kouzaki, K. Nishimura, F. Ogita and M. Miyachi. 1997. Metabolic Profile of High Intensity Intermittent Exercises, *Medicine & Science in Sports & Exercise*, 29(3): 390–395.

Taube, W., M. Gruber, S. Beck, M. Faist, A. Gollhofer and M. Schubert. 2007. Cortical and Spinal Adaptations Induced by Balance Training: Correlation between Stance Stability and Corticospinal Activation, *Acta Physiologica*, 189: 347–358.

Taube, W., C. Leukel, M. Schubert, M. Gruber, T. Rantalainen and A. Gollhofer. 2008. Differential Modulation of Spinal and Corticospinal Excitability during Drop Jumps, *Journal of Neurophysiology*, 99: 1243–1252.

Thompson, A., I.N. Bezodis and R.L. Jones. 2009. An In-Depth Assessment of Expert Sprint Coaches' Technical Knowledge, *Journal of Sports Sciences*, 27(8): 855–861.

Tong, T.K. and F.H. Fu. 2006. Effect of Specific Inspiratory Muscle Warm Up on Intense Intermittent Run to Exhaustion, *European Journal of Applied Physiology*, 97: 673–680.

Tricoli, V., L. Lamas, R. Carnevale and C. Urginowitsch. 2005. Short-Term Effects on Lower-Body Functional Power Development: Weightlifting vs. Vertical Jump Training Programs, *Journal of Strength & Conditioning Research*, 19(2): 433–437.

Tse, M.A., A.M. McManus and R.S.W. Masters. 2005. Development and Validation of a Core Endurance Intervention Program: Implications for Performance in College-Age Rowers, *Journal of Strength & Conditioning Research*, 19(3): 547–552.

Twist, P.W. and D. Benicky. 1996. Conditioning Lateral Movement for Multi-Sport Athletes: Practical Strength and Quickness Drills, *Strength & Conditioning*, 18(5): 10–19.

Tyler, T.F., S.J. Nicholas, R.J. Campbell and M.P. McHugh. 2001. The Association of Hip Strength and Flexibility with the Incidence of Adductor Muscle Strains in Professional Ice Hockey Players, *American Journal of Sports Medicine*, 29(2): 124–128.

Tyler, T.F., S.J. Nicholas, R.J. Campbell, S. Donnellan and M.P. McHugh. 2002. The Effectiveness of a Preseason Exercise Program to Prevent Adductor Muscle Strains in Professional Ice Hockey Players, *American Journal of Sports Medicine*, 30(5): 680–683.

van Beurden, E., A. Zask, L.M. Barnett and U.C. Dietrich. 2002. Fundamental Movement Skills: How Do Primary School Children Perform? The 'Move It Groove It' Program in Rural Australia, *Journal of Science & Medicine in Sport*, 5(3): 244–252.

van Ingen Schenau, J.J. de Koning and G. de Groot. 1994. Optimisation of Sprinting Performance in Running, Cycling and Speed Skating, *Sports Medicine*, 17(4): 259–275.

Vera-Garcia, F.J., S.G. Grenier and S.M. McGill. 2000. Abdominal Muscle Response during Curl-Ups on Both Stable and Labile Surfaces, *Physical Therapy*, 80: 564–569.

Vescovi, J.D. and M.R. McGuigan. 2008. Relationships between Sprinting, Agility and Jump Ability in Female Athletes, *Journal of Sports Sciences*, 26(1): 97–107.

Voliantis, S., A.K. McConnell, Y. Koutedakis and D.A. Jones. 1999. The Influence of Prior Activity upon Inspiratory Muscle Strength in Rowers and Non-Rowers, *International Journal of Sports Medicine*, 20: 542–547.

Vuorimaa, T. and J. Karvonen. 1988. Recovery Time in Interval Training for Increasing Aerobic Capacity, *Annals of Sports Medicine*, 3: 215–219.

Walklate, B.M., B.J. O'Brien, C.D. Paton and W. Young. 2009. Supplementing Regular Training with Short-Duration Sprint-Agility Training Leads to a Substantial Increase in Repeated Sprint-Agility Performance with National Level Badminton Players, *Journal of Strength & Conditioning Research*, 23(5): 1477–1481.

Wallace, B.J., T.W. Kernozek, J.M. White, D.E. Kline, G.A. Wright, H.T. Peng and C.-F. Huang. 2010. Quantification of Vertical Ground Reaction Forces of Popular Bilateral Plyometric Exercises, *Journal of Strength & Conditioning Research*, 24(1): 207–212.

Waryasz, G.R. 2010. Exercise Strategies to Prevent the Development of the Anterior Pelvic Tilt: Implications for Possible Prevention of Sports Hernias and Osteitis Pubis, *Strength & Conditioning Journal*, 32(4): 56–65.

Weyand, P. and M.W. Bundle. 2005. Energetics of High-Speed Running: Integrating Classical Theory and Contemporary Observations, *American Journal of Physiology: Regulatory, Integrative and Comparative Physiology*, 288: R956–R965.

Weyand, P.G., R.F. Sandell, D.N.L. Prime and M.W. Bundle. 2010. The Biological Limits to Running Speed Are Imposed from the Ground Up, *Journal of Applied Physiology*, 108(4): 950–961.

Wikstrom, E.A., M.D. Tillman, T.L. Chmielewski and P.A. Borsa. 2006. Measurement and Evaluation of Dynamic Joint Stability of the Knee and Ankle after Injury, *Sports Medicine*, 36(5): 393–410.

Wilkinson, D.M., J.L. Fallowfield and S.D. Myers. 1999. A Modified Incremental Shuttle Run Test Protocol for the Determination of Peak Shuttle Running Speed and the Prediction of Maximal Oxygen Uptake, *Journal of Sports Sciences*, 17: 413–419.

Willardson, J.M. 2007. Core Stability Training: Applications to Sports Conditioning Programs, *Journal of Strength & Conditioning Research*, 21(3): 979–985.

Wilmore, J.H. and D.L. Costill. 1999. Cardiorespiratory Adaptations to Training. In: J.H. Wilmore and D.L. Costill, eds, *Physiology of Sport and Exercise*, 2nd edn, Champaign, IL: Human Kinetics, pp. 277–308.

Wilson, G.J. and A.J. Murphy. 1996. Strength Diagnosis: The Use of Test Data to Determine Specific Strength Training, *Journal of Sports Sciences*, 14: 167–173.

Wilson, G.J., R.U. Newton, A.J. Murphy and B.J. Humphries. 1993. The Optimal Training Load for the Development of Dynamic Athletic Performance, *Medicine & Science in Sports & Exercise*, 25(11): 1279–1286.

Wilson, G.J., A.J. Murphy and J.F. Prior. 1994. Musculotendinous Stiffness: Its Relationship to Eccentric, Isometric and Concentric Performance, *Journal of Applied Physiology*, 76(6): 2714–2719.

Wilson, G.J., A.D. Lyttle, K.J. Ostrowski and A.J. Murphy. 1995. Assessing Dynamic Performance: A Comparison of Rate of Force Development Tests, *Journal of Strength & Conditioning Research*, 9(3): 176–181.

Wilson, G.J., A.J. Murphy and A. Giorgi. 1996. Weight and Plyometric Training: Effects on Eccentric and Concentric Force Production, *Canadian Journal of Applied Physiology*, 21(4): 301–315.

Wilson, J.M. and E.P. Flanagan. 2008. The Role of Elastic Energy in Activities with High Force and Power Requirements: A Brief Review, *Journal of Strength & Conditioning Research*, 22(5): 1705–1715.

Wilson, J.M., L.M. Hornbuckle, J.-S. Kim, C. Urginowitsch, S.-R. Lee, M.C. Zourdos, B. Sommer and L.B. Panton. 2010. Effects of Static Stretching on Energy Cost and Running Endurance Performance, *Journal of Strength & Conditioning Research*, 24(9): 2274–2279.

Winchester, J.B., J.M. McBride, M.A. Maher, R.P. Mikat, B.K. Allen, D.E. Kline and M.R. McGuigan. 2008. Eight Weeks of Ballistic Exercise Improves Power Independently of Changes in Strength and Muscle Fiber Type Expression, *Journal of Strength & Conditioning Research*, 22(6): 1728–1734.

Witvrouw, E., J. Bellemans, R. Lysens, L. Danneels and D. Cambier. 2001. Intrinsic Risk Factors for the Development of Patellar Tendinitis in an Athletic Population: A Two-Year Prospective Study, *American Journal of Sports Medicine*, 29(2): 190–195.

Witvrouw, E., L. Danneels, P. Asselman, T. D'have and D. Cambier. 2003. Muscle Flexibility as a Risk Factor for Developing Muscle Injuries in Male Professional Soccer Players, *American Journal of Sports Medicine*, 31(1): 41–46.

Witvrouw, E., N. Mahieu, L. Danneels and P. McNair. 2004. Stretching and Injury Prevention: An Obscure Relationship, *Sports Medicine*, 34(7): 443–449.

Woods, K., P. Bishop and E. Jones. 2007. Warm-Up and Stretching in the Prevention of Muscle Injury, *Sports Medicine*, 37(12): 1089–1099.

Workman, J.C., D. Docherty, K.C. Parfrey and D.G. Behm. 2008. Influence of Pelvis Position on the Activation of Abdominal and Hip Flexor Muscles, *Journal of Strength & Conditioning Research*, 22(5): 1563–1569.

Yaggie, J.A. and B.M. Campbell. 2006. Effects of Balance Training on Selected Skills, *Journal of Strength & Conditioning Research*, 20(2): 422–428.

Yamaguchi, T., K. Oshii, M. Yamanaka and K. Yasuda. 2006. Acute Effect of Static Stretching on Power Output during Concentric Dynamic Constant External Resistance Leg Extension, *Journal of Strength & Conditioning Research*, 20(4): 804–810.

Young, W.B. 2006. Transfer of Strength and Power Training to Sports Performance, *International Journal of Sports Physiology & Performance*, 1: 74–83.

Young, W. and D. Farrow. 2006. A Review of Agility: Practical Considerations for Strength and Conditioning, *Strength & Conditioning Journal*, 28(5): 24–29.

Young, W., B. McLean and J. Ardagna. 1995. Relationship between Strength Qualities and Sprinting Performance, *Journal of Sports Medicine & Physical Fitness*, 35(1): 13–19.

Young, W.B., A. Jenner and K. Griffiths. 1998. Acute Enhancement of Power Performance from Heavy Load Squats, *Journal of Strength & Conditioning Research*, 12(2): 82–84.

Young, W.B., C. MacDonald and M.A. Flowers. 2001a. Validity of Double- and Single-Leg Vertical Jumps as Tests of Leg Extensor Muscle Function, *Journal of Strength & Conditioning Research*, 15(1): 6–11.

Young, W.B., M.H. McDowell and B.J. Scarlett. 2001b. Specificity of Sprint and Agility Training Methods, *Journal of Strength & Conditioning Research*, 15(3): 315–319.

Young, W.B., R.U. Newton, T.L. Doyle. 2005. Physiological and Anthropometric Characteristics of Starters and Non-Starters in Elite Australian Rules Football: A Case Study, *Journal of Science & Medicine in Sport*, 8(3): 333–345.

Yu, B., R.M. Queen, A.N. Abbey, Y. Liu, C.T. Moorman and W.E. Garrett. 2008. Hamstring Muscle Kinematics and Activation during Overground Sprinting, *Journal of Biomechanics*, 41: 3121–3126.

Zatsiorsky, V.W. and W.J. Kraemer. 2006. Timing in Strength Training. In: *Science and Practice of Strength Training*, 2nd edn, Champaign, IL: Human Kinetics, pp. 89–108.

Zazulak, B.T., T.E. Hewett, N.P. Reeves, B. Goldberg and J. Cholewicki. 2007. Deficits in Neuromuscular Control of the Trunk Predict Knee Injury Risk: A Prospective Biomechanical–Epidemiological Study, *American Journal of Sports Medicine*, 35(7): 1123–1130.

Zuur, A.T., J. Lundbye-Jensen, C. Leukel, W. Taube, M.J. Grey, A. Gollhofer, J.B. Nielsen and M. Gruber. 2010. Contribution of Afferent Feedback and Descending Drive to Human Hopping, *Journal of Physiology*, 588(5): 799–807.

INDEX

acceleration 10, 24–5, 27, 49–51, 53, 55, 74, 77–8, 85, 88–90, 135, 137, 139–41, 143, 146–7, 150, 164; initial acceleration 13, 23, 27, 49, 74
aerobic: aerobic capacity 35, 38, 95–8; aerobic conditioning 98–9, 163–4; aerobic endurance 35–6, 96, 98, 100–1; aerobic interval training 99–102, 164–5; aerobic metabolism, oxidative metabolism 14–15, 92–7, 99, 100, 123; aerobic power, maximal oxygen uptake (VO_2max) 93, 98; maximal aerobic speed (MAS) 14, 35–6, 93, 99
agility 3–6, 7–16, 18, 19–23, 28–9, 31–2, 34–5, 37, 40–1, 43, 49, 51–3, 55, 57, 68, 72–4, 85, 92, 94–5, 98, 103–6, 108, 122–3, 126, 128, 141–7, 150–2, 157, 159, 161–2, 164–5; reactive agility 4, 28, 31–2, 144–6, 150–2, 164–5l; reactive agility test (RAT) 29, 32
agonist muscle, motor units 13, 61, 68, 81–3, 131
anaerobic: anaerobic capacity 35, 37, 93, 102; anaerobic endurance, fitness 29, 35, 100–1; anaerobic interval training 99–101, 164–5; anaerobic metabolism 14, 37, 92–3, 99–100; anaerobic power 22, 98; maximal anaerobic running speed 93
antagonist muscle, antagonist motor units 13, 61, 78, 83, 131
arm action, arm swing 137–8
athleticism 4, 27, 40
ATP (adenosine triphosphate) 14–15, 92–6

balance 27, 33, 40, 44–6, 68; balance assessment, balance testing 33, 45; balance training, sensorimotor training 44–6, 108–9; dynamic 33, 44–6; postural 33, 108; static 44–6
ballistic: ballistic action, movement 73, 77–8, 88; ballistic resistance training 23, 76–9, 81, 90, 164–5
bilateral 25–6, 52–6, 61, 76–7, 79, 83–4, 164

change of direction: movement 5, 10, 11–16, 28, 30, 34, 42–3, 51–2, 55, 57, 62, 65, 74–6, 78–9, 85, 89, 103, 105–7, 110, 112, 115, 118, 126, 142–3, 145–7, 151; Illinois 'agility' test 25, 29, 31; performance, speed 3–5, 7, 12–13, 20–2, 24–6, 29–30, 34–5, 41, 43, 49–52, 55, 57, 61, 68, 75, 77, 85, 107, 142, 145, 147, 151; pro 'agility' test 25, 29; tests, assessment, measures 13, 19, 21–2, 25–6, 28–32, 61, 107, 142; training 150, 163–5
concentric: concentric force production, force development 13, 52, 54, 77–8; concentric movement, action 9–13, 23, 25–6, 52, 74–9, 81, 85, 88–9, 143; concentric performance, force development 25, 49, 77–8, 140; concentric power, rate of force development, speed-strength 23, 34, 50, 75–7; concentric strength 22, 49, 50, 108
coordination, intermuscular 14, 73, 78, 135, 138; intramuscular 73, 75, 77, 81, 135; neuromuscular 13, 42, 55, 135–6, 138, 140; training 68, 88
core: endurance 107; musculature 11, 103, 106, 108, 110, 127; stability 34, 103, 105, 107–8, 110; strength 34–5, 68, 103, 105, 107–8, 110; training, exercises 103–4, 106, 107–8, 110, 115

countermovement 9, 51, 85, 146; horizontal jump 26; vertical jump 25, 81, 84, 89

deceleration 13, 52, 55, 74–5, 106, 143, 146, 150
decision-making 3–6, 15–16, 28, 32, 141, 146, 150–2, 154
drop jump 13, 25–7, 41–3, 81, 83–5
dynamic correspondence 52–3
dynamic stabilisation 14, 33–4, 44, 46

eccentric action, movement, phase 10, 12–13, 25–7, 50, 55, 74–9, 81, 89, 131; eccentric loading 51, 54, 79, 83, 85, 124; eccentric strength 22, 26, 49–52, 106, 108
ecological validity 32
economy, running economy, work economy 9–10, 74, 85, 97–8, 101, 125
elastic energy, storage, return 9–11, 13–14, 50, 74, 78, 81, 84, 129, 136; series elastic elements 9, 11, 78, 84
elasticity, tendon compliance 129–130
electronic timing 28
endurance: athletes 9, 74, 85, 90, 96, 98, 136, 159; performance 97–100, 102, 104; tests, assessment 34–6, 101, 107; training 12, 84, 98, 100, 104, 108, 112, 158, 163
enzymes 93, 96; enzyme adaptation 95–6
extensor muscles 11, 34, 50, 61, 89, 106, 125, 140, 144; ankle extensors, plantarflexors 12, 50, 77–9, 130, 138; hip extensors 12, 14, 50, 54, 138; knee extensors 11–12, 22–23, 50, 138

fatigue 15, 84, 89–90, 92–3, 95, 97–8, 100–1, 127–8, 157, 163; index 38
field-based assessment, testing 22, 32–9
field sports 32, 37–9, 95, 101, 159
flexibility 122, 128, 129–131; training, exercises 122, 126, 128–131
flexor 34, 61; hip flexors 50, 65, 110, 127, 138; knee flexors 23, 50, 54, 138
flight phase, swing phase 12–13, 50, 92, 106–7, 117, 135–6; flight time 27, 89, 137
foot 8, 13, 45, 50, 135–6, 138–9, 143–4; contact 8–9, 12–14, 20, 49–50, 74, 103, 106, 137–8; forefoot 136; midfoot 85, 136; rearfoot 136; strike 8–9, 11, 13, 50, 106, 135–9, 143
force 8–9, 11, 22–3, 25, 41, 43–4, 52–4, 68, 75, 78, 84, 89, 103–5, 136; braking forces 8, 13–14, 136, 138, 143; development 9–10, 12–14, 20, 22–3, 49, 51–5, 74, 76–9; ground reaction force 4, 8–10, 12, 14–15, 20, 22, 26–7, 33, 49–51, 54–5, 83–4, 136–7, 139–140, 143; output 9, 12–13, 20, 26, 39, 55, 78, 100, 124; propulsion forces 10, 13–14, 22–23, 74, 92, 103, 106, 136, 138–9
force–velocity relationship 11, 78
frequency of training 12, 65, 83, 130, 162–5

glycogen, muscle glycogen 96–7, 127
glycolysis, glycolytic metabolism 15, 93–7; glycolytic capacity 93; glycolytic system 14–15, 93, 95
ground contact time 9–10, 27, 73, 88, 137, 139

heart rate 35–6, 95, 99–102, 122, 128
high-intensity activity, effort 14–15, 36–8, 84, 92–98, 100–1, 123–4, 126–9, 163; high-intensity training 35, 96–9, 102, 160, 165
hip, hip girdle 11–12, 41, 51, 55, 57, 103–8, 110, 115, 117–18, 120, 138, 141
hydrogen ions, H^+ 15, 93–5

information processing 32
information–movement coupling 16, 152
intensity, training intensity, work intensity 35–7, 55, 65, 83–5, 94–5, 97–102, 107, 125–8, 159–160, 162–5
intermittent activity, exercise 15, 98, 123; intermittent fitness test 36–7; intermittent sports 14, 92, 94, 96, 101, 122, 142, 145
intervals: rest 39, 55, 89– 91, 99–101, 128; training, conditioning 12, 36, 97–102, 164–5; work 38, 96, 99–101

jump squat 23–4, 51, 75, 78– 80, 90

kinematic, kinematics 12, 15–16, 25, 27, 42, 49, 51–2, 74, 88–9, 137, 143
kinetics 15–16, 25, 27, 42, 49, 51–2, 85, 88, 103, 138, 142–3
kinetic chain, lower limb kinetic chain 8, 10, 14, 23, 49–50, 81, 103, 136, 138, 143

lactate 15, 37, 93–4, 97, 123; handling 93, 123; threshold 97–99
lumbar spine, lumbar vertebrae 10, 54–5, 104–5, 108
lumbo-pelvic-hip complex 11, 68, 103–7
lumbopelvic posture 10, 108, 127–8

macrocycle, training 53, 157, 161, 163
maturation 40–2
mesocycle, training 158–65
metabolic: conditioning 92, 95, 98, 100–2, 158, 161, 163–5; pathways, processes 4–5, 14–15, 35, 92–101, 123, 128
microcycle, training 159–61, 163
mobility 14, 40, 43–4, 52, 122, 126–30
morphology, morphological 11, 52–3; adaptations 11, 51, 53, 75, 77–9, 158
motor: control 68, 107–8, 145; cortex 76, 81; learning 6, 40, 143; patterns 40; skills 5–6, 40–1, 88, 140, 150; unit 52, 77–8, 81, 83–4, 89, 97, 124–5, 129
movement: competency 4–5, 32; dexterity 40; fundamental abilities 40, 44; fundamental

Index

movements 40–1, 43; response, strategy 3, 5, 15–16, 32, 143–7, 151–2, 154; screening, screens 43, 113, 129; skills, abilities 4–5, 40–3, 88, 141–2, 145–7, 150–2, 164; task 3–5, 8–16, 20–1, 23, 25, 27–33, 40, 42–6, 49, 51–53, 55, 57, 61, 68, 73–9, 81, 84, 89, 92, 94, 97–8, 101–3, 105–8, 110, 113, 115, 117, 123–6, 128–131, 137–147, 150–152, 154, 164–5

muscle: buffering capacity 15, 35, 93–4, 97–8; fascicle 11, 77–8, 81; fibre, cell 11–12, 15, 79, 89–90, 93–4, 97; muscle–tendon complex, musculotendinous unit 9–11, 73, 79, 81, 124–5, 129; oxidative capacity 15, 35, 94–8, 100; pennation angle 11–12; pH 15, 94, 97

neuromuscular adaptation 52, 73, 81, 97–8, 101; coordination, skill 13–14, 42, 61, 135–6, 138, 140; control 16, 41–2, 44–5, 65, 108; function, performance 3, 7, 14, 19–20, 40, 73, 75, 84, 97, 124–5; 'spurt' 41–2; training 41–2, 76, 97, 108

Olympic-style weightlifting 25, 76–8, 90, 164–5
oxidative capacity *see* muscle oxidative capacity
oxidative metabolism *see* aerobic metabolism
oxygen uptake kinetics, VO$_2$ kinetics 94, 123

pelvis 104–6, 110, 117, 127
perception, perceptual aspects 4–6, 15–16, 32, 123, 146, 150–2, 154; perception–action coupling 6, 150, 152, 154
periodisation 100, 157–165
phosphocreatine (PCr) 14–15, 93–6, 127
plantarflexor *see* extensors, ankle extensors

racquet sports 35, 39, 44, 76, 94, 96, 101–2, 129, 139–141, 144–5, 147, 150, 159
rate of force development (RFD) 10, 23, 77
recovery 12, 15, 37–9, 55, 93–6, 98–102, 123, 161; action, recovery phase (of sprinting action) 135, 138, 143; active 36, 95, 122
reflex: local spinal reflexes 9, 81, 129; 'stretch reflex' 9–10, 83, 125, 129–130
repeated sprint, sprints 14–15, 38–9, 92–5, 97–8, 100–1, 123; ability, performance 5, 15, 22, 35–6, 38, 94–5, 98, 101–2, 123; conditioning, sprint interval training 96–7, 100–2, 164–5

scheduling, schedule 53, 157–8, 161, 163
shuttle run test 29, 30–1, 36–8
speed development, training 4–7, 12, 35, 40–1, 51, 55, 68, 72, 74–5, 77, 129, 140–2, 157, 159, 161, 164–5
speed-endurance 22, 100, 102; speed-endurance conditioning 100, 102

speed–strength 13, 22–7, 50, 52–3, 73–6, 83, 88, 90–1, 158, 161–5; reactive 13, 25–7, 50, 73–5
split-step 51, 85, 139, 141, 144, 146, 150
spring–mass: characteristics 92; model 8–9, 11, 14, 103, 106, 136–8, 143
sprint interval training 12, 96,98, 100–1; *see also* repeated sprint conditioning
stability 10, 14, 27, 33–4, 40, 43–4, 52, 61–2, 65, 68, 103, 106, 110, 112; lumbopelvic 34, 44, 104–8, 112, 117, 138; postural 11, 14, 27, 33, 34, 55, 108; torsional 34, 62, 107, 112, 113, 115
stance phase 8, 13, 50, 54, 92, 107, 135–6, 138
stiffness 10–11, 14, 51, 61, 68, 79, 81, 92, 106, 108, 110, 124, 130, 136; joint 41, 123; lower limb 10, 12, 41, 50, 61, 97, 106, 129, 136, 138; musculotendinous 10, 74, 79, 81, 124–5, 129
strength 4, 7, 12–14, 20–3, 26–7, 34, 40–1, 49–53, 55–6, 61, 65, 68, 72–7, 90, 104–5, 107–8, 110, 112, 115, 162; concentric 22, 50, 108; eccentric 13, 22, 26, 49–51, 108; endurance 22; isometric 20, 50, 106, 108, 140; reactive 13, 27, 75; training, development 4, 12, 49, 51–57, 61–2, 65, 68, 72–6, 78, 83, 158, 161–5
stretch reflex 9–10, 83, 125, 129–30
stretching 122, 124–6, 128–31; ballistic 126, 130; dynamic flexibility exercises, dynamic range of motion exercises 126, 130; proprioceptive neuromuscular facilitation (PNF) 125, 129, 131; static 125, 126, 127, 128, 129, 130
stretch–shortening cycle (SSC) 9–11, 25–7, 73–4, 76, 79, 81, 83, 125, 129, 140, 162; fast 9–10, 13, 74, 76, 79, 81, 83–85, 129, 163, 165; slow 9, 10, 74, 76, 79, 81, 83, 84–5, 164–5
stride frequency, stride rate 8–9, 14, 88–9, 92, 138
stride length 5, 8, 88, 138
swing phase *see* flight phase

team sports 9, 13, 23, 25, 27, 30, 32, 35–6, 39, 51, 85, 90, 94, 96, 101–3, 112, 125, 140–2, 144–5, 150, 159–60
tendon 11, 73, 77–9, 81, 129–30, 136
toe-off 8, 10, 135, 137–9
transfer 5, 7, 52, 53, 68, 77, 79, 88, 107, 150; of training effects 5, 52–3, 56, 77, 135, 157; training 53, 56–7, 65, 68, 151, 160, 165
T-test 26, 30, 107

unilateral 25–6, 53–5, 61, 76, 79, 85, 113, 164–5

velocity 8, 11, 13–14, 21–2, 41, 50, 74–5, 77–9, 99, 107, 124, 140, 144, 146, 150, 152

VO$_2$max (maximal oxygen uptake) 35–7, 98–100, 102, 127
VO$_2$peak (peak oxygen uptake) 35–7, 97
vVO$_2$max (velocity at VO$_2$max) 14, 35–6, 93, 99

volume, training 55, 83–4, 90, 97, 100, 127–8, 159–160, 162–5
volume load 159–160, 163

warm up 122–9, 131

Taylor & Francis
eBooks
FOR LIBRARIES

ORDER YOUR FREE 30 DAY INSTITUTIONAL TRIAL TODAY!

Over 23,000 eBook titles in the Humanities, Social Sciences, STM and Law from some of the world's leading imprints.

Choose from a range of subject packages or create your own!

Benefits for you
- Free MARC records
- COUNTER-compliant usage statistics
- Flexible purchase and pricing options

Benefits for your user
- Off-site, anytime access via Athens or referring URL
- Print or copy pages or chapters
- Full content search
- Bookmark, highlight and annotate text
- Access to thousands of pages of quality research at the click of a button

For more information, pricing enquiries or to order a free trial, contact your local online sales team.

UK and Rest of World: **online.sales@tandf.co.uk**

US, Canada and Latin America:
e-reference@taylorandfrancis.com

www.ebooksubscriptions.com

ALPSP Award for BEST eBOOK PUBLISHER 2009 Finalist

Taylor & Francis eBooks
Taylor & Francis Group

A flexible and dynamic resource for teaching, learning and research.